Selected Titles in This Series

P9-CRA-477

Lectures on the Mathematics of Finance

Volume 8

CRM MONOGRAPH SERIES

Centre de Recherches Mathématiques
Université de Montréal

Lectures on the Mathematics of Finance

WAGGONER LIBRARY
DISCARD

Ioannis Karatzas

The Centre de Recherches Mathématiques (CRM) of the Université de Montréal was created in 1968 to promote research in pure and applied mathematics and related disciplines. Among its activities are special theme years, summer schools, workshops, postdoctoral programs, and publishing. The CRM is supported by the Université de Montréal, the Province of Québec (FCAR), and the Natural Sciences and Engineering Research Council of Canada. It is affiliated with the Institut des Sciences Mathématiques (ISM) of Montréal, whose constituent members are Concordia University, McGill University, the Université de Montréal, the Université du Québec à Montréal, and the Ecole Polytechnique.

American Mathematical Society
Providence, Rhode Island USA

WAGGONER LIBRARY
TREVECCA NAZARENE UNIVERSITY

The production of this volume was supported in part by the Fonds pour la Formation de Chercheurs et l'Aide à la Recherche (Fonds FCAR) and the Natural Sciences and Engineering Research Council of Canada (NSERC).

1991 *Mathematics Subject Classification.* Primary 90A09; Secondary 60H30, 93E20.

Library of Congress Cataloging-in-Publication Data

Karatzas, Ioannis.
    Lectures on the mathematics of finance / Ioannis Karatzas.
       p. cm. — (CRM monograph series, ISSN 1065-8599; v. 8)
    Includes bibliographical references.
    ISBN 0-8218-0637-8 (alk. paper)
    1. Business mathematics. I. Title. II. Series
HF5691.K338 1996
332′.01′51—dc20
                                        96-27511
                                            CIP

Copying and reprinting. Individual readers of this publication, and nonprofit libraries acting for them, are permitted to make fair use of the material, such as to copy a chapter for use in teaching or research. Permission is granted to quote brief passages from this publication in reviews, provided the customary acknowledgment of the source is given.

Republication, systematic copying, or multiple reproduction of any material in this publication (including abstracts) is permitted only under license from the American Mathematical Society. Requests for such permission should be addressed to the Assistant to the Publisher, American Mathematical Society, P. O. Box 6248, Providence, Rhode Island 02940-6248. Requests can also be made by e-mail to reprint-permission@ams.org.

© 1997 by the American Mathematical Society. All rights reserved.
Reprinted with corrections 1997.
The American Mathematical Society retains all rights
except those granted to the United States Government.
Printed in the United States of America.

♾ The paper used in this book is acid-free and falls within the guidelines
established to ensure permanence and durability.
This volume was typeset using $\mathcal{A}_{\mathcal{M}}\mathcal{S}$-LATEX,
the American Mathematical Society's TEX macro system,
and submitted to the American Mathematical Society in camera-ready
form by the Centre de Recherches Mathématiques.

10 9 8 7 6 5 4 3 2   02 01 00 99 98 97

Εἰς μνήμην τῶν γονέων μου
Χρίστου καὶ Εὐδοξίας

« Ὑμετέρης γενεῆς τε καὶ αἵματος εὔχομαι εἶναι »

I. K.

Contents

Preface

The "Mathematization" of the field of Finance has proceeded at a very rapid, sometimes explosive, pace during the last fifteen years. Ever since the role of the so-called equivalent martingale-measure was noticed, and its significance understood in the context of both pricing and portfolio optimization problems, powerful techniques from Stochastic Analysis and Stochastic Control have been brought to bear on almost all aspects of Mathematical Finance: the study of arbitrage, hedging, pricing, consumption/investment optimization, incomplete and/or constrained markets, equilibrium, differential information, the term-structure of interest rates, transaction costs, and so on. At the same time, the development of sophisticated Analytical and Numerical Methods, based primarily on partial differential equations and on their numerical solution, has helped to increase the relevance of these developments in the everyday practice of Finance.

The notes that follow are an attempt to put some of these developments in perspective, and to suggest questions that remain open. They are based on the André Aisenstadt Lectures delivered at the Centre de Recherches Mathématiques, Université de Montréal, in May 1996; their content reflects also the earlier survey paper [144], the lectures at a Winter School in Friedrichroda, Thuringia (March 1992), the lectures at the Institute of Mathematics and its Applications, University of Minnesota (June 1993) and the lectures at a Summer School in the Academia Sinica, Beijing (September 1994). To a large extent, that is, with the exception of Sections 2.5 and 2.6, Chapters 0-3 are an abridgement of the forthcoming monograph "Methods of Mathematical Finance" with S. E. Shreve (to be published by Springer-Verlag); Chapters 4-6 are based on the research papers [54], [55] and [146] with J. Cvitanić and S. G. Kou, and Chapter 7 on the recent paper [57] with J. Cvitanić.

The André Aisenstadt lectures were addressed to an audience consisting mostly of mathematicians, and presupposed little or no knowledge of Finance. They did assume familiarity with the elements of Stochastic Analysis and of parabolic Partial Differential Equations, at a level comparable to the first five chapters of the book [154] on "Brownian Motion and Stochastic Calculus".

At the end of the volume, the interested reader may find the "Historical Notes" helpful for understanding the evolution of this field, and for excursions into topics that are not touched here. These notes, as well as the bibliography that follows them, are not meant to be exhaustive; they reflect the limits of my knowledge, and I apologize for possible omissions. Similarly, the choice of topics treated in the lectures reflects my knowledge and interests, as well as limitations on the size of this volume.

I am deeply grateful to my colleagues Jakša Cvitanić, Jérôme Detemple, Nicole El Karoui, John Lehoczky and, foremost, Steven Shreve, who have taught me most of what I know about this field; and to my former students Abel Cadenillas, Steve Kou, Peter Lakner, Igor Pikovsky and Xing-Xiong Xue, from whom I have learned the rest.

I wish to thank my hosts at the Centre de Recherches Mathématiques, particularly Professors Martin Goldstein and Luc Vinet, as well as Louis Pelletier, for the invitation to the André Aisenstadt Chair and for making my stay in Montréal this month a most enjoyable one. Professors Daniel Dufresne, Anatole Joffe and Yannis Yatracos followed the lectures but also went out of their way to show me a great time in the city, and I am grateful. The participants A. Lazrak, D. Salopek and X. Zhao offered comments and corrections, which improved the text considerably. Louise Letendre typed the manuscript of my notes with unbelievable efficiency and speed, and with great cheer; qu'elle soit chaleureusement remerciée.

Ioannis Karatzas
Montréal
May 1996

CHAPTER 0

The model

0.1. Introduction

We shall deal, throughout these lectures, with the following model for a financial market $\mathcal{M}$, in which $n + 1$ assets (securities) are traded continuously. The first of these is an asset without systematic risk, called *bond* (or "bank account"), whose price $B(t)$ at time t evolves according to the equation

$$(0.1.1) \qquad dB(t) = B(t)r(t)\,dt, \quad B(0) = 1.$$

The remaining n assets are subject to systematic risk; we shall refer to them as *stocks*, and model the evolution of the price-per-share $P_i(t)$ of the ith stock at time t by the linear stochastic differential equation

$$(0.1.2) \quad dP_i(t) = P_i(t)\left[b_i(t)\,dt + \sum_{j=1}^{d}\sigma_{ij}(t)\,dW_j(t)\right], \qquad \begin{aligned} P_i(0) &= p_i \in (0,\infty), \\ i &= 1,\ldots,n. \end{aligned}$$

In this model, the sources of systematic risk are modelled by the independent components of a d-dimensional Brownian motion $W(t) = (W_1(t),\ldots,W_d(t))'$, $0 \leq t \leq T$. With this interpretation, the "volatility coefficient" $\sigma_{ij}(t)$ in (0.1.2) models the instantaneous intensity with which the jth source of uncertainty influences the price of the ith stock at time t. The Brownian motion W is defined on a given complete probability space $(\Omega, \mathcal{F}, \mathbb{P})$; we shall denote by $\mathbb{F} = \{\mathcal{F}(t), 0 \leq t \leq T\}$ the $\mathbb{P}$-augmentation of the natural filtration

$$(0.1.3) \qquad \mathcal{F}^W(t) = \sigma\big(W(s), 0 \leq s \leq t\big), \qquad 0 \leq t \leq T$$

generated by W. Unless otherwise stated explicitly, the time-horizon T will be considered finite.

The "interest rate" process $\{r(t), 0 \leq t \leq T\}$, the vector-process of "appreciation rates" $\{b(t) = (b_1(t),\ldots,b_n(t))', 0 \leq t \leq T\}$, and the matrix-process of "volatilities" $\{\sigma(t) = (\sigma_{ij}(t))_{\substack{1 \leq i \leq n \\ 1 \leq j \leq d}}, 0 \leq t \leq T\}$, will be referred to, collectively, as the *coefficients* of the model $\mathcal{M}$. We shall assume throughout these lectures that these coefficients are progressively measurable with respect to $\mathbb{F}$ and satisfy the mild condition

$$\int_0^T \left(|r(t)| + \|b(t)\| + \|\sigma(t)\|^2\right) dt < \infty, \text{ a.s.}$$

with $\|x\| = (x_1^2 + \cdots + x_m^2)^{1/2}$ the Euclidean norm in $\mathbb{R}^m$.

DISCUSSION. The model of (0.1.1), (0.1.2) is general enough to be interesting, and it can be further extended relatively easily to allow for dividends, for jumps in the stock-prices $P_i(\cdot)$, etc. At the same time, it is simple enough to provide concrete answers to many interesting questions, as we shall try to demonstrate in these lectures.

The requirement that the coefficients $r(t)$, $b(t)$, $\sigma(t)$ be adapted to $\mathbb{F}$, essentially makes them functionals of the Brownian path $\{W(s), 0 \leq s \leq t\}$ up to time t, for every $0 \leq t \leq T$. This assumption

  (i) precludes anticipation of the future, but
  (ii) allows for dependence on the past of the driving Brownian motion, or of the stock prices;

both these features are desirable.

In the special case when these coefficients are deterministic, or can be expressed at every $t \in [0, T]$ as given functions of t and $P(t) = \big(P_1(t), \dots, P_n(t)\big)'$, the stock-price process $\{P(t), 0 \leq t \leq T\}$ is *Markovian*, in fact a vector diffusion process.

0.2. Portfolio and consumption rules

Let us introduce now, in the market model $\mathcal{M}$ of the previous section, a *small investor*, that is, an economic agent who can decide, at each instant $t \in [0, T]$,

  (i) how much money $\pi_i(t)$ to invest in each of the available stocks $i = 1, \dots, n$, and
  (ii) what his cumulative consumption-to-date $C(t)$ should be.

Of course, these decisions must be made in a non-anticipative way, without fore-knowledge of future events; in other words, $C(t)$ and $\pi_i(t)$, $i = 1, \dots, n$ must be $\mathcal{F}(t)$-measurable random variables. And these decisions have no effect on market prices, whence the term "small investor".

If we denote by $X(t)$ the wealth of this agent at time t, then $X(t) - \sum_{i=1}^{n} \pi_i(t)$ is the amount invested in the bond, and thus the *wealth-process* $\{X(t), 0 \leq t \leq T\}$ obeys the equation

$$(0.2.1) \quad dX(t) = \sum_{i=1}^{n} \pi_i(t) \frac{dP_i(t)}{P_i(t)} + \left(X(t) - \sum_{i=1}^{n} \pi_i(t) \right) \frac{dB(t)}{B(t)} - dC(t)$$

$$= \sum_{i=1}^{n} \pi_i(t) \left[b_i(t)\, dt + \sum_{j=1}^{d} \sigma_{ij}(t)\, dW_j(t) \right]$$

$$+ \left(X(t) - \sum_{i=1}^{n} \pi_i(t) \right) r(t)\, dt - dC(t)$$

$$= r(t) X(t)\, dt + \pi'(t) \big[(b(t) - r(t)\mathbf{1}_n)\, dt + \sigma(t)\, dW(t) \big]$$
$$- dC(t), \quad X(0) = x$$

from (0.1.1), (0.1.2), where $x \in \mathbb{R}$ is the initial capital, $\mathbf{1}_n \triangleq (1, \dots, 1)' \in \mathbb{R}^n$, and prime ($'$) denotes transposition. The solution of this *linear stochastic differential equation with random coefficients* is not hard to write down:

$$(0.2.2) \quad \gamma(t) X(t) = x - \int_{(0,t]} \gamma(s)\, dC(s)$$

$$+ \int_0^t \gamma(s) \pi'(s) \big[\sigma(s)\, dW(s) + (b(s) - r(s)\mathbf{1}_n)\, ds \big],$$

$$0 \leq t \leq T,$$

where

$$(0.2.3) \qquad \gamma(t) \triangleq \frac{1}{B(t)} = \exp\left(-\int_0^t r(s)\,ds\right)$$

is the *discount factor in* $\mathcal{M}$.

After this heuristic discussion, let us make some precise definitions.

0.2.1. DEFINITION. (i) An $\mathbb{F}$-adapted process $C = \{C(t), 0 \leq t \leq T\}$ with increasing, right-continuous paths and $C(0) = 0$, $C(T) < \infty$ a.s. is called *cumulative consumption process*.

(ii) An $\mathbb{F}$-progressively measurable, $\mathbb{R}^n$-valued process $\pi = \{(\pi_1(t), \ldots, \pi_n(t))'$, $0 \leq t \leq T\}$ with

$$\int_0^T \|\pi'(t)\sigma(t)\|^2\,dt + \int_0^T |\pi'(t)(b(t) - r(t)\mathbf{1}_n)|\,dt < \infty, \quad \text{a.s.}$$

in called *portfolio process*.

(iii) For a given $x \in \mathbb{R}$ and (π, C) as above, the process $X(t) \equiv X^{x,\pi,C}(t)$, $0 \leq t \leq T$ of (0.2.1), (0.2.2) is called the *wealth process* corresponding to initial capital x, portfolio π, and cumulative consumption process C.

Notice that we are allowing both $\pi_i(t)$ ($i = 1, \ldots, n$) an $X(t) - \sum_{i=1}^n \pi_i(t)$ to take negative values; in other words, both short-selling of stocks, and borrowing at interest rate $r(\cdot)$, are permitted. Clearly then, we need to impose *some* restriction on admissible portfolios.

0.2.2. DEFINITION. We say that a given portfolio process $\pi(\cdot)$ is *tame*, if the associated "discounted gains process"

$$(0.2.4) \quad M^\pi(t) \triangleq \int_0^t \gamma(s)\pi'(s)[\sigma(s)\,dW(s) + (b(s) - r(s)\mathbf{1}_n)\,ds], \qquad 0 \leq t \leq T$$

is a.s. bounded from below by some real constant:

$$(0.2.5) \qquad \mathbb{P}[M^\pi(t) \geq q_\pi, \ \forall \ 0 \leq t \leq T] = 1, \quad \text{for some} \quad q_\pi \in \mathbb{R}.$$

In the absence of a condition like (0.2.5), it is not hard to construct *doubling strategies*, that is, portfolios that attain arbitrarily large values of wealth with probability one at $t = T$, starting with zero initial capital at $t = 0$! Indeed, take $n = d = 1$, $\sigma(\cdot) \equiv 1$, $r(\cdot) = b(\cdot) \equiv 0$; then for any $a > 0$ (say, $a = \$100$ Trillion) we can find a portfolio process $\pi(\cdot)$ such that

$$(0.2.6) \qquad X^{0,\pi,0}(T) = M^\pi(T) = a, \quad \text{a.s.}$$

To see this, consider the martingale

$$Q(t) \triangleq \int_0^t \frac{dW(s)}{\sqrt{T-s}}, \qquad 0 \leq t < T$$

with quadratic variation $\langle Q \rangle(t) = \int_0^t (ds)/(T-s) = \log(T/(T-t))$ and $\mathbb{E}\,Q(t) = 0$, $0 \leq t < T$. From Theorem 3.4.6 in Karatzas & Shreve (1991), have $Q(t) = B(\log(T/(T-t)))$, where $B(u) \triangleq Q(T - Te^{-u})$, $0 \leq u < \infty$ is Brownian motion. Therefore, the $\mathbb{F}$-stopping time $\tau_a \triangleq \inf\{t \in [0,T)/Q(t) = a\} \wedge T$ satisfies $\mathbb{P}(0 < \tau_a < T) = 1$; and the portfolio $\pi(t) \triangleq (1/\sqrt{T-t})\mathbf{1}_{\{t \leq \tau_a\}}$ has the properties $\int_0^T \pi^2(t)\,dt = \log(T/(T-\tau_a)) < \infty$, a.s. and $M^\pi(t) = \int_0^t (1/\sqrt{T-s})\mathbf{1}_{\{s \leq \tau_a\}}\,dW(s) = Q(t \wedge \tau_a)$, $0 \leq t \leq T$, so that (0.2.6) follows. Notice that (0.2.5) fails in this case;

for if it did not, we would have by Fatou's lemma $\mathbb{E}\,M^\pi(T) \le \underline{\lim}_{t\uparrow T}\mathbb{E}\,M^\pi(t) = 0$, contradicting (0.2.6). This example is due to S. E. Shreve.

Even among tame portfolios, however, there are some that contradict a basic tenet of the reality available to most of us, according to which "there is no free lunch".

0.2.3. DEFINITION. A tame portfolio $\pi(\cdot)$ that satisfies

$$(0.2.7) \qquad \mathbb{P}\big[M^\pi(T) \ge 0\big] = 1, \quad \mathbb{P}\big[M^\pi(T) > 0\big] > 0$$

is called an *arbitrage opportunity* (or "free-lunch"). We say that a market $\mathcal{M}$ is *arbitrage-free* if no such portfolios exist in it.

The "free-lunch" interpretation of (0.2.7) should be clear: starting with zero initial capital at $t = 0$, and employing the strategy $\pi(\cdot)$, we end up at time $t = T$ with wealth $X(T) = X^{0,\pi,0}(T) = B(T)M^\pi(T)$, no exposure to risk whatsoever $\big(X(T) \ge 0,$ a.s.$\big)$, and positive probability of gain $\big(\mathbb{P}\big(X(T) > 0\big) > 0\big)$.

Here is an example, due to A. V. Skorohod and communicated to me by S. Levental, of a *tame portfolio that satisfies* (0.2.7). Consider a market $\mathcal{M}$ with $n = d = 1$, $T = 1$, $r(\cdot) \equiv 0$, $\sigma(\cdot) \equiv 1$ and $b(\cdot) = 1/(R(\cdot))$, where $R(\cdot)$ is the Bessel process with drift

$$dR(t) = \left(\frac{1}{R(t)} - 2\right) dt + dW(t), \qquad R(0) = 1.$$

Now $R(\cdot)$ is ordinary Bessel process (with zero drift) under the probability measure

$$\tilde{\mathbb{P}}(A) = \mathbb{E}\left[e^{2(W(1)-1)}1_A\right], \quad A \in \mathcal{F}(1)$$

that makes $\tilde{W}(t) = W(t) - 2t$, $0 \le t \le 1$ a Brownian motion; therefore $\mathbb{P}\big[R(t) > 0,\ \forall\ 0 \le t \le 1\big] = \tilde{\mathbb{P}}\big[R(t) > 0,\ \forall\ 0 \le t \le 1\big] = 1$ (e.g. Karatzas & Shreve (1991), pp. 157–162). Clearly, the discounted gains process of the constant portfolio $\pi(\cdot) \equiv 1$ is

$$M^\pi(t) = W(t) + \int_0^t \frac{ds}{R(s)} = 2t - 1 + R(t), \qquad 0 \le t \le 1$$

so that $\mathbb{P}\big[M^\pi(t) \ge -1, \forall\ 0 \le t \le 1\big] = 1$ ($\pi(\cdot)$ is tame), and $\mathbb{P}\big[M^\pi(1) = 1+R(T) > 1\big] = 1$ ($\pi(\cdot)$ is an arbitrage opportunity). Thus, the market $\mathcal{M}$ of this example is *not* arbitrage-free.

Are there simple, easy-to-test criteria on the structure of a given market model $\mathcal{M}$, that can help us decide whether $\mathcal{M}$ contains arbitrage opportunities or not? The next is a result in this direction.

0.2.4. THEOREM. (i) *If $\mathcal{M}$ is arbitrage-free, then there exists a progressively measurable process $\theta\colon [0,T] \times \Omega \to \mathbb{R}^d$, called* market price of risk (*or* "relative-risk") *process, such that*

$$(0.2.8) \qquad b(t) - r(t)\mathbf{1}_n = \sigma(t)\theta(t), \qquad 0 \le t \le T \text{ a.s.}$$

(ii) *Conversely, if such a process $\theta(\cdot)$ exists and satisfies, in addition to the above requirements,*

$$(0.2.9) \qquad \int_0^T \big\|\theta(t)\big\|^2 dt < \infty, \text{ a.s.}$$

and

$$(0.2.10) \qquad \mathbb{E}\left[\exp\left\{-\int_0^T \theta'(t)\,dW(t) - \frac{1}{2}\int_0^T \|\theta(t)\|^2\,dt\right\}\right] = 1,$$

then $\mathcal{M}$ is arbitrage-free.

From Novikov's theorem (Proposition 3.5.12 in Karatzas & Shreve (1991)), the conditions (0.2.9), (0.2.10) are satisfied if $\mathbb{E}\left[\exp\{\frac{1}{2}\int_0^T \|\theta(t)\|^2\,dt\}\right] < \infty$ holds; in particular, if $\theta(\cdot)$ is bounded uniformly in (t, w).

0.2.5. DEFINITION. Consider a market model $\mathcal{M}$ with $n \leq d$, for which there exists an $\mathbb{F}$-progessively measurable process $\theta\colon [0, T] \times \Omega \to \mathbb{R}^d$ satisfying (0.2.8)–(0.2.10); then $\mathcal{M}$ will be called *standard*.

For a standard market $\mathcal{M}$, the exponential process

$$(0.2.11) \qquad Z_0(t) \triangleq \exp\left[-\int_0^t \theta'(s)\,dW(s) - \frac{1}{2}\int_0^t \|\theta(s)\|^2\,ds\right], \qquad 0 \leq t \leq T$$

is a martingale, and thus

$$(0.2.12) \qquad \mathbb{P}^0(A) \triangleq \mathbb{E}\left[Z_0(T)1_A\right], \quad A \in \mathcal{F}(T)$$

defines a probability measure which is equivalent (mutually absolutely continuous with respect) to $\mathbb{P}$, with likelihood ratio process

$$\frac{d\mathbb{P}^0}{d\mathbb{P}}\bigg|_{\mathcal{F}(t)} = Z_0(t), \qquad 0 \leq t \leq T.$$

This $\mathbb{P}^0$ is the so-called *risk-neutral* (or "yield-equating") *equivalent martingale measure*. Under $\mathbb{P}^0$, the process

$$(0.2.13) \qquad W^{(0)}(t) \triangleq W(t) + \int_0^t \theta(s)\,ds, \qquad 0 \leq t \leq T$$

is Brownian motion, by Girsanov (Theorem 3.5.1 in Karatzas & Shreve (1991)), and thus the equations of (0.1.2) become

$$(0.2.14) \qquad dP_i(t) = P_i(t)\left[r(t)\,dt + \sum_{j=1}^d \sigma_{ij}(t)\,dW_j^{(0)}(t)\right], \qquad i = 1,\ldots,n$$

or equivalently

$$(0.2.15) \qquad d\big(\gamma(t)P_i(t)\big) = \big(\gamma(t)P_i(t)\big)\sum_{j=1}^d \sigma_{ij}(t)\,dW_j^{(0)}(t), \qquad i = 1,\ldots,n.$$

In other words, under $\mathbb{P}^0$ the stock appreciation rates $b_i(\cdot)$ are replaced in (0.1.2) by the interest rate $r(\cdot)$, as in (0.2.14), whence the terminology "yield-equating" or "risk-neutral". Furthermore, (0.2.15) shows that the discounted stock-prices $\gamma(\cdot)P_i(\cdot)$ become local martingales under $\mathbb{P}^0$ (*martingales*, under the Novikov condition $\mathbb{E}\left[\exp\{\frac{1}{2}\int_0^T \|\sigma(t)\|^2\,dt\}\right] < \infty$), whence the term "martingale measure". Finally, the measures $\mathbb{P}$ and $\mathbb{P}^0$ are equivalent, whence the terminology "equivalent" martingale measure.

0.2.6. REMARK. The condition $n \leq d$ in Definition 0.2.5 is no real restriction, because otherwise the number of stocks can always be reduced, by duplicating some of them as "mutual funds" (that is, (t, w)-dependent linear combinations) of others.

If the volatility matrix $\sigma(t, w)$ has full (row) rank, then we may take

$$(0.2.16) \qquad \theta(t) = \sigma'(t)\big(\sigma(t)\sigma'(t)\big)^{-1}\big[b(t) - r(t)\mathbf{1}_n\big]$$

in (0.2.8).

0.2.7. REMARK. In an arbitrage-free market $\mathcal{M}$, the discounted gains process $M^\pi(\cdot)$ of (0.2.4) and the wealth-equation of (0.2.2) can be written, equivalently, as

$$M^\pi(t) = \int_0^t \gamma(s)\pi'(s)\sigma(s)\,dW^{(0)}(s)$$

$$(0.2.17) \qquad \gamma(t)X^{x,\pi,C}(t) = x - \int_{(0,t]} \gamma(s)\,dC(s) + \int_0^t \gamma(s)\pi'(s)\sigma(s)\,dW^{(0)}(s),$$

$$0 \leq t \leq T$$

respectively, in terms of the process $W^{(0)}(\cdot)$ of (0.2.13). In particular, *if $\mathcal{M}$ is standard*, then

$$(0.2.18) \qquad \left\{ \begin{array}{l} \gamma(t)X^{x,\pi,C}(t) + \displaystyle\int_{(0,t]} \gamma(s)\,dC(s) = x + M^\pi(t), \qquad 0 \leq t \leq T \\[2mm] \text{is a local martingale under the probability measure } \mathbb{P}^0 \text{ of (0.2.12)} \end{array} \right\}.$$

If the portfolio $\pi(\cdot)$ is tame, then this local martingale is bounded from below, hence is a *supermartingale*, and the optional sampling theorem gives

$$(0.2.19) \quad \mathbb{E}^0\left[\gamma(\tau)X^{x,\pi,C}(\tau) + \int_{(0,\tau]} \gamma(s)\,dC(s)\right] = x + \mathbb{E}^0 M^\pi(\tau) \leqq x, \ \forall \ \tau \in \mathcal{S}.$$

Here $\mathbb{E}^0$ denotes expectation with respect to the probability measure $\mathbb{P}^0$ of (0.2.12), and $\mathcal{S}$ is the class of $\mathbb{F}$-stopping times with values in $[0, T]$.

SKETCH OF PROOF FOR THEOREM 0.2.4. Let $\pi(\cdot)$ be a tame portfolio.

(a) Suppose that $\mathcal{M}$ is standard, i.e., that (0.2.8)–(0.2.10) are satisfied for some $\theta \colon [0, T] \times \Omega \to \mathbb{R}^n$ progressively measurable. If $\pi(\cdot)$ is an arbitrage opportunity, we have $M^\pi(T) \geq 0$ a.s. from (0.2.7), as well as $\mathbb{E}^0 M^\pi(T) \leq 0$ from (0.2.19); therefore $M^\pi(T) = 0$ a.s., which contradicts $\mathbb{P}\big[M^\pi(T) > 0\big] > 0$ of (0.2.7).

(b) Recall the definition (0.2.4) of the discounted gains process, and suppose there exists a set $A \subseteq [0, T] \times \Omega$ with positive product measure $(\lambda \otimes \mathbb{P})(A) > 0$, where λ denotes Lebesgue measure, such that we have

$$(0.2.20) \qquad \left\{ \begin{array}{ll} \sigma'\pi = \mathbf{0}; & \text{(no exposure to risk)} \\[1mm] \pi'(b - r\mathbf{1}_n) \neq 0; & \text{(non-zero rate)} \end{array} \right\}$$

on A. For an arbitrary $k > 0$, construct a new portfolio process

$$\hat{\pi} \triangleq \left\{ \begin{array}{ll} k\,\mathrm{sgn}\big(\pi'(b - r\mathbf{1}_n)\big)\pi; & \text{on } A \\[1mm] 0; & \text{on } A^c \end{array} \right\}$$

so that, from (0.2.4),

$$M^{\hat{\pi}}(T) = \begin{cases} k \displaystyle\int_0^T \gamma(s) \big| \pi'(s) \big(b(s) - r(s) \mathbf{1}_n \big) \big| \, ds > 0; & \text{on } B \\ 0; & \text{on } B^c \end{cases}$$

for some $B \in \mathcal{F}(T)$ with $\mathbb{P}(B) > 0$.

Clearly, $\hat{\pi}(\cdot)$ is then an arbitrage opportunity; in order to rule it out we must have, by (0.2.20), that *every vector in* $Kernel\big(\sigma'(t,w)\big)$ *must be orthogonal to* $b(t,w) - r(t,w)\mathbf{1}_n$, for a.e. (t,w). Thus $b(t,w) - r(t,w)\mathbf{1}_n$ should belong to $\big(Kernel\big(\sigma'(t,w)\big)\big)^{\perp} = Range\big(\sigma(t,w)\big)$, which is precisely (0.2.8). It can then be shown that $\theta(\cdot)$ can be selected in (0.2.8) so as to be progressively measurable. $\square$

0.2.8. REMARK. One may replace the process $C(\cdot)$ in (0.2.1), (0.2.2) and in (0.2.17)–(0.2.19) by $C(\cdot) - E(\cdot)$, where $E(\cdot)$ is another increasing, adapted process with right-continuous paths and $E(0) = 0$, $E(T) < \infty$ a.s. Then $E(t)$ has the interpretation of *cumulative endowment* (income) up to time t. We shall use this setup in Chapter 3, as well as in Section 1.4, where we shall also employ the notation $X^{x,\pi,C-E}(\cdot)$ for the solution of the analogue

$$(0.2.21) \qquad \gamma(t)X(t) \equiv x + \int_{(0,t]} \gamma(s)dE(s) - \int_{(0,t]} \gamma(s)\,dC(s)$$
$$+ \int_0^t \gamma(s)\pi'(s)\sigma(s)\,dW^{(0)}(s), \qquad 0 \le t \le T$$

of (0.2.17).

0.3. Completeness

Let us place ourselves in the context of a *standard* market model $\mathcal{M}$, as in Definition 0.2.5. We shall call *contingent claim* any $\mathcal{F}(T)$-measurable random variable $Y \colon \Omega \to [0, \infty)$ with

$$(0.3.1) \qquad u_0 \triangleq \mathbb{E}^0\big[\gamma(T)Y\big] = \mathbb{E}\big[\gamma(T)Z_0(T)Y\big] < \infty.$$

As a typical example let $Y = \varphi\big(P(T)\big)$, where $\varphi \colon (0,\infty)^d \to [0,\infty)$ is a given function and $P(T) = \big(P_1(T), \dots, P_d(T)\big)'$ is the vector of stock prices at time T. Here the value $Y(w)$ is *contingent* on the value of the random vector $P(T,w)$ at the terminal time $t = T$, which of course is not known in advance at $t = 0$.

0.3.1. DEFINITION. A contingent claim Y is called *attainable*, if there exists a tame portfolio $\pi(\cdot)$ with

$$(0.3.2) \qquad X^{u_0,\pi,0}(T) = Y, \text{ a.s.}$$

The standard market model $\mathcal{M}$ is called *complete*, if every contingent claim is attainable; otherwise it is called *incomplete*.

0.3.2. EXERCISE. In the Definition 0.3.1 of attainability, the requirement of "tameness" can be replaced by the requirement that "$M^{\pi}(\cdot)$ is a $\mathbb{P}^0$-martingale".

$\big($*Hint*: Indeed, suppose we have $\gamma(T)Y = u_0 + M^{\pi}(T)$ for some portfolio $\pi(\cdot)$. If $\pi(\cdot)$ is tame, then $M^{\pi}(\cdot)$ is a $\mathbb{P}^0$-supermartingale from Remark 0.2.7, with $\mathbb{E}^0 M^{\pi}(T) = \mathbb{E}^0\big(\gamma(T)Y\big) - u_0 = 0 = \mathbb{E}^0 M^{\pi}(0)$, hence a $\mathbb{P}^0$-martingale. If $M^{\pi}(\cdot)$

is a $\mathbb{P}^0$-martingale, then $M^\pi(t) = \mathbb{E}^0\big[M^\pi(T) \mid \mathcal{F}(t)\big] = \mathbb{E}^0\big[\gamma(T)Y \mid \mathcal{F}(t)\big] - u_0 \geq -u_0 > -\infty$, $\forall\, 0 \leq t \leq T$, so $\pi(\cdot)$ is tame.)

0.3.3. EXERCISE. If $x < u_0$, there can be no tame portfolio $\pi(\cdot)$ with $X^{x,\pi,0}(T) \geq Y$, a.s.

(Hint: For suppose there were; then $u_0 = \mathbb{E}^0\big[\gamma(T)Y\big] \leq x$, from (0.2.19).)

0.3.4. EXERCISE. If $x > u_0$, there can be no tame portfolio $\pi(\cdot)$ with $X^{x,\pi,0}(T) = Y$ a.s. and such that $M^\pi(\cdot)$ is a martingale.

For our standard market model $\mathcal{M}$, there is a very simple criterion to decide whether $\mathcal{M}$ is complete; it requires that there be exactly as many stocks as "sources of uncertainty"; and that these latter "should appear in the driving terms of all the equations (0.1.2), in a non-singular fashion".

0.3.5. THEOREM. *A standard market model $\mathcal{M}$ is complete, if and only if*
(i) *$n = d$, and*
(ii) *$\sigma(t,w)$ is non-singular, for $(\lambda \otimes \mathbb{P}) -$ a.e. $(t,w) \in [0,T] \times \Omega$.*

PROOF OF SUFFICIENCY. Suppose that the conditions (i), (ii) hold and, for an arbitrary contingent claim Y, consider the $\mathbb{P}^0$-martingale $\hat{M}(t) \triangleq \mathbb{E}^0\big[\gamma(T)Y \mid \mathcal{F}(t)\big]$, $0 \leq t \leq T$. From the representation of Brownian martingales as stochastic integrals, it can be shown that there exists a progressively measurable $\varphi\colon [0,T] \times \Omega \to \mathbb{R}^n$ with $\int_0^T \|\varphi(t)\|^2\, dt < \infty$ and

$$(0.3.3) \qquad \hat{M}(t) = u_0 + \int_0^t \varphi'(s)\, dW^{(0)}(s), \qquad 0 \leq t \leq T$$

almost surely (cf. Exercise 0.3.6 below). Now define a process $\hat{\pi}\colon [0,T] \times \Omega \to \mathbb{R}^n$ by $\hat{\pi}'(t) \triangleq B(t)\varphi'(t)\sigma^{-1}(t)$; it is not hard to check that $\hat{\pi}(\cdot)$ satisfies the requirements of Definition 0.2.1(ii) for a portfolio process, and that we have

$$(0.3.4) \quad \hat{M}(t) = u_0 + \int_0^t \gamma(s)\hat{\pi}'(s)\sigma(s)\, dW^{(0)}(s) = u_0 + M^{\hat{\pi}}(t) = \gamma(t)X^{u_0,\hat{\pi},0}(t),$$
$$0 \leq t \leq T$$

(in particular, $X^{u_0,\hat{\pi},0}(T) = \hat{M}(T)/\gamma(T) = Y$) a.s. Clearly the process $M^{\hat{\pi}}(\cdot)$ is a $\mathbb{P}^0$-martingale, and is bounded from below by $-u_0$, so $\hat{\pi}(\cdot)$ is a tame portfolio. Thus Y is attainable, and $\mathcal{M}$ is complete. $\square$

PROOF OF NECESSITY (argument due to S. E. Shreve). Let us suppose that the market $\mathcal{M}$ is complete, and consider the bounded, $\mathbb{F}$-adapted process $\psi(t) \triangleq f\big(\sigma(t)\big)$, $0 \leq t \leq T$ where f is the mapping of Exercise 0.3.7 below, as well as the $\mathcal{F}(T)$-measurable random variable

$$Y \triangleq B(T)\left[1 + \int_0^T \psi'(s)\, dW^{(0)}(s)\right] = Y^+ - Y^-.$$

We have $\mathbb{E}^0\big[\gamma(T)|Y|\big] = \mathbb{E}^0\big[\gamma(T)(Y^+ + Y^-)\big] < \infty$, $\mathbb{E}^0\big[\gamma(T)Y\big] = \mathbb{E}^0\big[\gamma(T) \times (Y^+ - Y^-)\big] = 1$. Since $Y^\pm$ are attainable, there exist portfolios $\pi_\pm(\cdot)$ such that $M^{\pi_\pm}(\cdot)$ are $\mathbb{P}^0$-martingales (Exercise 0.3.2) and

$$M^{\pi_\pm}(T) = \int_0^T \gamma(s)\pi_\pm'(s)\sigma(s)\, dW^{(0)}(s) = \gamma(T)Y^\pm - E^0\big[\gamma(T)Y^\pm\big], \text{ a.s.}$$

Then with $\pi \triangleq \pi_+ - \pi_-$, the process $M^\pi = M^{\pi+} - M^{\pi-}$ is also a $\mathbb{P}^0$-martingale, and

$$M^\pi(T) = \int_0^T \gamma(s)\pi'(s)\sigma(s)\,dW^{(0)}(s) = \gamma(T)Y - \mathbb{E}^0\big(\gamma(T)Y\big)$$

$$= \gamma(T)Y - 1 = \int_0^T \psi'(s)\,dW^{(0)}(s).$$

But $\int_0^\cdot \psi'(s)\,dW^{(0)}(s)$ is also a $\mathbb{P}^0$-martingale, so we deduce

$$\int_0^t \gamma(s)\pi'(s)\sigma(s)\,dW^{(0)}(s) = \int_0^t \psi'(s)\,dW^{(0)}(s), \qquad 0 \leq t \leq T$$

almost surely, as well as

$$\psi(t,w) = \gamma(t,w)\sigma'(t,w)\pi(t,w) \in Range\big(\sigma'(t,w)\big) = \big(Kernel\big(\sigma(t,w)\big)\big)^\perp,$$

$(\lambda \otimes \mathbb{P})$ - a.e. on $[0,T] \times \Omega$. But $\psi(t,w) \in Kernel\big(\sigma(t,w)\big)$, and $\psi(t,w) \neq \mathbf{0}$ if $Kernel\big(\sigma(t,w)\big) \neq \{\mathbf{0}\}$ (Exercise 0.3.7). We deduce that $Kernel\big(\sigma(t,w)\big) = \{\mathbf{0}\}$, and conditions (i), (ii) follow. $\qquad\square$

Under the conditions of Theorem 0.3.5, there is only one process $\theta(\cdot)$ satisfying (0.2.8), namely

$$(0.3.5) \qquad \theta(t) = \sigma^{-1}(t)\big[b(t) - r(t)\mathbf{1}_d\big], \qquad 0 \leq t \leq T.$$

0.3.6. EXERCISE. Justify the representation (0.3.3).

(*Hint*: Use the martingale representation Theorem 3.4.15, as well as Problem 3.4.16, in Karatzas & Shreve (1991). Use also the "Bayes rule"

$$(0.3.6) \qquad \mathbb{E}^0\big[Q \mid \mathcal{F}(s)\big] = \frac{\mathbb{E}\big[QZ_0(t) \mid \mathcal{F}(s)\big]}{Z_0(s)}, \quad \text{a.s.}$$

which is valid for $0 \leq s \leq t \leq T$ and any $\mathcal{F}(t)$-measurable random variable $Q\colon \Omega \to [0,\infty).$)

0.3.7. EXERCISE. There exists a bounded, measurable function $f\colon L(\mathbb{R}^d;\mathbb{R}^n) \to \mathbb{R}^d$ such that: $f(\sigma) \in Kernel(\sigma)$, $f(\sigma) \neq \mathbf{0}$ if $Kernel(\sigma) \neq \{\mathbf{0}\}$, hold for every $\sigma \in L(\mathbb{R}^d;\mathbb{R}^n)$.

(*Hint*: Just let $\mathbf{e}_1,\ldots,\mathbf{e}_d$ be basis vectors in $\mathbb{R}^d$, and set $m(\sigma) \triangleq 1$ if $Kernel(\sigma) = \{\mathbf{0}\}$, $m(\sigma) \triangleq \min\{i = 1,\ldots,d/\operatorname{proj}_{Kernel(\sigma)}(\mathbf{e}_i) \neq \mathbf{0}\}$ otherwise. Then $f(\sigma) \triangleq \operatorname{proj}_{Kernel(\sigma)}(\mathbf{e}_{m(\sigma)})$ can be shown to be Borel-measurable.)

0.3.8. EXERCISE. In a *standard, complete* market-model $\mathcal{M}$, suppose that the coefficients $r(\cdot)$, $b_i(\cdot)$, $\sigma_{ij}(\cdot)$, $1 \leq i, j \leq d$ are of the form $\Gamma\big(t, P(\cdot)\big)$, $0 \leq t \leq T$, where $P(\cdot) = \big(P_1(\cdot),\ldots,P_d(\cdot)\big)'$ is the vector of stock-price processes and $\Gamma\colon [0,T] \times C\big([0,T];\mathbb{R}^d\big) \to \mathbb{R}$ a progressively measurable functional (Definition 3.5.15 and pp. 302–311 in Karatzas & Shreve (1991)). In other words, assume that the coefficients are (nonanticipative) functionals of past and present stock-prices. If the resulting system of Stochastic (Functional-) Differential Equations (0.1.2) has a pathwise unique, strong solution, argue that the augmentation of the filtration

$$(0.3.7) \qquad \mathcal{F}^P(t) = \sigma\big(P(s), 0 \leq s \leq t\big), \qquad 0 \leq t \leq T$$

generated by the stock-prices coincides then with the filtration $\mathbb{F}$ of (0.1.3). If, furthermore, the resulting system of equations (0.2.14) also has a pathwise unique, strong solution, then $\mathbb{F}$ coincides as well with the (augmented) filtration generated by the process $W^{(0)}(\cdot)$ of (0.2.13); and in this case, the representation (0.3.3) follows directly from the "classical" martingale representation property of the Brownian motion, without additional arguments as in Exercise 0.3.6.

The first part of these lectures (Chapters 1–3) will deal exclusively with *complete markets*. Part II (Chapters 4–6) will discuss various aspects of *incomplete markets* (and more generally, markets with constraints on portfolio choice), including transaction costs (Chapter 7).

0.4. Hedging

Let us place ourselves within the context of a standard, complete market model $\mathcal{M}$, as in Definition 0.2.5 and Theorem 0.3.5, and recall the notion of contingent claim from the beginning of Section 3.

Consider the following situation: two agents enter at time $t = 0$ into an agreement. One of them, called the *seller*, agrees to provide the second agent with a (random) payment $Y(w) \geq 0$ at time $t = T$, where Y is a contingent claim: a nonnegative, $\mathcal{F}(T)$-measurable random variable satisfying (0.3.1). In return for this commitment, the second agent, called the *buyer*, agrees to pay to the seller a certain amount $x \geq 0$ at time $t = 0$. *What should this amount be?* In other words, what is the "fair price", at the initial time $t = 0$, for the promise to deliver the random amount $Y(w)$ at the "expiration time" $t = T$?

In order to answer this question, we have to consider the situations of the two agents separately.

The seller's objective is, starting with the amount $x \geq 0$ that he receives at time $t = 0$, to find a portfolio/consumption strategy $(\hat{\pi}, \hat{C})$ which enables him to make good on his commitment, i.e., to "hedge" the contingent claim Y at time $t = T$ in the sense that his capital will have grown by then enough to cover his obligation:

$$(0.4.1) \qquad\qquad X^{x,\hat{\pi},\hat{C}}(T) - Y \geq 0, \text{ a.s.}$$

The least initial amount $x \geq 0$ which enables the seller to achieve this, is called *upper hedging price* for the contingent claim Y at time $t = 0$, and is denoted by

$$(0.4.2) \qquad h_{\text{up}} \triangleq \inf\big\{ x \geq 0 \;/\; \exists (\hat{\pi}, \hat{C}) \text{ with } \hat{\pi}(\cdot) \text{ tame}, X^{x,\hat{\pi},\hat{C}}(T) \geq Y \text{ a.s.} \big\}.$$

This is the smallest price that the seller can accept from the buyer at time $t = 0$, which enables the seller to cover his obligation at $t = T$ *without risk*, in the sense of (0.4.1).

The buyer's objective is, starting with the initial amount $-x$ (a debt, as he pays $x \geq 0$ to the seller!), to find a portfolio/consumption strategy $(\check{\pi}, \check{C})$ so that the payment Y, which he receives at time $t = T$, makes it possible for him to cover the debt that he incurred at time $t = 0$ by purchasing the contingent claim:

$$(0.4.3) \qquad\qquad X^{-x,\check{\pi},\check{C}}(T) + Y \geq 0, \text{ a.s.}$$

The largest amount $x \geq 0$ that enables the buyer to achieve this, is called *lower hedging price* for the contingent claim Y at time $t = 0$, and is denoted by

$$(0.4.4) \qquad h_{\text{low}} \triangleq \sup \left\{ x \geq 0 \ \middle/ \ \begin{array}{l} \exists (\tilde{\pi}, \check{C}) \text{ with } M^{\tilde{\pi}}(\cdot) \text{ a } \mathbb{P}^0\text{-supermartingale,} \\ \text{and } X^{-x, \tilde{\pi}, \check{C}}(T) \geq -Y \text{ a.s.} \end{array} \right\}$$

(recall Remark 0.2.7, Exercise 0.3.2, and see Remark 4.6.6). This is the highest price that the buyer can afford to pay at time $t = 0$, which guarantees that he will be in a position to cover his debt at time $t = T$ *without risk*, in the sense of (0.4.3).

The following result justifies the terminology "upper" and "lower" hedging price.

0.4.1. PROPOSITION. *With $u_0 = \mathbb{E}\left[\gamma(T) Z_0(T) Y \right] < \infty$ as in (0.3.1), we have*

$$(0.4.5) \qquad\qquad\qquad 0 \leq h_{\text{low}} \leq u_0 \leq h_{\text{up}} \leq \infty.$$

PROOF. If the set of (0.4.2) is empty, then $h_{\text{up}} = \infty > u_0$; if not, then for any x in this set we have from (0.2.19), (0.4.1):

$$x \geq \mathbb{E}^0 \left[\gamma(T) X^{x, \tilde{\pi}, \hat{C}}(T) \right] \geq \mathbb{E}^0 \left[\gamma(T) Y \right] = u_0, \text{ thus } h_{\text{up}} \geq u_0.$$

On the other hand, the set of (0.4.4) is nonempty (it contains the origin), and for any $x \geq 0$ in this set:

$$-x \geq \mathbb{E}^0 \left[\gamma(T) X^{-x, \tilde{\pi}, \check{C}}(T) + \int_{(0,T]} \gamma(t) d\check{C}(t) \right] \geq -\mathbb{E}^0 \left[\gamma(T) Y \right] = -u_0$$

from (0.4.3), (0.2.19). Thus every element of the set in (0.4.4) is dominated by u_0, so $h_{\text{low}} \leq u_0$. $\qquad\square$

As we shall see in Theorem 1.2.1, we have in fact

$$(0.4.6) \qquad\qquad\qquad h_{\text{low}} = u_0 = h_{\text{up}}$$

for any contingent claim Y, if the market $\mathcal{M}$ is *complete*.

The corresponding situation for an incomplete (or, more generally, constrained) market, will be discussed in Sections 4.4, 4.6; in that case h_{up} and h_{low} will typically be different, and will be characterized in terms of *auxiliary stochastic control problems*.

0.4.2. REMARK. It can be shown that every price outside $[h_{\text{low}}, h_{\text{up}}]$ leads to an arbitrage opportunity, while no price in the interior of this interval does; see Exercise 4.3.3 and the discussion preceding it.

Part 1

Complete markets

CHAPTER 1

Pricing

1.1. Introduction

We shall take up in this Chapter the problem of *Pricing* (valuation) *for Contingent Claims*, or contractual obligations between a buyer and a seller, that we broached briefly in *Section* 0.4. This is an ancient problem, as old perhaps as economic history itself. Here we shall place ourselves in the context of a *complete market* where, as it turns out, the problem admits a very satisfactory solution.

Namely, as we shall see in *Section* 1.2, the upper- and lower-hedging prices of (0.4.2), (0.4.4), respectively, are the same in this context, and are equal to the expected discounted value $u_0 = \mathbb{E}^0\big[\gamma(T)Y\big]$ of the contingent claim Y under the equivalent martingale measure of (0.2.12). For a "European" call-option, this leads to the famous Black & Scholes (1973) formulae (1.3.13), (1.3.14). We discuss in *Section* 1.3 additional examples of "European" contingent claims (that can be exercised by their buyer only at a fixed time $t = T$), for which more-or-less explicit computations are possible: put-options, barrier options, average (or "Asian") options, and exchange options.

In *Section* 1.4 we take up the case of "American" contingent claims, which can be exercised by their holder (buyer) at any stopping time during a given time-interval $[0,T]$, the "lifetime" of the contingent claim. This feature makes the valuation problem much harder for such claims, as it involves the solution to a problem of *optimal stopping*: if $Y(\cdot)$ is the payoff of this contingent claim, then again the upper- and lower-hedging prices are the same, and equal to $\sup_{\tau \in \mathcal{S}} \mathbb{E}^0\big[\gamma(\tau)Y(\tau)\big]$, the maximal expected discounted value of the contingent claim under the equivalent martingale measure, over all stopping times $\tau \colon \Omega \to [0,T]$ (Theorem 1.4.3). Very few examples can now be computed in closed form; we discuss the "American" versions of the call-option, the put-option on an infinite horizon (for which the associated optimal stopping problem admits an explicit solution), and the put-option on a finite-horizon (whose solution reduces to a genuine moving-boundary problem).

1.2. European contingent claims

We shall place ourselves within the context of a *standard market model* $\mathcal{M}$ as in Definition 0.2.5, namely

$$(1.2.1) \qquad\qquad dB(t) = B(t)r(t)\,dt$$

$$(1.2.2) \quad dP_i(t) = P_i(t)\Big[b_i(t)\,dt + \sum_{j=1}^{d}\sigma_{ij}(t)\,dW_j(t)\Big], \quad P_i(0) = p_i \in (0,\infty)$$
$$\text{for } i = 1,\dots,d$$

which is also *complete*; that is, the number n of stocks is equal to the dimension d of the driving Brownian motion $W = (W_1, \ldots, W_d)'$, and the volatility matrix $\sigma(\cdot) = \{\sigma_{ij}(\cdot)\}_{1 \le i,j \le d}$ is invertible (Theorem 0.3.5). This model will be employed throughout the chapter.

A *European Contingent Claim* (ECC) will be for us, throughout this chapter, just an $\mathcal{F}(T)$-measurable random variable $Y: \Omega \to [0, \infty)$ with

$$(1.2.3) \qquad u_0 \triangleq \mathbb{E}^0\big[\gamma(T)Y\big] = \mathbb{E}\big[\gamma(T)Z_0(T)Y\big] \in (0, \infty),$$

as in the beginning of Section 0.3. The number u_0 of (1.2.3) is the expected discounted value of the contingent claim under the equivalent martingale measure $\mathbb{P}^0$ of (0.2.12).

Just as in Section 0.4, $Y(w)$ represents the size of a (random) payment that an agent, called the *seller*, undertakes to make to another agent, called the *buyer*, at the contractually specified time $t = T$. The size of this payment typically depends on the price of one of the underlying assets, at time T or during the entire interval $[0, T]$, as in the examples at the end of this section. And just as in Section 0.4, the question here again is *how much the buyer should pay at time $t = 0$ to the seller, in return for this obligation.*

We discussed in Section 0.4 the *upper* (h_{up}) and *lower* (h_{low}) *hedging prices* for Y in a general standard, complete market model $\mathcal{M}$. We observed that the interval $[h_{\text{low}}, h_{\text{up}}]$ contains the number u_0 of (1.2.3), and remarked that any price outside this interval leads to an arbitrage opportunity (Proposition 0.4.1 and Remark 0.4.2). For a *complete* market $\mathcal{M}$, as in the model considered here, the interval $[h_{\text{low}}, h_{\text{up}}]$ actually collapses to the point $\{u_0\}$, thus providing a complete answer to the pricing question.

1.2.1. THEOREM. *For a standard, complete market model $\mathcal{M}$ as in (1.2.1), (1.2.2), the infimum of (0.4.2) and the supremum of (0.4.4) are both attained, and equal*

$$(1.2.4) \qquad h_{\text{up}} = h_{\text{low}} = u_0 = \mathbb{E}^0\big[\gamma(T)Y\big] \in (0, \infty),$$

for any European Contingent Claim Y. Furthermore, there exists a tame portfolio $\hat{\pi}(\cdot)$ such that, with $\check{\pi}(\cdot) \triangleq -\hat{\pi}(\cdot)$ and

$$(1.2.5) \qquad \hat{X}(t) \triangleq \frac{1}{\gamma(t)}\mathbb{E}^0\big[\gamma(T)Y \mid \mathcal{F}(t)\big], \qquad 0 \le t \le T,$$

we have a.s.

$$(1.2.6) \qquad X^{u_0, \hat{\pi}, 0}(t) = -X^{-u_0, \check{\pi}, 0}(t) = \hat{X}(t), \qquad 0 \le t \le T.$$

PROOF. We already know that $h_{\text{low}} \le u_0 \le h_{\text{up}}$ from Proposition 0.4.1, so in order to prove (1.2.4) and the other claims of the theorem, *it suffices to exhibit a tame portfolio $\hat{\pi}(\cdot)$ such that, with $\check{\pi}(\cdot) \triangleq -\hat{\pi}(\cdot)$, $M^{\check{\pi}}(\cdot)$ is a $\mathbb{P}^0$-martingale and* (1.2.6) *holds.* Because then $X^{u_0, \hat{\pi}, 0}(T) = -X^{-u_0, \check{\pi}, 0}(T) = Y$ and thus u_0 belongs to both the sets of (0.4.2), (0.4.4)-meaning that we have also the inequalities $h_{\text{up}} \le u_0 \le h_{\text{low}}$.

In order to do this, just repeat verbatim the sufficiency proof of Theorem 0.3.5 and obtain

$$(1.2.7) \qquad \gamma(t)\hat{X}(t) = \hat{M}(t) \triangleq \mathbb{E}^0\big[\gamma(T)Y \mid \mathcal{F}(t)\big]$$

$$= u_0 + \int_0^t \gamma(s)\hat{\pi}'(s)\sigma(s)\,dW^{(0)}(s), \qquad 0 \le t \le T$$

as in (0.3.3), (0.3.4), from the martingale representation theorem (cf. Exercise 0.3.6) and the invertibility of the volatility matrix $\sigma(\cdot)$

Clearly $M^{\hat{\pi}}(\cdot) = -M^{\tilde{\pi}}(\cdot) = \hat{M}(\cdot) - u_0$ is a $\mathbb{P}^0$-martingale and is bounded from below by $-u_0 > -\infty$; thus $\hat{\pi}(\cdot)$ is a tame portfolio, and (1.2.6) holds. $\qquad \square$

The tame portfolio $\hat{\pi}(\cdot)$ is the *optimal hedging portfolio for the seller*, and $\tilde{\pi}(\cdot) = -\hat{\pi}(\cdot)$ the *optimal hedging portfolio for the buyer*. The process $\hat{X}(\cdot)$ of (1.2.5) is called the *price-process for the contingent claim, during the interval* $[0,T]$.

Here are some examples of European Contingent Claims.

1.2.2. EXAMPLE (European Call-Option). $Y = \big(P_m(T)-q\big)^+$ with "maturity" $T > 0$ and "exercise price" $q > 0$, $m = 1,\ldots,d$. The *buyer* of this contract has the option to buy, at time $t = T$, one share of the mth stock at the specified price $q > 0$; if $P_m(T) \le q$, the contract is worthless to him and he does not exercise his option. But if $P_m(T) > q$, the *seller* is obligated to sell at the price q, and thus the buyer can make a profit of $P_m(T) - q$ by selling then the share at its market price. Thus, this contract effectively obligates the seller to a payment of $Y = \big(P_m(T) - q\big)^+$ at time $t = T$.

1.2.3. EXAMPLE (European Put-Option). $Y = \big(q - P_m(T)\big)^+$ with "maturity" $T > 0$ and "exercise price" $q > 0$, $m = 1,\ldots,d$.

Similar to Example 1.2.2, except now the *buyer* of the contract has the option to sell at the specified price $q > 0$, and the *seller* of the contract the obligation to buy at this price (should the option be exercised).

1.2.4. EXAMPLE. $Y = \varphi\big(P_m(T)\big)$ where $\varphi : (0,\infty) \to [0,\infty)$ is convex increasing and satisfies a polynomial growth condition in $\|p\|$, and $m = 1,\ldots,d$. This is a generalization of Example 1.2.2.

1.2.5. EXAMPLE. $Y = \varphi\big(P(T)\big)$, for some function $\varphi : (0,\infty)^d \to [0,\infty)$, which is continuous, and with $P(t) = \big(P_1(t),\ldots,P_d(t)\big)'$ the vector of stock prices. This is a generalization of Examples 1.2.2–1.2.4.

1.2.6. EXAMPLE (Path-dependent option). $Y = \big(\max_{T-\delta \le t \le T} P_m(t) - q\big)^+$ for some $q \ge 0$, $0 < \delta \le T$, $m = 1,\ldots,d$.

1.2.7. EXAMPLE (Barrier option). $Y = \big(P_m(T) - q\big)^+ 1_{\{\tau_h \le T\}}$, for some $h > q > 0$, $h > p_m = P_m(0)$, $m = 1,\ldots,d$ and with $\tau_h \triangleq \inf\{t \in [0,\infty) \,/\, P_m(t) \ge h\}$. This is similar to the European call-option of Example 1.2.2, except that now the stock-price process $P_m(\cdot)$ has to reach a certain "barrier" level $h > q \vee p_m$ for the option to become "activated".

1.2.8. EXAMPLE (Asian Option). $Y = \big(\frac{1}{T}\int_0^T P_m(t)\,dt - q\big)^+$ on the mth stock, $m = 1,\ldots,d$. This is similar to a European call-option with exercise price $q > 0$ and maturity $T > 0$, except that now the "average stock-price" $\frac{1}{T}\int_0^T P_m(t)\,dt$, over the interval $[0,T]$, is used in place of the "terminal stock-price" $P_m(T)$.

1.2.9. EXAMPLE (Option to exchange asset 2 for asset 1 at time $t = T$). $Y = \big(P_1(T) - P_2(T)\big)^+$. This is similar to the European call-option of Example 1.2.2 with $m = 1$, except that now we replace the exercise price $q > 0$ by the price $P_2(T)$ of the second stock at time $t = T$.

1.3. Examples

We shall assume in this section that *the coefficients* $r(\cdot)$, $\sigma(\cdot) = \{\sigma_{ij}(\cdot)\}_{1\le i,j\le d}$ *are given constants* namely $r(\cdot) \equiv r \ge 0$, $\sigma(\cdot) \equiv \sigma \in L(\mathbb{R}^d; \mathbb{R}^d)$ a nonsingular $(d\times d)$ matrix, and we shall set $a \triangleq \sigma\sigma'$. Then the equations of (1.2.1), (1.2.2) become

$$(1.3.1) \qquad dB(t) = B(t)r\,dt, \quad B(0) = 1$$

$$(1.3.2) \qquad dP_i(t) = P_i(t)\left[b_i(t)\,dt + \sum_{j=1}^d \sigma_{ij}\,dW_j(t)\right]$$

$$= P_i(t)\left[r\,dt + \sum_{j=1}^d \sigma_{ij}\,dW_j^{(0)}(t)\right],$$

$$P_i(0) = p_i \in (0,\infty), \qquad i = 1,\dots,d$$

in the notation of (0.2.11)–(0.2.14) and (0.3.5). In particular, $B(t) = 1/\gamma(t) = e^{rt}$ and

$$(1.3.3) \quad P_i(t) = H_i\big(t - s, P(s), \sigma\big(W^{(0)}(t) - W^{(0)}(s)\big)\big);$$
$$0 \le s \le t \le T, \qquad i = 1,\dots d,$$

where the function $H = (H_1,\dots,H_d)\colon [0,\infty) \times (0,\infty)^d \times \mathbb{R}^d \to (0,\infty)$ is defined by

$$(1.3.4) \qquad H_i(u,p,y) \triangleq p_i \exp\left[u\left(r - \frac{1}{2}a_{ii}\right) + y_i\right], \qquad i = 1,\dots d$$

and

$$(1.3.5) \qquad P(t) = \big(P_1(t),\dots,P_d(t)\big)', \qquad 0 \le t \le T.$$

1.3.1. EXAMPLE. In the case $Y = \varphi\big(P(T)\big)$ of Example 1.2.5 with $\varphi\colon (0,\infty)^d \to [0,\infty)$ continuous and satisfying polynomial growth conditions in both $\|p\|$ and $1/\|p\|$, we have from (1.2.5), (1.3.3):

$$\hat{X}(t) = \mathbb{E}^0\big[e^{-r(T-t)}\varphi\big(P(T)\big) \mid \mathcal{F}(t)\big]$$
$$= e^{-r(T-t)}\mathbb{E}^0\big[(\varphi \circ H)\big(T - t, P(t), \sigma\big(W^{(0)}(T) - W^0(t)\big)\big) \mid \mathcal{F}(t)\big]$$
$$= e^{-r(T-t)}\int_{\mathbb{R}^d} (\varphi \circ H)(T - t, P(t), \sigma\xi)G_{T-t}(\xi)\,d\xi, \qquad 0 \le t < T$$

and $\hat{X}(T) = \varphi\big(P(T)\big)$, where

$$(1.3.6) \qquad G_s(\xi) \triangleq (2\pi s)^{-d/2}\exp\left(-\frac{\|\xi\|^2}{2s}\right); \qquad s > 0, \quad \xi \in \mathbb{R}^d.$$

In other words, with

$$(1.3.7) \quad U(s,p) \triangleq \begin{cases} e^{-rs}\int_{\mathbb{R}^d}(\varphi \circ H)(s,p,\sigma\xi)G_s(\xi)\,d\xi; & s > 0, \quad p \in (0,\infty)^d \\ \varphi(p); & s = 0, \quad p \in (0,\infty)^d, \end{cases}$$

the price-process of the European Contingent Claim $Y = \varphi(P(T))$ *is given by*

$$(1.3.8) \qquad \hat{X}(t) = U(T - t, P(t)), \qquad 0 \le t \le T.$$

Now from the Feynman-Kac theorem (e.g. Karatzas & Shreve (1991), p. 366) the function of (1.3.7) is also the unique solution of the *Cauchy problem*

$$(1.3.9) \qquad \begin{cases} \frac{\partial U}{\partial s} = \frac{1}{2}p'\sigma(D^2U)\sigma'p + rp'DU - rU; & s > 0, \quad p \in (0, \infty)^d \\ U(0, p) = \varphi(p); & p \in (0, \infty)^d \end{cases}$$

where the vector $DU = (\partial U/\partial x_1, \ldots, \partial U/\partial x_d)'$ is the gradient of U, and the matrix $D^2U = \{\partial^2 U/\partial x_i \partial x_j\}_{1 \le i,j \le d}$ the Hessian; see Friedman (1964) for the general theory of linear, parabolic partial differential equations.

From (1.3.8), (1.3.9) and (1.3.2), it develops with the help of Itô's rule that the process $\hat{X}(\cdot)$ satisfies the equation (1.2.7), namely

$$d\hat{X}(t) = r\hat{X}(t)\, dt + \hat{\pi}'(t)\sigma\, dW^{(0)}(t), \quad \hat{X}(0) = U(T, P(0))$$

with $\hat{\pi}(\cdot) = (\hat{\pi}_1(\cdot), \ldots, \hat{\pi}_d(\cdot))'$ given by

$$(1.3.10) \qquad \hat{\pi}_i(t) = P_i(t) \cdot \frac{\partial U}{\partial p_i}(T - t, P_i(t)); \qquad 0 \le t < T, \qquad i = 1, \ldots, d.$$

In other words, the portfolio $\hat{\pi}(\cdot)$ of (1.3.10) is the *optimal hedging portfolio of* Theorem 1.2.1; at any given time t, it holds $(\partial U/\partial p_i)(T - t, P_i(t))$ shares of the ith stock, $i = 1, \ldots, d$. Clearly, the price u_0 of the contingent claim at time $t = 0$ is given by

$$(1.3.11) \qquad u_0 = \hat{X}(0) = U(T, P(0)), \quad \text{as in (1.3.7).}$$

1.3.2. EUROPEAN CALL-OPTION. If we take $d = 1$, $\sigma = \sigma_{11} > 0$ and $\varphi(p) = (p - q)^+$, $0 < p < \infty$ in the previous example, we recover the *European Call-Option*

$$(1.3.12) \qquad Y = (P_1(T) - q)^+$$

with exercise price $q > 0$. In this case, the Gaussian integration of (1.3.7) can be carried out very explicitly, yielding the famous *Black & Scholes* (1973) *formula*

$$(1.3.13) \quad U(s, p; q)$$

$$= \begin{cases} p\Phi(\mu_+(s, p; q)) - qe^{-rs}\Phi(\mu_-(s, p; q)); & s > 0, \ 0 < p < \infty \\ (p - q)^+; & s = 0, \ 0 < p < \infty \end{cases}$$

with

$$(1.3.14) \qquad \mu_\pm(s, p; q) \triangleq \frac{1}{\sigma\sqrt{s}}\left[\log\left(\frac{p}{q}\right) + \left(r \pm \frac{\sigma^2}{2}\right)s\right],$$

$$\Phi(z) \triangleq \frac{1}{\sqrt{2\pi}}\int_{-\infty}^{z} e^{-u^2/2}\, du.$$

A particularly attractive feature of this celebrated formula, which accounts to considerable extent for its use in the everyday practice of finance, is that *it does not involve the stock appreciation rate* $b(\cdot)$ *at all*. This rate is, in practice, very hard to compute or estimate. By contrast, the interest rate $r(\cdot)$ is directly observable, and the volatility $\sigma(\cdot)$ can in principle be estimated (although with some difficulty) on the basis of historical data for stock-prices.

1.3.3. EUROPEAN PUT-OPTION. $Y = \bigl(q - P_1(T)\bigr)^+$ with $d = 1$, $\sigma = \sigma_{11} > 0$. The price-process of this option can be computed easily from that of the European Call-Option, since $P_1(t)e^{-rt}$ is a $\mathbb{P}^0$-martingale:

$$\hat{X}(t) = \mathbb{E}^0\bigl[e^{-r(T-t)}\bigl(q - P_1(T)\bigr)^+ \mid \mathcal{F}(t)\bigr]$$

$$= e^{-r(T-t)}\mathbb{E}^0\bigl[\bigl(q - P_1(T)\bigr) + \bigl(P_1(T) - q\bigr)^+ \mid \mathcal{F}(t)\bigr]$$

$$= qe^{-r(T-t)} - P_1(t) + U\bigl(T - t, P_1(t); q\bigr), \qquad 0 \le t \le T,$$

or equivalently $\hat{X}(t) = \tilde{U}\bigl(T - t, P_1(t); q\bigr)$, where

$$(1.3.15) \quad \tilde{U}(s, p; q)$$

$$\triangleq \left\{ \begin{array}{ll} qe^{-rs}\Phi\bigl(-\mu_-(s, p; q)\bigr) - p\Phi\bigl(-\mu_+(s, p; q)\bigr); & s > 0, \; 0 < p < \infty \\ (q - p)^+; & s = 0, \; 0 < p < \infty \end{array} \right\}$$

in the notation of (1.3.13), (1.3.14).

1.3.4. EXAMPLE. $Y = \varphi\bigl(P_1(T)\bigr)$ with $d = 1$, $\sigma = \sigma_{11} > 0$, where $\varphi\colon [0, \infty) \to [0, \infty)$ is convex, increasing and satisfies a polynomial growth condition in $\|p\|$, as in Example 1.2.4.

Such a function has right-hand derivative $\varphi'(\cdot)$ which exists and is increasing everywhere on $[0, \infty)$, with $\varphi'(0) \ge 0$; furthermore, suppose that $\varphi(\cdot)$ is of class C^2 piecewise on $(0, \infty)$. Thus, integration by parts gives

$$\varphi(p) = \varphi(0) + \int_0^p \varphi'(q)\,dq = \varphi(0) + \int_0^\infty 1_{[0,p)}(q)\varphi'(q)\,dq$$

$$= \varphi(0) + \varphi'(0)p + \int_0^\infty (p - q)^+ \varphi''(q)\,dq, \qquad 0 \le p < \infty.$$

From (1.2.5) and Fubini's theorem, it follows that the price-process for this contingent claim is given as

$$(1.3.16) \qquad \hat{X}(t) = \mathbb{E}^0\bigl[e^{-r(T-t)}\varphi\bigl(P_1(T)\bigr) \mid \mathcal{F}(t)\bigr]$$

$$= e^{-r(T-t)}\varphi(0)$$

$$+ \varphi'(0)e^{rt} \cdot \mathbb{E}^0\bigl[e^{-rT}P_1(T) \mid \mathcal{F}(t)\bigr]$$

$$+ \int_0^\infty \mathbb{E}^0\bigl[e^{-r(T-t)}\bigl(P_1(T) - q\bigr)^+ \mid \mathcal{F}(t)\bigr]\varphi''(q)\,dq$$

$$= \varphi(0)e^{-r(T-t)} + \varphi'(0)P_1(t)$$

$$+ \int_0^\infty U\bigl(T - t, P_1(t); q\bigr)\varphi''(q)\,dq, \qquad 0 \le t \le T$$

in the notation of (1.3.13), (1.3.14). In other words,

$$(1.3.17) \qquad \hat{X}(t) = U\bigl(T - t, P_1(t)\bigr), \qquad 0 \le t \le T$$

where

$$(1.3.18) \qquad U(s, p) = e^{-rs}\int_{\mathbb{R}} \varphi\bigl(pe^{(r - \sigma^2/2)s + \sigma\xi}\bigr)\frac{e^{-\xi^2/2s}}{\sqrt{2\pi s}}\,d\xi$$

$$= \varphi(0)e^{-rs} + \varphi'(0)p + \int_0^\infty U(s, p; q)\varphi''(q)\,dq$$

for $s > 0$, and $U(0, p) = \varphi(p)$, $0 < p < \infty$ (from (1.3.6)–(1.3.8) and (1.3.16)).

Just as in (1.3.10), the optimal hedging portfolio $\hat{\pi}_1(\cdot)$ of Theorem 1.2.1 is given here again as

$$(1.3.19) \qquad \hat{\pi}_1(t) = P_1(t)\frac{\partial U}{\partial p}(T - t, P_1(t)) = Q(T - t, P_1(t)), \qquad 0 \le t < T$$

where

$$(1.3.20) \qquad Q(s, p) \triangleq p \cdot \frac{\partial U}{\partial p}(s, p) = \int_{\mathbb{R}} \psi\left(pe^{(r - \sigma^2/2)s + \sigma\xi}\right)\frac{e^{-\xi^2/2s}}{\sqrt{2\pi s}}\,d\xi$$

and $\psi(p) \triangleq p\varphi'(p)$, for $0 < p, s < \infty$.

1.3.5. REMARK. Let us suppose now that $\psi(p) = p\varphi'(p) \ge \varphi(p)$ holds everywhere on $[0, \infty)$, with strict inequality on a set of positive Lebesgue measure; for instance, this is the case for the European Call-Option of Example 1.3.2, where $\varphi(p) = (p - q)^+$, $0 \le p < \infty$. Then (1.3.18), (1.3.20) give $Q(s, p) > U(s, p)$ for $0 < s < p < \infty$, whence

$$(1.3.21) \qquad \hat{\pi}_1(t) > \hat{X}(t), \qquad 0 \le t < T$$

from (1.3.17), (1.3.19). In other words, *the optimal hedging portfolio for the European call-option always borrows.*

1.3.6. BARRIER OPTION. $Y = \left(P_1(T) - q\right)^+ 1_{\{\tau_h \le T\}}$ as in Example 1.2.7 with $\tau_h = \inf\{t \ge 0 \, / \, P_1(t) \ge h\}$, $0 < p, q < h < \infty$, $d = 1$, $\sigma = \sigma_{11} > 0$, $P_1(0) = p$.

In order to compute the price process $\hat{X}(\cdot)$ of this option we write $P_1(t) = p\exp\{\sigma\tilde{W}(t)\}$, where $\tilde{W}(t) \triangleq W^{(0)}(t) + \nu t$, $t \ge 0$ is Brownian motion with drift $\nu \triangleq r/\sigma - \sigma/2$ under the equivalent probability measure $\mathbb{P}^0$. Clearly $\{\tau_h \le t\} = \{\tilde{M}(t) \ge m\}$, where $m \triangleq \frac{1}{\sigma}\log(h/p)$ and $\tilde{M}(t) \triangleq \max_{0 \le s \le t}\tilde{W}(s)$, and the joint distribution (under $\mathbb{P}^0$) of $\tilde{W}(t)$, $\tilde{M}(t)$ is well-known, from the reflection principle (e.g. Karatzas & Shreve (1991), Proposition 2.8.1) and the Girsanov theorem:

$$(1.3.22) \quad \mathbb{P}^0\left[\tilde{W}(t) \in da; \tilde{M}(t) \in d\xi\right] = e^{\nu a - (\nu^2 t)/2} \cdot \frac{2(2\xi - a)}{\sqrt{2\pi t^3}}e^{-(2\xi - a)^2/2t}\,da\,d\xi;$$

$$\xi > 0, \quad a \le \xi.$$

In particular

$$(1.3.23) \quad \mathbb{P}^0\left[\tilde{W}(t) \in da; \tilde{M}(t) \ge \tilde{m}\right] = \begin{cases} \frac{1}{\sqrt{2\pi t}}e^{-(a - \nu t)^2/2t}\,da; & a \ge \tilde{m} \\ \frac{1}{\sqrt{2\pi t}}e^{-(a - \nu t - 2\tilde{m})^2/2t + 2\tilde{m}\nu}\,da; & a < \tilde{m} \end{cases}$$

for $\tilde{m} \ge 0$. We have then from (1.2.5), (1.3.8), (1.3.13):

$$(1.3.24) \quad \tilde{X}(t) = \mathbb{E}^0\left[e^{-r(T-t)}\left(P_1(T) - q\right)^+ 1_{\{\tau_h \le T\}} \mid \mathcal{F}(t)\right]$$

$$= 1_{\{\tau_h \le t\}} \cdot U\left(T - t, P_1(t); q\right)$$

$$+ 1_{\{\tau_h > t\}} \cdot \mathbb{E}^0\left[e^{-r(T-t)}\left(pe^{\sigma\tilde{W}(T)} - q\right)^+ 1_{\{\tilde{M}(T) \ge m\}} \mid \mathcal{F}(t)\right].$$

From the Markov property, this last expectation is equal to

$$(1.3.25) \quad e^{-rs} \cdot \mathbb{E}^0\left[\left(pe^{\sigma(b+\tilde{W}(s))} - q\right)1_{\{b+\tilde{W}(s)\geq\ell;\ \tilde{M}(s)\geq m-b\}}\right]\Bigg|_{s=T-t,\ b=\tilde{W}(t)}$$

$$= e^{-rs} \cdot \mathbb{E}^0\left[\left(pe^{\sigma b}e^{\sigma\tilde{W}(s)} - q\right)1_{\{\tilde{W}(s)\geq\tilde{\ell};\ \tilde{M}(s)\geq\tilde{m}\}}\right]\Bigg|_{\substack{s=T-t,\ b=\tilde{W}(t) \\ \tilde{m}=m-b,\ \tilde{\ell}=\ell-b}}$$

where $\ell \triangleq \frac{1}{\sigma}\log(q/p)$; it should be noted that, on $\{\tau_h > t\} = \{\tilde{M}(t) < m\}$, we have $m > \tilde{W}(t) = b$ so that $\tilde{m} = m - b > 0$.

Thanks to (1.3.23), the expression of (1.3.25) can be computed explicitly as

$$(1.3.26) \quad Q(s,b;p,q)$$

$$\triangleq pe^{\sigma b}\left\{e^{2\mu(m-b)}\left[\Phi\left(\frac{2m-b-\ell}{\sqrt{s}} + \mu\sqrt{s}\right) - \Phi\left(\frac{m-b}{\sqrt{s}} + \mu\sqrt{s}\right)\right]\right.$$

$$\left. + \Phi\left(\frac{b-m}{\sqrt{s}} + \mu\sqrt{s}\right)\right\}$$

$$- qe^{-rs}\left\{e^{2\nu(m-b)}\left[\Phi\left(\frac{2m-b-\ell}{\sqrt{s}} + \nu\sqrt{s}\right) - \Phi\left(\frac{m-b}{\sqrt{s}} + \nu\sqrt{s}\right)\right]\right.$$

$$\left. + \Phi\left(\frac{b-m}{\sqrt{s}} + \nu\sqrt{s}\right)\right\}; \qquad b < m, \quad s > 0$$

with $\mu \triangleq \frac{r}{\sigma} + \frac{\sigma}{2}$ and $\Phi(\cdot)$ as in (1.3.14). We deduce from (1.3.24)

$$(1.3.27) \quad \hat{X}(t) = Q\left(T-t, \tilde{W}(t); P_1(0), q\right)1_{\{\tau_h > t\}}$$

$$+ U\left(T-t, pe^{\sigma\tilde{W}(t)}; q\right)1_{\{\tau_h \leq t\}}, \qquad 0 \leq t \leq T.$$

In particular, the fair price of (1.2.4) is

$$u_0 = \hat{X}(0) = Q\left(T, 0; P_1(0), q\right).$$

1.3.7. PATH-DEPENDENT OPTION. $Y = \max_{0\leq t\leq T} P_1(t)$ as in Example 1.2.6 with $\delta = T$, $q = 0$ and $d = 1$, $\sigma = \sigma_{11} > 0$.

In the notation of the previous Example 1.3.6 on the Barrier Option, and with

$$(1.3.28) \quad f(s,b;\rho) \triangleq 1 - \Phi\left(\frac{b-\rho s}{\sqrt{s}}\right) + e^{2\nu b}\left[1 - \Phi\left(\frac{b+\rho s}{\sqrt{s}}\right)\right];$$

$$b \geq 0, \quad s > 0, \quad \rho \in \mathbb{R},$$

we have:

$$(1.3.29) \quad \hat{X}(t) = \mathbb{E}^0\left[e^{-r(T-t)}pe^{\sigma\tilde{M}(T)} \mid \mathcal{F}(t)\right]$$

$$= pe^{-r(T-t)}\left[e^{\sigma\tilde{M}(t)} + \sigma e^{\sigma\tilde{W}(t)}\int_{\tilde{M}(t)-\tilde{W}(t)}^{\infty} f(T-t,\xi;\nu)e^{\sigma\xi}\,d\xi\right]$$

for the value process of (1.2.5), and

$$\hat{\pi}_1(t) = pe^{-r(T-t)}\left[e^{\sigma\tilde{M}(t)}f\big(T-t,\tilde{M}(t)-\tilde{W}(t);\nu\big)\right.$$
$$\left. + \sigma e^{\sigma\tilde{W}(t)}\int_{\tilde{M}(t)-\tilde{W}(t)}^{\infty} f(T-t,\xi;\nu)e^{\sigma\xi}\,d\xi\right], \qquad 0 \le t \le T$$

for the corresponding optimal hedging portfolio of (1.2.7). For the details of these derivations, see Karatzas & Shreve (1997), Appendix E and Example 2.4.5.

1.3.8. ASIAN OPTION. $Y = \left(\int_0^T P_1(t)f(t)\,dt - q\right)^+$ with $d=1$, $\sigma = \sigma_{11} > 0$ and $f\colon [0,T] \to [0,\infty)$ Hölder continuous with $\int_0^T f(t)\,dt = 1$ (if $f(\cdot) \equiv \frac{1}{T}$, then we have the setup of Example 1.2.8).

Clearly $\hat{X}(t) = \mathbb{E}^0\big[e^{-r(T-t)}Y \mid \mathcal{F}(t)\big] = e^{-r(T-t)}M(t)$, where

$$(1.3.30) \quad M(t) \triangleq \mathbb{E}^0\left[\left(\int_0^T P_1(u)f(u)\,du - q\right)^+ \Bigg| \mathcal{F}(t)\right]$$
$$= P_1(t)\mathbb{E}^0\left[\left(\int_t^T \frac{P_1(u)}{P_1(t)}f(u)\,du - \frac{q-\int_0^t P_1(u)f(u)\,du}{P_1(t)}\right)^+ \Bigg| \mathcal{F}(t)\right]$$
$$= P_1(t)\varphi\big(t,\Lambda(t)\big), \qquad 0 \le t \le T$$

is a $\mathbb{P}^0$-martingale. We have set $\Lambda(t) \triangleq \big(q - \int_0^t P_1(u)f(u)\,du\big)/P_1(t)$, $0 \le t \le T$ and

$$(1.3.31) \quad \varphi(t,x) \triangleq \mathbb{E}^0\left[\left(\int_t^T P_1(u)f(u)\,du - x\right)^+ \Bigg| P_1(t) = 1\right]$$
$$= \mathbb{E}^0\left(\int_t^T e^{(r-\sigma^2/2)(u-t)+\sigma(W^{(0)}(u)-W^{(0)}(t))}f(u)\,du - x\right)^+;$$
$$(t,x) \in [0,T] \times \mathbb{R}.$$

This function is continuous on $[0,T] \times \mathbb{R}$, of class $C^{1,2}$ on $(0,T) \times \mathbb{R}$, and convex decreasing in x. An application of Itô's rule shows that

$$dM(t) = P_1(t)\left[\frac{\partial\varphi}{\partial t} + \frac{\sigma^2}{2}\Lambda^2(t)\frac{\partial^2\varphi}{\partial x^2} - \big(f(t)+r\Lambda(t)\big)\frac{\partial\varphi}{\partial x} + r\varphi\right]\big(t,\Lambda(t)\big)\,dt$$
$$+ \sigma P_1(t)\left[\varphi - \Lambda(t)\frac{\partial\varphi}{\partial x}\right]\big(t,\Lambda(t)\big)\,dW^{(0)}(t),$$

and thus that φ solves the Cauchy problem

$$(1.3.32) \quad \frac{\partial\varphi}{\partial t} + \frac{\sigma^2}{2}x^2\frac{\partial^2\varphi}{\partial x^2} - \big(f(t)+rx\big)\frac{\partial\varphi}{\partial x} + r\varphi = 0; \qquad 0 \le t < T, \quad x \in \mathbb{R}$$
$$(1.3.33) \qquad\qquad\qquad \varphi(T,x) = x^-;$$

for the *linear* equation of (1.3.32). This equation is quite simple, and can be solved numerically; see Rogers & Shi (1994).

Then the price-process $\hat{X}(\cdot)$ of (1.2.5), and the associated hedging portfolio $\hat{\pi}(\cdot)$ of (1.2.7), are given as

$$(1.3.34) \qquad \hat{X}(t) = e^{-r(T-t)}P_1(t)\varphi\big(t,\Lambda(t)\big), \quad \Lambda(t) = \frac{q-\int_0^t P_1(u)f(u)\,du}{P_1(t)}$$
$$(1.3.35) \qquad\qquad \hat{\pi}(t) = e^{-r(T-t)}P_1(t)\psi\big(t,\Lambda(t)\big), \qquad 0 \le t \le T,$$

respectively, where $\psi(t,x) \triangleq \varphi(t,x) - x(\partial\varphi/\partial x)(t,x)$. In particular, $u_0 = \hat{X}(0) = P_1(0)e^{-rT}\varphi(0, q/P_1(0))$ in (1.2.3).

1.3.9. EXCHANGE OPTION. $Y = (P_1(T) - P_2(T))^+$ as in Example 1.2.9, with constant volatility matrix $\sigma = (\sigma_{ij})_{1 \le i,j \le d}$. In this case, (1.2.3) gives

$$(1.3.36) \quad u_0 = \mathbb{E}^0\big[\gamma(T)(P_1(T) - P_2(T))^+\big]$$

$$= P_2(0)\mathbb{E}^0\left[\frac{\gamma(T)P_2(T)}{P_2(0)}\left(\frac{P_1(T)}{P_2(T)} - 1\right)^+\right] = P_2(0) \cdot \mathbb{E}^{\mathbb{Q}}\left(\frac{P_1(T)}{P_2(T)} - 1\right)^+,$$

where $\mathbb{Q}$ is the *probability* measure given by

$$(1.3.37) \qquad \frac{d\mathbb{Q}}{d\mathbb{P}^0} \triangleq \frac{\gamma(T)P_2(T)}{P_2(0)} = \exp\left\{\sum_{k=1}^d \sigma_{2k}W_k^{(0)}(T) - \frac{T}{2}\sum_{k=1}^d \sigma_{2k}^2\right\}.$$

We have used here (0.2.15) in the form

$$\gamma(t)P_i(t) = P_i(0) \cdot \exp\left\{\sum_{k=1}^d \sigma_{ik}W_k^{(0)}(t) - \frac{t}{2}\sum_{k=1}^d \sigma_{ik}^2\right\}; \qquad 0 \le t \le T, \quad i = 1,\ldots,d,$$

which also gives

$$(1.3.38) \quad d\left(\frac{P_1(t)}{P_2(t)}\right)$$

$$= \left(\frac{P_1(t)}{P_2(t)}\right)\left[\sum_{k=1}^d (\sigma_{1k} - \sigma_{2k})\,dW_k^{(0)}(t) + \sum_{k=1}^d \sigma_{2k}(\sigma_{2k} - \sigma_{1k}) \cdot dt\right]$$

But by Girsanov's theorem, the process $\tilde{W} = (\tilde{W}_1, \ldots, \tilde{W}_d)$ defined by

$$\tilde{W}_k(t) \triangleq W_k^{(0)}(t) - \sigma_{2k}t; \qquad 0 \le t \le T, \quad k = 1,\ldots,d$$

is Brownian motion under the probability measure $\mathbb{Q}$ of (1.3.37), and in terms of it we may re-write (1.3.38) as

$$(1.3.39) \qquad d\left(\frac{P_1(t)}{P_2(t)}\right) = \left(\frac{P_1(t)}{P_2(t)}\right) \cdot \sum_{k=1}^d (\sigma_{1k} - \sigma_{2k})d\tilde{W}_k(t) = \frac{P_1(t)}{P_2(t)} \cdot \sigma d\tilde{B}(t).$$

Here $\sigma \triangleq \sqrt{\sum_{k=1}^d (\sigma_{1k} - \sigma_{2k})^2}$, and $\tilde{B}(\cdot)$ is standard, one-dimensional Brownian motion under $\mathbb{Q}$.

It follows from (1.3.36), (1.3.39) that the price u_0 at time $t = 0$ for this exchange-option, is given by $P_2(0)$, multiplied by the Black-Scholes price of (1.3.13), (1.3.14) $U(T, (P_1(0))/(P_2(0)); 1)$ with $p = (P_1(0))/(P_2(0))$, $q = 1$ and $r \equiv 0$:

$$(1.3.40) \qquad u_0 = P_2(0)\left[\frac{P_1(0)}{P_2(0)} \cdot \Phi\left(\mu_+\left(T, \frac{P_1(0)}{P_2(0)}\right)\right) - \Phi\left(\mu_-\left(T, \frac{P_1(0)}{P_2(0)}\right)\right)\right]$$

$$= P_1(0) \cdot \Phi\left(\mu_+\left(T, \frac{P_1(0)}{P_2(0)}\right)\right) - P_2(0) \cdot \Phi\left(\mu_-\left(T, \frac{P_1(0)}{P_2(0)}\right)\right)$$

where $\mu_\pm(s,p) = (\log p \pm (\sigma^2/2)s)/(\sigma\sqrt{s})$ for $s > 0$, $p > 0$.

1.4. American contingent claims

Consider a standard, complete market model $\mathcal{M}$, as in (1.2.1), (1.2.2).

1.4.1. DEFINITION. An American Contingent Claim (ACC) is an $\mathbb{F}$-adapted process $Y: [0,T] \times \Omega \to [0,\infty)$ with continuous sample paths and

$$(1.4.1) \qquad \mathbb{E}^0 \left[\sup_{0 \le t \le T} \left(\gamma(t) Y(t) \right) \right] < \infty.$$

By analogy with Sections 0.4 and 1.2, consider now the following situation: at time $t = 0$, two agents (the "buyer" and the "seller") enter into an agreement. The *seller* agrees to provide the buyer with the random payment $Y(\tau(w), w)$ at time $t = \tau(w)$, where $\tau: \Omega \to [0,T]$ is a stopping time and *at the disposal of the buyer*. What is the amount of money $x \ge 0$ that the buyer should pay (to the seller) at time $t = 0$, in return for this commitment?

Clearly, the *seller's objective* is, starting with the amount $x \ge 0$ that he receives at $t = 0$, to find a portfolio/consumption strategy $(\hat{\pi}, \hat{C})$ which enables him to fulfil his obligation, *no matter when the seller decides to ask for the payment*. In other words,

$$(1.4.2) \qquad X^{x,\hat{\pi},\hat{C}}(\tau) \ge Y(\tau), \text{ a.s.} \qquad (\forall\, \tau \in \mathcal{S}),$$

where $\mathcal{S}$ is the class of stopping times $\tau: \Omega \to [0,T]$. Then, by analogy with (0.4.2), the *upper hedging price* for the ACC is

$$(1.4.3) \quad H_{\text{up}} \triangleq \inf\{ x \ge 0 \,/\, \exists\, (\hat{\pi}, \hat{C}) \text{ with } \hat{\pi}(\cdot) \text{ tame, and}$$

$$X^{x,\hat{\pi},\hat{C}}(\tau) \ge Y(\tau) \text{ a.s. } (\forall\, \tau \in \mathcal{S})\}.$$

On the other hand, the *buyer's objective* is, starting with the initial amount $-x$, to find a portfolio/cumulative endowment strategy $(\check{\pi}, \check{E})$ *and a stopping time* $\check{\tau} \in \mathcal{S}$ (his "exercise time"), such that the payment he receives at $t = \check{\tau}(w)$ allows him to cover the debt be incurred at $t = 0$ by purchasing the ACC:

$$(1.4.4) \qquad \check{E}(\check{\tau}) = 0, \quad X^{-x,\check{\pi},-\check{E}}(\check{\tau}) + Y(\check{\tau}) \ge 0, \text{ a.s.}$$

in the notation of Remark 0.2.8. Thus, the *lower hedging price* for the ACC is

$$(1.4.5) \quad H_{\text{low}} \triangleq \sup\{ x \ge 0 \,/\, \exists\, (\check{\pi}, \check{E}) \text{ with } M^{\check{\pi}} \text{ a } \mathbb{P}^0\text{-supermartingale and}$$

$$\check{E}(\check{\tau}) = 0, \, X^{-x,\check{\pi},-\check{E}}(\check{\tau}) \ge -Y(\check{\tau}) \text{ a.s. , for some } \check{\tau} \in \mathcal{S}\}.$$

We obtain the following analogues of Proposition 0.4.1 and Theorem 1.2.1.

1.4.2. PROPOSITION. *With* $v(0) \triangleq \sup_{\tau \in \mathcal{S}} \mathbb{E}^0 \left[\gamma(\tau) Y(\tau) \right]$, *we have*

$$(1.4.6) \qquad Y(0) \le H_{\text{low}} \le v(0) \le H_{\text{up}} \le \infty.$$

PROOF. If the set of (1.4.3) is empty, then $H_{\text{up}} = \infty \ge v(0)$; if not, and x belongs to this set, we have

$$x \ge \mathbb{E}^0 \left[\gamma(\tau) X^{x,\hat{\pi},\hat{C}}(\tau) \right] \ge \mathbb{E}^0 \left[\gamma(\tau) Y(\tau) \right], \qquad \forall\, \tau \in \mathcal{S}$$

from (0.2.19) and (1.4.2), so that $x \ge v(0)$ and thus $H_{\text{up}} \ge v(0)$.

On the other hand, the set of (1.4.5) clearly contains the number $Y(0)$, so $Y(0) \le H_{\text{low}}$; for an arbitrary number $x \ge 0$ in this set, the properties (0.2.18) and

(0.2.21), the supermartingale property of $M^{\check{\pi}}(\cdot)$, the optional sampling theorem, and (1.4.4), imply

$$-x \geq \mathbb{E}^0\left[\gamma(\check{\tau})X^{-x,\check{\pi},-\check{E}}(\check{\tau}) - \int_{(0,\check{\tau}]} \gamma(t)d\check{E}(t)\right] \geq -\mathbb{E}^0\left[\gamma(\check{\tau})Y(\check{\tau})\right],$$

whence $x \leq \mathbb{E}^0\left[\gamma(\check{\tau})Y(\check{\tau})\right] \leq v(0)$ and $H_{\text{low}} \leq v(0)$.   □

1.4.3. THEOREM. *In a standard, complete market model $\mathcal{M}$ as in* (1.2.1), (1.2.2), *the infimum of* (1.4.3) *and the supremum of* (1.4.5) *are both attained, and are equal*

$$(1.4.7) \qquad H_{\text{up}} = H_{\text{low}} = v(0) \triangleq \sup_{\tau \in \mathcal{S}} \mathbb{E}^0\left[\gamma(\tau)Y(\tau)\right] < \infty.$$

Furthermore, there exist a tame portfolio $\hat{\pi}(\cdot)$ and a consumption process $\hat{C}(\cdot)$ such that, with $\check{\pi}(\cdot) \equiv -\hat{\pi}(\cdot)$, $\check{E}(\cdot) \equiv \hat{C}(\cdot)$ and

$$(1.4.8) \qquad \hat{X}(t) \triangleq \frac{1}{\gamma(t)} \operatorname*{ess\,sup}_{\tau \in \mathcal{S}_{t,T}} \mathbb{E}^0\left[\gamma(\tau)Y(\tau) \mid \mathcal{F}(t)\right], \qquad 0 \leq t \leq T,$$

we have

$$(1.4.9) \qquad X^{v(0),\hat{\pi},\hat{C}}(t) = -X^{-v(0),\check{\pi},-\check{E}}(t) = \hat{X}(t) \geq Y(t), \qquad 0 \leq t \leq T$$

and $\hat{X}(T) = Y(T)$, almost surely; finally, the stopping time

$$(1.4.10) \qquad \check{\tau} \triangleq \inf\left\{t \in [0,T) \;/\; \hat{X}(t) = Y(t)\right\} \wedge T$$

attains the supremum in (1.4.7), *and satisfies*

$$(1.4.11) \qquad \check{E}(\check{\tau}) = 0, \quad X^{-v(0),\check{\pi},-\check{E}}(\check{\tau}) = X^{-v(0),\check{\pi},0}(\check{\tau}) = -Y(\check{\tau}), \text{ a.s.}$$

The portfolio $\hat{\pi}(\cdot)$ (resp. $\check{\pi}(\cdot)$) is the *optimal hedging portfolio* for the seller (resp., the buyer). The process $\hat{X}(\cdot)$ of (1.4.8) is called the *price-process of the* ACC in the interval $[0,T]$; and the stopping time $\check{\tau}$ of (1.4.10) is the *optimal exercise time for the buyer*. We have denoted by $\mathcal{S}_{t,T}$ the class of $\mathbb{F}$-stopping times $\tau \colon \Omega \to [t,T]$ with $0 \leq t \leq T$.

In order to prove this result, we need to recall a few facts about the *Optimal Stopping of Continuous-Time Processes*; these are listed in Theorem 1.4.4 below. The reader is referred to El Karoui (1981) or Karatzas (1993) for proofs and further details.

1.4.4. THEOREM (Results on Optimal Stopping). *There exists a nonnegative* $(\mathbb{F},\mathbb{P}^0)$-*supermartingale* $Z(\cdot) = \left\{Z(t), 0 \leq t \leq T\right\}$ *with* RCLL *paths (right continuous on $[0,T)$, with left-limits on $(0,T]$), called the "Snell envelope" of $\gamma(\cdot)Y(\cdot)$ under $\mathbb{P}^0$, with the following properties:*

(i) *$Z(\cdot)$ is the smallest $\mathbb{P}^0$-supermartingale that dominates the process $\gamma(\cdot)Y(\cdot)$.*
(ii) *For every $t \in [0,T]$, we have:*

$$(1.4.12) \qquad Z(t) = \operatorname*{ess\,sup}_{\tau \in \mathcal{S}_{t,T}} \mathbb{E}^0\left[\gamma(\tau)Y(\tau) \mid \mathcal{F}(t)\right], \text{ a.s.}$$

$$(1.4.13) \qquad \mathbb{E}\,Z(t) = v(t) \triangleq \sup_{\tau \in \mathcal{S}_{t,T}} \mathbb{E}^0\left[\gamma(\tau)Y(\tau)\right] = \mathbb{E}^0\left[\gamma(\check{\tau}_t)Y(\check{\tau}_t)\right],$$

where

$$(1.4.14) \qquad \check{\tau}_t \triangleq \inf\left\{\theta \in [t,T) \;/\; Z(\theta) = \gamma(\theta)Y(\theta)\right\} \wedge T$$

is a stopping time in $\mathcal{S}_{t,\theta}$, and

(1.4.15) $\left\{Z(\theta \wedge \check{\tau}_t), \mathcal{F}(\theta); t \le \theta \le T\right\}$ *is a* $\mathbb{P}^0$*-martingale.*

(iii) *The* $\mathbb{P}^0$*-supermartingale* $Z(\cdot)$ *is of class* $D[0,T]$ *(i.e.,* $\{Z(\tau)\}_{\tau \in \mathcal{S}}$ *is uniformly integrable) and* regular *(i.e.,* $\lim_{n \to \infty} \mathbb{E}^0 Z(\sigma_n) = \mathbb{E}^0 Z(\sigma)$ *for every monotone sequence* $\{\sigma_n\} \subseteq \mathcal{S}$ *with* $\lim_n \sigma_n = \sigma \in \mathcal{S}$*). Therefore,* $Z(\cdot)$ *admits the Doob-Meyer decomposition*

(1.4.16) $Z(t) = v(0) + M(t) - A(t), \qquad 0 \le t \le T$

where $M(\cdot)$ *is a uniformly integrable* $(\mathbb{F}, \mathbb{P}^0)$*-martingale, and* $A(\cdot)$ *a continuous, increasing,* $\mathbb{F}$*-adapted process with* $\mathbb{E}^0 A(T) < \infty$ *and* $A(0) = M(0) = 0$*.*

(iv) *The process* $A(\cdot)$ *is flat off the set* $\{0 \le t \le T \ / \ Z(t) = \gamma(t) Y(t)\}$*, i.e.*

(1.4.17) $$\int_0^T \big(Z(t) - \gamma(t) Y(t)\big)\, dA(t) = 0, \ \text{a.s.}$$

In particular, we have a.s.

(1.4.18) $A(\check{\tau}_t) = A(t), \qquad 0 \le t \le T.$

We obtain then from (1.4.8), (1.4.12) and (1.4.10), (1.4.14):

(1.4.19) $Z(\cdot) = \gamma(\cdot)\hat{X}(\cdot) \ge \gamma(\cdot) Y(\cdot), \quad \check{\tau} = \check{\tau}_0, \quad \hat{X}(\check{\tau}) = Y(\check{\tau})$

almost surely. The intuitive meaning for the random variable $A(t)$ is that of a "regret", for not having stopped by time $t \in [0,T]$ in the Problem of (1.4.13) with value $v(0) = \sup_{\tau \in \mathcal{S}} \mathbb{E}^0 \big[\gamma(\tau) Y(\tau)\big]$; of course, this regret is equal to $A(\check{\tau}) = A(0) = 0$ at the stopping time $\check{\tau}$ of (1.4.10), which is optimal for this problem.

PROOF OF THEOREM 1.4.3. In view of (1.4.6), it suffices to exhibit

(i) a tame portfolio $\hat{\pi}(\cdot)$, such that $M^{\hat{\pi}}(\cdot)$ is a $\mathbb{P}^0$-martingale, and

(ii) a consumption process $\hat{C}(\cdot)$, such that (1.4.9), (1.4.11) hold, with $\check{\pi}(\cdot) \equiv -\hat{\pi}(\cdot)$, $\check{E}(\cdot) \equiv \hat{C}(\cdot)$ and $\check{\tau}$ as in (1.4.10).

Arguing as in (1.2.7), we represent the $\mathbb{P}^0$-martingale $M(\cdot)$ of (1.4.16) as a stochastic integral

(1.4.20) $M(t) = \mathbb{E}^0\big[M(T) \mid \mathcal{F}(t)\big] = \mathbb{E}^0\big[Z(T) + A(T) \mid \mathcal{F}(t)\big] - v(0)$

$$= \int_0^t \gamma(s)\hat{\pi}'(s)\sigma(s)\, dW^{(0)}(s), \qquad 0 \le t \le T$$

for some portfolio process $\hat{\pi}(\cdot)$ (thanks to the martingale representation result in Exercise 0.3.6 and the invertibility of $\sigma(\cdot)$). Clearly, $M^{\hat{\pi}}(\cdot) = M(\cdot) \ge -v(0) > -\infty$, so $\hat{\pi}(\cdot)$ is tame. We also introduce the adapted, continuous increasing process

(1.4.21) $\hat{C}(t) \triangleq \int_0^t B(s)\, dA(s), \qquad 0 \le t \le T.$

From (1.4.19)–(1.4.21), the decomposition (1.4.16) takes the form

$$\gamma(t)\hat{X}(t) = v(0) + \int_0^t \gamma(s)\hat{\pi}'(s)\sigma(s)\, dW^{(0)}(s) - \int_0^t \gamma(s)\, d\hat{C}(s), \qquad 0 \le t \le T$$

of (0.2.17), and (1.4.9) follows. On the other hand, $\hat{X}(T) = Y(T)$ a.s. from (1.4.8), and

(1.4.22) $X^{v(0),\hat{\pi},\hat{C}}(\check{\tau}) = \hat{X}(\check{\tau}) = Y(\check{\tau}), \quad \hat{C}(\check{\tau}) = 0 \ \text{a.s.}$

from (1.4.10), (1.4.19) and (1.4.18), (1.4.21); thus (1.4.11) follows as well.   □

1.4.5. REMARK. The difference

$$(1.4.23) \quad \mathfrak{e}(t) \triangleq \frac{1}{\gamma(t)}\left\{ \sup_{\tau \in \mathcal{S}_{t,T}} \mathbb{E}^0\big[\gamma(\tau)Y(\tau) \mid \mathcal{F}(t)\big] - \mathbb{E}^0\big[\gamma(T)Y(T) \mid \mathcal{F}(t)\big]\right\},$$
$$0 \le t \le T$$

between the prices of the ACC $Y(\cdot)$, and the ECC $Y(T)$, at time t, is called the *early exercise premium* at $t \in [0,T]$. From (1.4.12), (1.4.16) and $\gamma(T)Y(T) = Z(T) = v(0) + M(T) - A(T)$, this can be written as

$$(1.4.24) \quad \mathfrak{e}(t) = \frac{1}{\gamma(t)}\mathbb{E}^0\big[A(T) - A(t) \mid \mathcal{F}(t)\big] = \frac{1}{\gamma(t)}\mathbb{E}^0\left[\int_t^T \gamma(s)\, d\hat{C}(s) \,\bigg|\, \mathcal{F}(t)\right].$$

In other words, the consumption process $\hat{C}(\cdot)$ of (1.4.21) has the interpretation of a "cash-flow", whose expected discounted value $\mathbb{E}^0\int_0^T \gamma(s)\, d\hat{C}(s)$ gives the early exercise premium $\mathfrak{e}(0)$ at $t = 0$.

In yet another interpretation, the triple of *adapted* processes $\big(\hat{X}(\cdot), \hat{\pi}, \hat{C}(\cdot)\big)$ solves the *Backwards Stochastic Differential Equation with Reflection*

$$\left\{ \begin{array}{l} \hat{X}(t) = Y(T) - \displaystyle\int_t^T r(u)\hat{X}(u)\, du - \int_t^T \hat{\pi}'(u)\sigma(u)\, dW^{(0)}(u) + \hat{C}(T) - \hat{C}(t), \\[4pt] \hspace{6cm} 0 \le t \le T \\[8pt] \hat{X}(t) \ge Y(t), \quad \forall\, 0 \le t \le T \quad \text{and} \quad \displaystyle\int_0^T \big(\hat{X}(t) - Y(t)\big)\, d\hat{C}(t) = 0 \end{array} \right\}$$

almost surely; see El Karoui et al. (1996) for the theory of such equations. The role of the process $\hat{C}(\cdot)$ here, is to avoid "overshooting the terminal target condition" (i.e., to achieve exactly $\hat{X}(T) = Y(T)$ a.s.), and to "effect the reflection $\hat{X}(\cdot) \ge Y(\cdot)$ in a minimal way" (i.e., with $\hat{C}(\cdot)$ flat off the set $\{t \in [0,T] \,/\, \hat{X}(t) = Y(t)\}$).

1.4.6. REMARK. From the optional sampling theorem, $\mathfrak{e}(\cdot) \equiv 0$ *if* $\gamma(\cdot)Y(\cdot)$ *is a* $\mathbb{P}^0$-*submartingale*. In this case, the ACC $Y(\cdot)$ is equivalent to the ECC $Y(T)$, and the ACC is exercised at expiration: $\check{\tau} = T$ a.s., in (1.4.10).

1.4.7. EXAMPLE (American call-option). By analogy with the European call-option of Example 1.2.2, we have here the ACC $Y(t) = \big(P_m(t) - q\big)^+$, $0 \le t \le T$ on the mth stock, with $r(\cdot) \ge 0$ and $\sigma(\cdot)$ bounded. This contract is of interest to a *buyer* who needs to acquire an asset by a given date $t = T$; an American call-option on this asset guarantees to him that he will not need to pay more than the exercise price q for the asset, when he decides to exercise his option.

The process $\gamma(\cdot)P_m(\cdot)$ is a $\mathbb{P}^0$-martingale (recall (0.2.15) and the discussion following it) and $q\gamma(\cdot)$ is decreasing, so that $\gamma(\cdot)\big(P_m(\cdot) - q\big)$ is a $\mathbb{P}^0$-submartingale. But then the same is true of $\gamma(\cdot)Y(\cdot)$ by Jensen's inequality, and

$$\check{\tau} = T, \quad \mathfrak{e}(\cdot) \equiv 0,$$

from Remark 1.4.6: *the American Call-Option is equivalent to the European Call-Option of* Example 1.2.2. We also have the a.s. bounds

$$P_m(t) \geq \frac{1}{\gamma(t)} \mathbb{E}^0 \big[\gamma(T) \big(P_m(T) - q \big)^+ \mid \mathcal{F}(t) \big]$$

$$=: \hat{X}^{(T)}(t) \geq P_m(t) - q \mathbb{E}^0 \big[e^{-\int_t^T r(s)\,ds} \mid \mathcal{F}(t) \big]$$

so that, if $\int_0^\infty r(s)\,ds = \infty$ a.s., we have $\lim_{T \to \infty} \hat{X}^{(T)}(t) = P_m(t)$: "as the horizon T increases to infinity, the value of the American call-option converges to the price of the underlying stock".

1.4.8. EXAMPLE (American put-option). $Y(t) = \big(q - P(t) \big)^+$, $0 \leq t < \infty$ *on an infinite horizon* $(T = \infty)$ *with* $d = 1$, $P(\cdot) \equiv P_1(\cdot)$ *and constant* $r > 0$, $\sigma = \sigma_{11} > 0$, $q > 0$.

This process $Y(\cdot)$ is continuous, adapted and bounded $\big(0 \leq Y(\cdot) \leq q \big)$, so that (1.4.1) is satisfied rather trivially. From Theorem 1.4.3, the price-process is given as

$$(1.4.25) \quad \hat{X}(t) = \operatorname*{ess\,sup}_{\tau \in \mathcal{S}_t} \mathbb{E}^0 \big[e^{-r(\tau - t)} \big(q - P(\tau) \big)^+ \mid \mathcal{F}(t) \big] = G\big(P(t) \big),$$

$$0 \leq t < \infty$$

where

$$(1.4.26) \qquad G(x) \triangleq \sup_{\tau \in \mathcal{S}_0} \mathbb{E}^0 \big[e^{-r\tau} \big(q - P(\tau) \big)^+ \mid P(0) = x \big], \qquad 0 < x < \infty$$

and $\mathcal{S}_t \triangleq \mathcal{S}_{t,\infty}$, for $0 \leq t < \infty$.

In order to compute the function of (1.4.26), and find a stopping time $\check{\tau}$ that attains the supremum, we shall look first at *hitting times* of the form

$$(1.4.27) \qquad \tau_a \triangleq \inf \big\{ t \geq 0 \,/\, P(t) \leq a \big\}, \qquad 0 < a < q.$$

We shall try to find an optimal stopping time in this restricted class, and then show that this time is also optimal in $\mathcal{S}_0$.

Let us start by noticing that with $P(0) = x > a$, the time τ_a of (1.4.27) is the first-passage-time to the level $y \triangleq \frac{1}{\sigma} \log \big(\frac{a}{x} \big) < 0$ by the Brownian motion $W^{(0)}(t) + \nu t$, $0 \leq t < \infty$ with drift $\nu \triangleq \frac{r}{\sigma} - \frac{\sigma}{2}$. From p. 197 in Karatzas & Shreve (1991),

$$\mathbb{E}^0 (e^{-r\tau_a}) = \exp \big[\nu y - |y| \sqrt{\nu^2 + 2r} \big] = \Big(\frac{a}{x} \Big)^\gamma, \qquad x > a$$

where $\gamma \triangleq \big(\nu + \sqrt{\nu^2 + 2r} \big) / \sigma$; consequently, for every $0 < a < q$ we have

$$(1.4.28) \quad g_a(x)$$

$$\triangleq \mathbb{E}^0 \big[e^{-r\tau_a} \big(q - P(\tau_a) \big)^+ \mid P(0) = x \big] = \left\{ \begin{array}{ll} (q - a)\big(\frac{a}{x} \big)^\gamma; & x > a \\[2mm] q - x; & 0 \leq x \leq a \end{array} \right\}$$

as well as

$$(1.4.29) \qquad g(x) \triangleq \sup_{0 < a < q} g_a(x) = g_b(x), \quad \text{where} \quad b \triangleq \frac{q\gamma}{1 + \gamma}.$$

Notice from (1.4.28) that $g_a'(a-) = -1$, $g_a'(a+) = -\gamma\big(\frac{q}{a} - 1 \big)$ are equal, if and only if $a = b$ as in (1.4.29). In other words, only this choice leads to the "smooth fit" condition $g_a'(a-) = g_a'(a+)$, thus making $g_a(\cdot)$ of class $C^1(0, \infty)$.

In particular, the function $g(\cdot) = g_b(\cdot)$ is of class $C^1(0, \infty) \cap C^2\big((0,\infty)\backslash\{b\}\big)$, decreasing, convex and satisfies $0 \le -g'(\cdot) \le 1$ as well as

(1.4.30)
$$\begin{cases} \frac{1}{2}\sigma^2 x^2 g''(x) + rx g'(x) - rg(x) = 0; & x > b \\ \frac{1}{2}\sigma^2 x^2 g''(x) + rx g'(x) - rg(x) = -rq < 0; & 0 < x < b \\ g(x) > (q-x)^+; & x > b \\ g(x) = q - x; & 0 \le x \le b. \end{cases}$$

It is now very straightforward, to see that *the function of* (1.4.26) *is given by*

(1.4.31) $G(\cdot) = g(\cdot) = g_b(\cdot)$ as in (1.4.28)–(1.4.30),

and the supremum in (1.4.26) *is achieved by the stopping time*

(1.4.32) $\check{\tau} = \tau_b \triangleq \inf\{t \ge 0 \;/\; P(t) \le b\}$ with $b = \dfrac{q\gamma}{1+\gamma}.$

Indeed, for any stopping time $\tau \in \mathcal{S}_0$ and with $P(0) = x > 0$ we have, from (1.4.30), the dynamics $dP(t) = P(t)\big[r\,dt + \sigma\,dW^{(0)}\big]$, and Itô's rule:

$$e^{-r(\tau \wedge n)} g\big(P(\tau \wedge n)\big) - g(x) \le \sigma \int_0^{\tau \wedge n} e^{-rt} P(t) g'\big(P(t)\big)\,dW^{(0)}(t), \quad \text{a.s.}$$

for every $n \in \mathbb{N}$. The $\mathbb{P}^0$-expectation of the stochastic integral on the right-hand side is equal to zero, thus

$$g(x) \ge \mathbb{E}^0\big[e^{-r(\tau \wedge n)} g\big(P(\tau \wedge n)\big)\big] \ge \mathbb{E}^0\big[e^{-r(\tau \wedge n)}\big(q - P(\tau \wedge n)^+\big)\big], \qquad \forall\, n \in \mathbb{N}.$$

Letting now $n \to \infty$, we have by bounded convergence:

$$\mathbb{E}^0\big[e^{-r\tau_b}\big(q - P(\tau_b)\big)^+\big] = g(x) \ge \mathbb{E}^0\big[e^{-r\tau}\big(q - P(\tau)\big)^+\big], \qquad \forall\, \tau \in \mathcal{S}_0,$$

proving the claims of (1.4.31)–(1.4.32).

Thus $\hat{X}(\cdot) = G\big(P(\cdot)\big)$ and $\check{\tau}$ of (1.4.25), (1.4.32) are, respectively, the *price-process* and *optimal exercise time* (of the buyer), for this American put-option. From (1.4.30) and Itô's rule, it is possible also to obtain the optimal hedging portfolio (for the seller)

(1.4.33) $\hat{\pi}(t) = P(t)G'\big(P(t)\big) = \left\{\begin{array}{ll} -\gamma \hat{X}(t); & \hat{X}(t) > b \\ -\hat{X}(t); & \hat{X}(t) \le b \end{array}\right\}, \qquad 0 \le t < \infty,$

as well as the *cash-flow process* in (1.4.24)

(1.4.34) $\hat{C}(t) = rq \int_0^t \mathbf{1}_{\{P(u)<b\}}\,du, \qquad 0 \le t \le T.$

1.4.9. EXAMPLE (American Put-Option). By analogy with the European put-option of Example 1.2.3, we have here the ACC $Y(t) = \big(q - P(t)\big)^+$, $0 \le t \le T$ on a *finite horizon* $(T < \infty)$ with $d = 1$, $P(\cdot) = P_1(\cdot)$ and constant $r > 0$, $\sigma = \sigma_{11} > 0$, $q > 0$. This contract is of interest to a *buyer* who owns an asset, but intends to sell it by a given date $t = T$; an American put-option on this asset guarantees him at least the exercise price q, when he decides to exercise the option.

In this case the price-process of (1.4.8) is given by

$$\hat{X}(t) = \operatorname*{ess\,sup}_{\tau \in \mathcal{S}_{t,T}} \mathbb{E}^0\big[e^{-r(\tau-t)}\big(q - P(\tau)\big)^+ \mid \mathcal{F}(t)\big] = G\big(T - t, P(t)\big), \qquad 0 \le t \le T$$

where the function $G\colon (0,\infty) \times [0,\infty) \to (0,q]$ of

$$G(s,x) \triangleq \sup_{\tau \in \mathcal{S}_{0,s}} \mathbb{E}^0\big[e^{-r\tau}\big(q - P(\tau)\big)^+ \mid P(0) = x\big]$$

is continuous, and has the following properties:

  (i) $s \mapsto G(s,x)$ is increasing, $\forall\, x > 0$;
  (ii) $x \mapsto G(s,x)$ is decreasing, convex and of class $C^1(0,\infty)$ (smooth-fit), $\forall\, s > 0$;
  (iii) $x \mapsto x + G(s,x)$ is increasing, $\forall\, s > 0$.

Furthermore, if we consider the open *continuation region* $\mathcal{C} \triangleq \big\{(s,x) \in (0,\infty)^2\ /$ $G(s,x) > (q-x)^+\big\}$, then $\mathcal{C}_s = \big(b(s),\infty\big)$ for some $b(s) \in (0,q)$, $\forall\, s > 0$. It can be shown that the resulting function $b(\cdot)$ is continuous and decreasing, with

$$b(0+) \triangleq \lim_{s \downarrow 0} b(s) = q \quad \text{and} \quad b(\infty) \triangleq \lim_{s \to \infty} b(s) = b = \frac{q\gamma}{1+\gamma}$$

$$\lim_{s \to \infty} G(s,x) = g(x) = g_b(x), \qquad \forall\, x \in (0,\infty)$$

in the notation of (1.4.28) and (1.4.29). In addition, $G(\cdot,\cdot)$ satisfies the analogue of (1.4.30)

$$\begin{cases} -\frac{\partial G}{\partial s} + \frac{\sigma^2}{2}x^2\frac{\partial^2 G}{\partial x^2} + rx\frac{\partial G}{\partial x} - rG = 0; & \text{in } \mathcal{C} \\[4pt] -\frac{\partial G}{\partial s} + \frac{\sigma^2}{2}x^2\frac{\partial^2 G}{\partial x^2} + rx\frac{\partial G}{\partial x} - rG = -rq < 0; & \text{in } 0 < x < b(s), \quad s > 0 \\[4pt] G(s,x) > (q-x)^+; & \text{in } \mathcal{C} \\[4pt] G(s,x) = q - x; & \text{in } x > b(s), \quad s \geq 0. \end{cases}$$

Unlike the infinite-horizon case, neither the moving boundary nor the function $G(\cdot,\cdot)$ can now be computed explicitly; however, they can be calculated numerically. The function $b(\cdot)$ is the unique solution of the *integral equation*

$$q - x = qe^{-rs}\cdot\Phi\big(-\mu_-(s,x;q)\big) - x\cdot\Phi\big(-\mu_+(s,x;q)\big)$$
$$+ rq\int_0^s e^{-ru}\Phi\big(-\mu_-(s,x;b(s-u))\big)\,du; \qquad \forall\, x \leq b(s), \quad s > 0,$$

in the notation of (1.3.13)–(1.3.15). And in terms of $b(\cdot)$, we have the explicit representation

$$G(s,x) = \begin{cases} qe^{-rs}\cdot\Phi\big(-\mu_-(s,x;q)\big) - x\cdot\Phi\big(-\mu_+(s,x;q)\big) \\ \quad + rq\int_0^s e^{-ru}\Phi\big(-\mu_-\big(s,x;b(s-u)\big)\big)\,du; & x \geq 0, \quad s > 0\,, \\[4pt] (q-x)^+; & x \geq 0, \quad s = 0 \end{cases}$$

which should be compared with (1.3.15). We also have the following analogues of (1.4.32)–(1.4.34):

$$\check{\tau} = \inf\big\{t \in [0,T)\,/\,P(t) \leq b(T-t)\big\} \wedge T$$

for the *optimal exercise time* of the buyer;

$$\hat{\pi}(t) = P(t)\cdot\frac{\partial G}{\partial x}\big(T-t,P(t)\big), \qquad 0 \leq t \leq T$$

for the *optimal hedging portfolio* of the seller;

$$\hat{C}(t) = rq\int_0^t \mathbf{1}_{\{P(u) \leq b(T-u)\}}\,du, \qquad 0 \leq t \leq T$$

for the *cash-flow process* of (1.4.24); and

$$\mathfrak{e}(t) = rq \int_t^T e^{-r(u-t)} \Phi\big(-\mu_-(u-t, P(t); b(T-u))\big) \, du, \qquad 0 \le t \le T$$

for the *early exercise premium* of (1.4.24). For the details of all these derivations, the reader is referred to Section 2.7 of Karatzas & Shreve (1997).

1.4.10. EXAMPLE (American Exchange-Option). By analogy with the Example 1.2.9 we consider $Y(t) = \big(P_1(t) - P_2(t)\big)^+$, $0 \le t \le T$, the "American" counterpart of the European Exchange Option 1.3.9. From (0.2.15) the process $\gamma(\cdot)Y(\cdot) = \big(\gamma(\cdot)P_1(\cdot) - \gamma(\cdot)P_2(\cdot)\big)^+$ is a $\mathbb{P}^0$-submartingale if the volatility matrix $\sigma(\cdot)$ is bounded, and Remark 1.4.6 says that this option should only be exercised at expiration: $\check{\tau} = T$, a.s. In particular, if $\sigma(\cdot) \equiv \sigma$ is a constant matrix, the value $v(0)$ of the option is given by (1.3.40).

1.4.11. QUESTION. What can be said about the "American" version $Y(t) = \big(\frac{1}{t} \int_0^t P_1(u) \, du - q\big)^+$, $0 < t \le T$ of the Asian Option 1.3.8 (Example 1.2.8)?

CHAPTER 2

Optimization

2.1. Introduction

We shall place ourselves throughout this Chapter in the context of a financial market model $\mathcal{M}$ given by

$$(2.1.1) \qquad\qquad dB(t) = B(t)r(t)\, dt$$

$$(2.1.2) \qquad dP_i(t) = P_i(t)\left[b_i(t)\, dt + \sum_{j=1}^{d} \sigma_{ij}(t)\, dW_j(t)\right], \quad P_i(0) = p_i \in (0, \infty),$$
$$i = 1, \ldots d$$

as in Section 0.1 with $n = d$. It will be assumed that the volatility matrix $\sigma(\cdot) = \{\sigma_{ij}(\cdot)\}_{1 \le i,j \le d}$ is *invertible* a.e. on $[0, T] \times \Omega$, and that the interest rate $r(\cdot)$ and the relative risk process $\theta(\cdot) = \sigma^{-1}(\cdot)[b(\cdot) - r(\cdot)\mathbf{1}_d]$ of (0.3.5) satisfy

$$(2.1.3) \quad \mathbb{E}\int_0^T \left(\left\|\theta(t)\right\|^2 + r(t)\right) dt < \infty, \quad \mathbb{P}[r(t) \ge -\eta, \ \forall\, 0 \le t \le T] = 1$$

$$\text{for some } \eta \ge 0.$$

Under these conditions, the exponential process $Z_0(\cdot)$ of (0.2.11) is only a *local martingale* (hence also supermartingale).

2.1.1. DEFINITION. A pair (π, C) of portfolio/consumption processes is called *admissible* for the initial capital $x \ge 0$, if we have

$$(2.1.4) \qquad\qquad X(t) \equiv X^{x,\pi,C}(t) \ge 0, \qquad \forall\, 0 \le t \le T$$

almost surely. The class of all such pairs will be denoted by $\mathcal{A}(x)$. Clearly, for any pair in the class, the portfolio $\pi(\cdot)$ is tame.

It will be convenient to introduce the positive semimartingale

$$(2.1.5) \qquad\qquad H_0(t) \triangleq \gamma(t)Z_0(t), \quad 0 \le t \le T,$$

called *state-price-density process*, and notice (by applying the product rule to $Z_0(t) \cdot \gamma(t)X(t)$) that (0.2.18), (0.2.19) give now

$$(2.1.6) \quad H_0(t)X(t) + \int_{(0,t]} H_0(s)\, dC(s)$$
$$= x + \int_0^t H_0(s)\big(\sigma'(s)\pi(s) - X(s)\theta(s)\big)'\, dW(s), \quad 0 \le t \le T$$

$$(2.1.7) \qquad \mathbb{E}\left[H_0(T)X(T) + \int_{(0,T]} H_0(t)\, dC(t)\right] \le x, \qquad \forall\, (\pi, C) \in \mathcal{A}(x).$$

The key observation here is that, for $(\pi, C) \in \mathcal{A}(x)$, the process of (2.1.6) is a $\mathbb{P}$-local martingale and nonnegative, thus also a $\mathbb{P}$-*supermartingale*. But then so is the process $H_0(\cdot)X(\cdot)$, and thus

$$(2.1.8) \qquad X(s) \equiv 0 \quad \text{for all } s \geq \tau_0 \triangleq \inf\{t \in [0, T)/X(t) = 0\} \wedge T$$

(cf. Karatzas & Shreve (1991), Problem 1.3.29); on the other hand, the optional sampling theorem, applied to the supermartingale of (2.1.6), gives $\mathbb{E}\left[H_0(T)X(T) + \int_{(\tau_0, T]} H_0(s) \, dC(s)\right] \leq H_0(\tau_0)X(\tau_0)$, a.s. and thus also

$$(2.1.9) \qquad C(t) = C(t \wedge \tau_0), \qquad \forall \, 0 \leq t \leq T \quad \text{almost surely,}$$

$$(2.1.10) \qquad \mathbb{P}\left[\pi(t) = 0, \lambda - \text{ a.e. } t \in (\tau_0, T)\right] = 1.$$

In other words, "bankrupty is an absorbing state" for $(\pi, C) \in \mathcal{A}(x)$: if the wealth becomes equal to zero before T, it stays there until the end of the horizon; no further consumption takes place, and no further investment either.

In this chapter, we shall consider exclusively consuption processes of the form

$$(2.1.11) \qquad C(t) = \int_0^t c(s) \, ds, \quad 0 \leq t \leq T$$

for some $\mathbb{F}$-progressively measurable *consumption rate process* $c \colon [0, T] \times \Omega \to [0, \infty)$. Our object will be the study of *optimization problems*; in order to formulate these, we need the concept of utility function.

2.1.2. DEFINITION. Consider a continuous function $U \colon (0, \infty) \to \mathbb{R}$ which is strictly increasing, strictly concave and continuously differentiable, with $U'(\infty) \triangleq \lim_{x \to \infty} U'(x) = 0$ and $U'(0+) \triangleq \lim_{x \downarrow 0} U'(x) = \infty$. Such a function will be called a *utility function*.

Primary examples of utility functions are $U(x) = \log x$ and $U_\alpha(x) = x^\alpha/\alpha$ for some $\alpha \in (-\infty, 1) \backslash \{0\}$, $0 < x < \infty$. For every utility function $U(\cdot)$, we shall denote by $I(\cdot)$ the inverse of the derivative $U'(\cdot)$; both these functions are continuous, strictly decreasing, and map $(0, \infty)$ onto itself with $I(0+) = U'(0+) = \infty$, $I(\infty) = U'(\infty) = 0$. We shall consider also the *convex dual*

$$(2.1.12) \qquad \tilde{U}(y) \triangleq \max_{0 < x < \infty} [U(x) - xy] = U(I(y)) - yI(y), \quad 0 < y < \infty$$

of $U(\cdot)$: a convex decreasing function, which is continuously differentiable on $(0, \infty)$ and satisfies

$$(2.1.13) \qquad \tilde{U}'(y) = -I(y), \quad 0 < y < \infty$$

$$(2.1.14) \qquad U(x) \triangleq \min_{0 < y < \infty} [\tilde{U}(y) + xy] = \tilde{U}(U'(x)) + xU'(x), \quad 0 < x < \infty$$

$$(2.1.15) \qquad \tilde{U}(\infty) = U(0+), \quad \tilde{U}(0+) = U(\infty).$$

These properties are not hard to verify, and are left as exercises.

2.1.3. DEFINITION. Consider a function $U \colon [0, T] \times (0, \infty) \to \mathbb{R}$ which is continuous and of class $C^{0,1}$ on its domain, and such that $U(t, \cdot)$ is a utility function in the sense of Definition 2.1.2 for every $t \in [0, T]$. Such a function will be called a *time-dependent utility function*. Just as in (2.1.12)–(2.1.14), we shall denote by $I(t, \cdot)$ the inverse of $U'(t, \cdot)$, and by $\tilde{U}(t, \cdot)$ the convex dual of $U(t, \cdot)$, $\forall \, t \in [0, T]$.

We are now in a position to introduce the *stochastic control problems* that we shall treat in this chapter. These concern a small investor in the market $\mathcal{M}$ of (2.1.1), (2.1.2), who starts with initial capital $x > 0$, acts as a price-taker, and has at his disposal portfolio/consumption rules $(\pi, C) \in \mathcal{A}(x)$ as in Definition 2.1.1.

2.1.4. PROBLEM (Utility from consumption). Given a time-dependent utility function $U_1(\cdot, \cdot)$ as in Definition 2.1.3, maximize the expected utility from consumption $\mathbb{E} \int_0^T U_1\big(t, c(t)\big) \, dt$, over the class

(2.1.16) $\mathcal{A}_1(x)$

$$\triangleq \left\{ (\pi, C) \in \mathcal{A}(x) \,/\, C(\cdot) \text{ as in } (2.1.11), \ \mathbb{E} \int_0^T U_1^-\big(t, c(t)\big) \, dt < \infty \right\}.$$

2.1.5. PROBLEM (Utility from terminal wealth). Given a utility function $U_2(\cdot)$ as in Definition 2.1.2, maximize the expected utility derived from terminal wealth $\mathbb{E} \, U_2\big(X^{x,\pi,C}(T)\big)$, over the class

(2.1.17) $\mathcal{A}_2(x) \triangleq \big\{ (\pi, C) \in \mathcal{A}(x) \,/\, \mathbb{E} \, U_2^-\big(X^{x,\pi,C}(T)\big) < \infty \big\}.$

2.1.6. PROBLEM (Utility from both consumption and terminal wealth). Let $U_1(\cdot, \cdot)$, $U_2(\cdot)$ be two given utility functions as above, and maximize the expected utility from consumption and terminal wealth $\mathbb{E} \big[\int_0^T U_1\big(t, c(t)\big) \, dt + U_2\big(X^{x,\pi,C}(T)\big) \big]$, over the class

(2.1.18) $\mathcal{A}_0(x) \triangleq \mathcal{A}_1(x) \cap \mathcal{A}_2(x).$

In the next three sections, we shall strive to compute the *value functions*

(2.1.19) $V_1(x) \triangleq \sup_{(\pi, C) \in \mathcal{A}_1(x)} \mathbb{E} \int_0^T U_1\big(t, c(t)\big) \, dt,$

$$V_2(x) \triangleq \sup_{(\pi, C) \in \mathcal{A}_2(x)} \mathbb{E} \, U_2\big(X^{x,\pi,C}(T)\big)$$

(2.1.20) $V_0(x) \triangleq \sup_{(\pi, C) \in \mathcal{A}_0(x)} \mathbb{E} \left[\int_0^T U_1\big(t, c(t)\big) \, dt + U_2\big(X^{x,\pi,C}(T)\big) \right]$

of these problems, and to find an *optimal pair* $(\hat{\pi}_i, \hat{C}_i) \in \mathcal{A}_i(x)$ $i = 0, 1, 2$ for each of them (i.e., a pair that attains the corresponding supremum). We shall deal with Problem 2.1.6 in Section 2.2 (general theory) and in Section 2.4 (explicit results for constant coefficients r, b, σ), whereas in Section 2.3 we shall study Problems 2.1.4, 2.1.5 and the relations they bear to Problem 2.1.6.

In Section 2.3 we also discuss the problem of *maximizing the long-term growth rate from investment* (Proposition 2.3.5). Section 2.5 deals with the problem of "portfolio insurance" in the form of *drawdown constraints*, whereby admissible portfolios are constrained in such a way that wealth is never allowed to fall below a certain given fraction of its maximum-to-date. "Goal problems", in which one strives to reach a prespecified level of wealth by a given time T, are studied in Section 2.6, along with the related problem of maximizing the probability of a perfect hedge.

2.2. Martingale methods

We shall devote this section to the study of Problem 2.1.6. In order to make headway with this problem, let us remind ourselves that *condition* (2.1.7) *has to hold for every pair* $(\pi, C) \in \mathcal{A}(x)$. We have in this regard the following result, analogue of the sufficiency part in Theorem 0.3.5, with the difference that we do not require here the exponential process $Z_0(\cdot)$ of (0.2.11) to be a martingale.

2.2.1. PROPOSITION. *In the context of the market model* $\mathcal{M}$ *of* (2.1.1)–(2.1.3), *consider a contingent claim* ξ *and a consumption process* $C(\cdot)$ *that satisfy*

$$(2.2.1) \qquad \mathbb{E}\left[H_0(T)\xi + \int_{(0,T]} H_0(t)\, dC(t)\right] = x > 0.$$

There exists then a portfolio process $\pi(\cdot)$, *such that* $(\pi, C) \in \mathcal{A}(x)$ *and* $X^{x,\pi,C}(T) = \xi$, *a.s.; in particular*

$$(2.2.2) \quad X^{x,\pi,C}(t) = \frac{1}{H_0(t)}\mathbb{E}\left[H_0(T)\xi + \int_{(t,T]} H_0(s)\, dC(s)\ \middle|\ \mathcal{F}(t)\right], \quad 0 \leq t \leq T.$$

The proof is, by now, fairly straightforward (recall also Theorem 1.2.1): one introduces the martingale

$$(2.2.3) \qquad M(t) \triangleq \mathbb{E}\left[H_0(T)\xi + \int_{(0,T]} H_0(s)\, dC(s)\ \middle|\ \mathcal{F}(t)\right], \quad 0 \leq t \leq T,$$

and invokes the martingale representation property of the Brownian filtration (e.g. Theorem 3.4.15 and Problem 3.4.16 in Karatzas & Shreve (1991)) to write it as a stochastic integral with respect to the Brownian motion,

$$(2.2.4) \qquad M(t) = x + \int_0^t \psi'(s)\, dW(s), \quad 0 \leq t \leq T$$

for a suitable progressively measurable $\psi \colon [0,T] \times \Omega \to \mathbb{R}^d$ with $\mathbb{P}\big(\int_0^T \|\psi(t)\|^2\, dt < \infty\big) = 1$. One then identifies

$$(2.2.5) \quad X(t) \triangleq \frac{1}{H_0(t)}\left[M(t) - \int_{(0,t]} H_0(s)\, dC(s)\right] \quad \text{as } X^{x,\pi,C}(t), \quad 0 \leq t \leq T,$$

the wealth process corresponding to $C(\cdot)$ and to the portfolio

$$(2.2.6) \qquad \pi(\cdot) \triangleq \big(\sigma^{-1}(\cdot)\big)'\left[X(\cdot)\theta(\cdot) + \frac{1}{H_0(\cdot)}\psi(\cdot)\right].$$

These remarks suggest that the Problem 2.1.6 is "equivalent" to *the problem of maximizing* $\mathbb{E}\big[\int_0^T U_1\big(t, c(t)\big)\, dt + U_2(\xi)\big]$ *over all pairs* (ξ, c) *of contingent claims and consumption-rate processes that satisfy the constraint*

$$(2.2.7) \qquad \mathbb{E}\left[H_0(T)\xi + \int_0^T H_0(t)c(t)\, dt\right] = x.$$

Now, with $y > 0$ a "Lagrange multiplier", whose role is to impose the constraint (2.2.7), we are led to look at

$$(2.2.8) \quad \mathbb{E}\left[\int_0^T U_1\big(t, c(t)\big)\, dt + U_2(\xi)\right] + y\left\{x - \mathbb{E}\left[H_0(T)\xi + \int_0^T H_0(t)c(t)\, dt\right]\right\}$$

$$= \mathbb{E}\int_0^T \big[U_1\big(t, c(t)\big) - yH_0(t) \cdot c(t)\big]\, dt + \mathbb{E}\big[U_2(\xi) - yH_0(T) \cdot \xi\big] + xy$$

$$\leq \mathbb{E}\left[\int_0^T \tilde{U}_1\big(t, yH_0(t)\big)\, dt + \tilde{U}_2\big(yH_0(T)\big)\right] + xy,$$

and to notice from (2.1.12) that *the last inequality holds as equality if and only if* ξ, $c(\cdot)$ *are given as*

(2.2.9) $\xi_0 \triangleq I_2(yH_0(T))$ and $c_0(t) \triangleq I_1(t, yH_0(t))$, $0 \leq t \leq T$

respectively. Then, we determine the Lagrange multiplier $y > 0$ by substituting the quantities of (2.2.9) back into (2.2.7):

(2.2.10) $\mathcal{X}_0(y) \triangleq \mathbb{E}\left[H_0(T)I_2(yH_0(T)) + \int_0^T H_0(t)I_1(t, yH_0(t))\, dt\right] = x.$

Indeed, suppose that the function $\mathcal{X}_0(\cdot)$ of (2.2.10) is real-valued, that is

(2.2.11) $\mathcal{X}_0(y) < \infty$, $\forall\, 0 < y < \infty$.

Then $\mathcal{X}_0(\cdot)$ maps $(0, \infty)$ onto itself and is continuous, strictly decreasing with $\mathcal{X}_0(0+) \triangleq \lim_{y \downarrow 0} \mathcal{X}_0(y) = \infty$, $\mathcal{X}_0(\infty) \triangleq \lim_{y \to \infty} \mathcal{X}_0(y) = 0$. If we denote the inverse of this function by $\mathcal{Y}_0(\cdot) \triangleq \mathcal{X}_0^{-1}(\cdot)$, then the Lagrange multiplier $y > 0$ is uniquely determined by (2.2.10) as

(2.2.12) $y = \mathcal{Y}_0(x).$

We can now formalize all of this, as follows.

2.2.2. THEOREM. *Suppose that* (2.2.11) *and*

(2.2.13) $V_0(x) < \infty$, $\forall\, 0 < x < \infty$

hold. For any given $x > 0$, consider the Problem 2.1.6 *with value $V_0(x)$ as in* (2.1.20), *and define ξ_0, $c_0(\cdot)$ as in* (2.2.9), (2.2.12). *There exists then a portfolio process $\pi_0(\cdot)$ such that the pair (π_0, C_0) belongs to the class $\mathcal{A}_0(x)$ of* (2.1.18) *and attains the supremum in* (2.1.20); *i.e., is* optimal for Problem 2.1.6. *The wealth process corresponding to this pair is, by* (2.2.2), (2.2.9):

$$X_0(t) \equiv X^{x, \pi_0, C_0}(t)$$
$$= \frac{1}{H_0(t)}\mathbb{E}\left[\int_t^T H_0(s)I_1(s, \mathcal{Y}_0(x)H_0(s))\, ds\right.$$
$$\left. + H_0(T)I_2(\mathcal{Y}_0(x)H_0(T)) \,\middle|\, \mathcal{F}(t)\right], \quad 0 \leq t \leq T.$$

The value *of this problem is given as*

(2.2.14) $V_0(x) = G_0(\mathcal{Y}_0(x)),$

where

$$G_0(y) \triangleq \mathbb{E}\left[\int_0^T U_1(t, I_1(t, yH_0(t)))\, dt + U_2(I_2(yH_0(t)))\right], \quad 0 < y < \infty$$

and the convex dual

(2.2.15) $\tilde{V}_0(y) \triangleq \sup_{x > 0}[V_0(x) - xy]$, $0 < y < \infty$

of the function $V_0(\cdot)$ is

(2.2.16) $\tilde{V}_0(y) = G_0(y) - y\mathcal{X}_0(y) = \mathbb{E}\left[\int_0^T \tilde{U}_1(t, yH_0(t))\, dt + \tilde{U}_2(yH_0(T))\right].$

PROOF. The pair (ξ_0, c_0) satisfies (2.2.7) by construction, as well as $U_1\big(t, c_0(t)\big) \geq U_1(t, 1) + \mathcal{Y}_0(x) H_0(t)\big(c_0(t) - 1\big)$, $0 \leq t \leq T$ and $U_2(\xi_0) \geq U_2(1) + \mathcal{Y}_0(x) H_0(T)(\xi_0 - 1)$, almost surely from (2.1.12). Therefore

$$(2.2.17) \quad \mathbb{E}\left[\int_0^T U_1^-\big(t, c_0(t)\big)\, dt + U_2^-(\xi_0)\right] \leq |U_2(1)| + \int_0^T |U_1(t, 1)|\, dt$$

$$+ \mathcal{Y}_0(x) \cdot \mathbb{E}\left[H_0(T) + \int_0^T H_0(t)\, dt\right] < \infty,$$

since $\mathbb{E}\, H_0(t) \leq e^{\eta t}$, $0 \leq t \leq T$ (recall (2.1.3) and the supermartingale property of $Z_0(\cdot)$). From Proposition 2.2.1 we know that there exists a portfolio $\pi_0(\cdot)$ with (π_0, C_0) in $\mathcal{A}(x)$ (thus also in the class $\mathcal{A}_0(x)$ of (2.1.18), thanks to (2.2.17)), and $X^{x, \pi_0, C_0}(T) = \xi_0$ a.s.

Now take arbitrary $x > 0$, $(\pi, C) \in \mathcal{A}_0(x)$ and $y > 0$; from (2.1.7), (2.2.8) and (2.2.16) we have

$$(2.2.18) \quad \mathbb{E}\left[\int_0^T U_1\big(t, c(t)\big)\, dt + U_2\big(X^{x, \pi, C}(T)\big)\right]$$

$$\leq \mathbb{E}\left[\int_0^T U_1\big(t, c(t)\big)\, dt + U_2\big(X^{x, \pi, C}(T)\big)\right]$$

$$+ y\left\{x - \mathbb{E}\left(H_0(T) X^{x, \pi, C}(T) + \int_0^T H_0(t) c(t)\, dt\right)\right\}$$

$$\leq Q(y) + xy,$$

where

$$Q(y) \triangleq \mathbb{E}\left(\int_0^T \tilde{U}_1(t, y H_0(t)\, dt + \tilde{U}_2\big(y H_0(T)\big)\right) = G_0(y) - y \mathcal{X}_0(y).$$

In particular, it follows from (2.2.18): $V_0(x) \leq Q(y) + xy$, $\forall\, x > 0$ whence

$$(2.2.19) \qquad \tilde{V}_0(y) \equiv \sup_{x > 0}\big[V_0(x) - xy\big] \leq Q(y), \quad \text{for every } y > 0.$$

On the other hand, (2.2.18) holds as equality if and only if $y = \mathcal{Y}_0(x)$ and $(\pi, C) = (\pi_0, C_0)$, so that

$$(2.2.20) \quad \mathbb{E}\left[\int_0^T U_1\big(t, c_0(t)\big)\, dt + U_2\big(X^{x, \pi_0, C_0}(T)\big)\right]$$

$$= Q\big(\mathcal{Y}_0(x)\big) + x \mathcal{Y}_0(x) = G_0\big(\mathcal{Y}_0(x)\big).$$

Now $V_0(x) = G_0\big(\mathcal{Y}_0(x)\big)$ follows from (2.2.18), (2.2.20); on the other hand, (2.2.20) also gives

$$Q(y) = V_0\big(\mathcal{X}_0(y)\big) - y \mathcal{X}_0(y) \leq \sup_{x > 0}\big[V_0(x) - xy\big]$$

for every given $y > 0$, and in conjunction with (2.2.19) we obtain (2.2.16). $\square$

2.2.3. EXERCISE. Under the assumptions of Theorem 2.2.2, the functions $V_0(\cdot)$ and $\tilde{V}_0(\cdot)$ of (2.2.14)–(2.2.16) are continuously differentiable, with

$$(2.2.21) \qquad \tilde{V}_0'(\cdot) = -\mathcal{X}_0(\cdot), \quad V_0'(\cdot) = \mathcal{Y}_0(\cdot) \quad \text{on } (0, \infty).$$

(*Hint:* It suffices to show $\tilde{V}_0(y_2) - \tilde{V}_0(y_1) = -\int_{y_1}^{y_2} \mathcal{X}_0(u)\,du$, or equivalently $y_2\mathcal{X}_0(y_2) - y_1\mathcal{X}_0(y_1) - \int_{y_1}^{y_2} \mathcal{X}_0(u)\,du = G_0(y_2) - G_0(y_1)$, for any $0 < y_1 < y_2 < \infty$. Recall also (2.1.13), in the form $U\big(I(y_2)\big) - U\big(I(y_1)\big) = y_2 I(y_2) - y_1 I(y_1) - \int_{y_1}^{y_2} I(u)\,du.$)

2.2.4. EXAMPLE (Logarithmic utility functions). $U_1(t,x) = U_2(x) = \log x$ *for* $(t,x) \in [0,T] \times (0,\infty)$. In this case we have $I_1(t,y) = I_2(y) = \frac{1}{y}$ and $\mathcal{X}_0(y) = (T+1)/y$ for $0 < y < \infty$ (in particular, the condition (2.2.11) is satisfied), as well as $\mathcal{Y}_0(x) = (T+1)/x$ for $0 < x < \infty$. The optimal terminal wealth ξ_0 and the optimal consumption-rate process $c_0(\cdot)$ are given by

$$\xi_0 = \frac{x}{T+1}\frac{1}{H_0(T)} \quad \text{and} \quad c_0(t) = \frac{x}{T+1}\frac{1}{H_0(t)}, \quad 0 \le t \le T$$

respectively (from (2.2.9), (2.2.12)), and the corresponding optimal wealth process is given by (2.2.2) as

$$X_0(t) = \frac{x}{T+1}\frac{1+T-t}{H_0(t)}, \quad 0 \le t \le T.$$

In particular, the martingale of (2.2.3) is $M_0(\cdot) \equiv x$, and thus $\psi_0(\cdot) \equiv 0$ in (2.2.4),

$$\pi_0(t) = \big(\sigma^{-1}(t)\big)'\theta(t)X_0(t) = \big(\sigma(t)\sigma'(t)\big)^{-1}\big[b(t) - r(t)\mathbf{1}_d\big]X_0(t), \quad 0 \le t \le T$$

in (2.2.6). Furthermore, the value-function of (2.1.20) is

$$V_0(x) = (1+T)\cdot\log\left(\frac{x}{1+T}\right) + \int_0^T \rho(t)\,dt + \rho(T), \quad 0 < x < \infty,$$

where $\rho(t) \triangleq \mathbb{E}\int_0^t \big(r(s) + \frac{1}{2}\|\theta(s)\|^2\big)\,ds, 0 \le t \le T$ is well-defined and finite, thanks to the conditions of (2.1.3). In particular, the assumption (2.2.13) is satisfied.

2.2.5. EXAMPLE. *Deterministic* $r(\cdot)$, $\theta(\cdot)$ *and* $U_1(t,x) = U_2(x) = (x^\alpha)/\alpha$, $(t,x) \in [0,T] \times (0,\infty)$ *with* $\alpha \in (-\infty,1)\backslash\{0\}$. In this case $I_1(t,y) = I_2(y) = y^{-1/(1-\alpha)}$ and, with

$$m(t) \triangleq \exp\left\{\frac{\alpha}{1-\alpha}\int_0^t r(s)\,ds + \frac{\alpha}{2(1-\alpha)^2}\int_0^t \|\theta(s)\|^2\,ds\right\},$$

$$N(t) \triangleq \int_0^t m(s)\,ds + m(t), \quad 0 \le t \le T,$$

we obtain $\mathcal{X}_0(y) = y^{-1/(1-\alpha)}N(T)$, $\mathcal{Y}_0(x) = \big(N(T)/x\big)^{1-\alpha}$ and thus

$$\xi_0 = \frac{x}{N(T)}\big(H_0(T)\big)^{-1/(1-\alpha)}, \quad c_0(t) = \frac{x}{N(T)}\big(H_0(t)\big)^{-1/(1-\alpha)}, \quad 0 \le t \le T.$$

On the other hand $\big(H_0(t)\big)^{-\alpha/(1-\alpha)} = m(t)A(t)$, where

$$A(t) \triangleq \exp\left\{\frac{\alpha}{1-\alpha}\int_0^t \theta'(s)\,dW(s) - \frac{\alpha^2}{2(1-\alpha)^2}\int_0^t \|\theta(s)\|^2\,ds\right\}$$

is a martingale. Thus, the optimal wealth process $X_0(\cdot) \equiv X^{x,\pi_0,C_0}(\cdot)$ is given by (2.2.2) as

$$X_0(t) = \frac{x}{N(T)}\frac{A(t)}{H_0(t)}\left\{m(T) + \int_t^T m(s)\,ds\right\} \quad \text{and} \quad c_0(t) = \frac{m(t)\cdot X_0(t)}{m(T) + \int_t^T m(s)\,ds}.$$

On the other hand, the martingale $M_0(\cdot)$ of (2.2.3)–(2.2.5) is computed as

$$M_0(t) = \frac{x}{N(T)} \left[A(t) \left\{ m(T) + \int_t^T m(s)\,ds \right\} + \int_0^t m(s)A(s)\,ds \right],$$

and thus satisfies $dM_0(t) = H_0(t)X_0(t)(\alpha/(1-\alpha))\theta'(t)\,dW(t)$, $M_0(0) = x$. This last expression yields the optimal portfolio $\pi_0(\cdot)$, as in (2.2.4), (2.2.6), in the form

$$\pi_0(t) = \frac{(\sigma(t)\sigma'(t))^{-1}}{1-\alpha} \left[b(t) - r(t)\mathbf{1}_d \right] X_0(t), \quad 0 \le t \le T.$$

Finally, the functions $G_0(\cdot)$ and $V_0(\cdot)$ are given as

$$G_0(y) = \frac{y^{-\alpha/(1-\alpha)}}{\alpha} N(T), \quad V_0(x) = \frac{x^\alpha}{\alpha} (N(T))^{1-\alpha}.$$

and so the assumptions (2.2.11), (2.2.13) are obviously satisfied.

2.2.6. EXERCISE. Use the results of Example 2.2.5 to show that the *assumption* (2.2.13) is satisfied, provided that the processes $r(\cdot)$, $\theta(\cdot)$ are bounded uniformly in (t, w), and that the utility functions $U_1(\cdot, \cdot)$, $U_2(\cdot)$ satisfy the conditions

$$(2.2.22) \qquad -k \le U_1(t, x), \; U_2(x) \le K(1 + x^\alpha), \qquad \forall\, (t, x) \in [0, T] \times (0, \infty)$$

for some constants $K \in (0, \infty)$, $k \in [0, \infty)$, $\alpha \in (0, 1)$.

2.2.7. EXERCISE. Show that the *assumption* (2.2.11) is satisfied, provided that for some real constants $K > 0$, $\rho > 0$ we have

$$(2.2.23) \qquad \sup_{0 \le t \le T} I_1(t, y) + I_2(y) \le Ky^{-\rho}, \qquad \forall\, y \in (0, \infty)$$

as well as *one* of the following conditions:

  (i) $0 < \rho \le 1$, or
  (ii) $r(\cdot)$, $\theta(\cdot)$ deterministic, or
  (iii) $r(\cdot)$, $\theta(\cdot)$ bounded uniformly in (t, w).

2.2.8. EXERCISE. Suppose that there exist constants $\beta \in (0, 1)$, $\gamma \in (1, \infty)$, such that the utility functions $U_1(t, \cdot)$, $U_2(\cdot)$ satisfy the condition

$$(2.2.24) \qquad \beta U'(x) \ge U'(\gamma x), \qquad \forall\, 0 < x < \infty,$$

or equivalently

$$(2.2.24') \qquad I(\beta y) \le \gamma I(y), \qquad \forall\, 0 < y < \infty,$$

uniformly in $t \in [0, T]$. Suppose also that $\mathcal{X}_0(y_*) < \infty$ for *some* $y_* \in (0, \infty)$. Show then that the assumption (2.2.11) is satisfied.

2.3. Ramifications

Let us consider now briefly the Problems 2.1.4 and 2.1.5, in the manner of the previous section and under the assumptions (2.2.11), (2.2.13). By analogy with the notation of (2.2.10) and (2.2.14), we introduce the functions

$$(2.3.1) \quad \mathcal{X}_1(y) \triangleq \mathbb{E} \int_0^T H_0(t) I_1\big(t, y H_0(t)\big)\, dt, \quad \mathcal{X}_2(y) \triangleq \mathbb{E}\big[H_0(T) I_2\big(y H_0(T)\big)\big],$$

$$0 < y < \infty$$

$$(2.3.2) \quad G_1(y) \triangleq \mathbb{E} \int_0^T U_1\big(t, I_1\big(t, y H_0(t)\big)\big)\, dt, \quad G_2(y) \triangleq \mathbb{E}\, U_2\big(I_2\big(y H_0(T)\big)\big),$$

$$0 < y < \infty$$

so that $\mathcal{X}_0(\cdot) = \mathcal{X}_1(\cdot) + \mathcal{X}_2(\cdot)$ and $G_0(\cdot) = G_1(\cdot) + G_2(\cdot)$. We also denote by $\mathcal{Y}_i(\cdot)$ the inverse of the continuous, strictly decreasing functions $\mathcal{X}_i(\cdot)$, $i = 1, 2$. We have the following results, analogues of Theorem 2.2.2.

2.3.1. THEOREM (Maximizing expected utility from consumption). *For any x > 0, consider the* Problem 2.1.4 *and introduce the consumption-rate process*

$$(2.3.3) \quad c_1(t) \triangleq I_1\big(t, \mathcal{Y}_1(x) H_0(t)\big), \quad 0 \le t \le T.$$

There exists a portfolio process $\pi_1(\cdot)$, such that the pair (π_1, C_1) is optimal, in the class $\mathcal{A}_1(x)$ of (2.1.16), for Problem 2.1.4 *(i.e., attains the supremum in (2.1.19) over this class). The corresponding optimal wealth-process $X_1(\cdot) \triangleq X^{x,\pi_1,C_1}(\cdot)$ is given by*

$$(2.3.4) \quad X_1(t) = \frac{1}{H_0(t)} \mathbb{E}\left[\int_t^T H_0(s) c_1(s)\, ds \;\middle|\; \mathcal{F}(t)\right], \quad 0 \le t \le T$$

and the optimal portfolio $\pi_1(\cdot)$ by

$$(2.3.5) \quad \sigma'(t)\pi_1(t) = \frac{\psi_1(t)}{H_0(t)} + X_1(t)\theta(t), \quad 0 \le t \le T$$

where $\psi_1(\cdot)$ is the integrand in the stochastic integral representation $M_1(t) = x + \int_0^t \psi_1'(s)\, dW(s)$ of the martingale $M_1(t) \triangleq \mathbb{E}\left[\int_0^T H_0(s) c_1(s)\, ds \;\middle|\; \mathcal{F}(t)\right], 0 \le t < T$.

2.3.2. THEOREM (Maximizing expected utility from terminal wealth). *Given initial capital $x > 0$, consider the* Problem 2.1.5 *and introduce the contingent claim*

$$(2.3.6) \quad \xi_2 \triangleq I_2\big(\mathcal{Y}_2(x) H_0(T)\big).$$

There exists a portfolio $\pi_2(\cdot)$, such that the pair $(\pi_2, 0)$ is optimal in $\mathcal{A}_2(x)$ for Problem 2.1.5 *(i.e., atains the supremum in (2.1.19) over this class). The corresponding optimal wealth process $X_2(\cdot) \triangleq X^{x,\pi_2,0}(\cdot)$ is given as*

$$(2.3.7) \quad X_2(t) = \frac{1}{H_0(t)} \mathbb{E}\big[H_0(T)\xi_2 \mid \mathcal{F}(t)\big], \quad 0 \le t \le T,$$

and the optimal portfolio $\pi_2(\cdot)$ by

$$(2.3.8) \quad \sigma'(t)\pi_2(t) = \frac{\psi_2(t)}{H_0(t)} + X_2(t)\theta(t), \quad 0 \le t \le T$$

where $\psi_2(\cdot)$ is the integrand in the martingale representation $H_0(t) X_2(t) = x + \int_0^t \psi_2'(s)\, dW(s), 0 \le t \le T$.

2.3.3. PROPOSITION. *The value functions $V_1(\cdot)$, $V_2(\cdot)$ of Problems 2.1.4, 2.1.5 are given as*

$$(2.3.9) \qquad\qquad V_i(x) = G_i\big(\mathcal{Y}_i(x)\big), \quad i = 1, 2$$

and their convex duals $\tilde{V}_i(y) \triangleq \sup_{x>0}\big[V_i(x) - xy\big]$ as

$$(2.3.10) \quad \tilde{V}_1(y) = \mathbb{E}\int_0^T \tilde{U}_1\big(t, yH_0(t)\big)\, dt, \quad \tilde{V}_2(y) = \mathbb{E}\,\tilde{U}_2\big(yH_0(T)\big), \quad 0 < y < \infty$$

respectively. In particular, $\tilde{V}_0(\cdot) = \tilde{V}_1(\cdot) + \tilde{V}_2(\cdot)$, and we have

$$(2.3.11) \qquad \tilde{V}_i'(\cdot) = -\mathcal{X}_i(\cdot), \quad V_i'(\cdot) = \mathcal{Y}_i(\cdot) \quad on\ (0,\infty), \quad i = 1, 2$$

by analogy with (2.2.21), as well as

$$(2.3.12) \quad V_0(x) = \max_{\substack{0 < x_1, x_2 < x \\ x_1 + x_2 = x}} \big[V_1(x_1) + V_2(x_2)\big] = \big(V_1\big(\mathcal{X}_1(y)\big) + V_2\big(\mathcal{X}_2(y)\big)\big)_{y=\mathcal{Y}_0(x)}.$$

The last equality suggests that a small investor, with initial wealth $x > 0$ and faced with Problem 2.1.6, might decompose at time $t = 0$ his wealth as $x = x_1^* + x_2^*$ with $x_i^* = \mathcal{X}_i\big(\mathcal{Y}_0(x)\big)$, $i = 1, 2$, and then:

(i) With initial capital x_1^*, solve Problem 2.1.4 (optimal strategies $\pi_1(\cdot)$ and $c_1(\cdot)$, optimal wealth $X_1(\cdot)$ as in (2.3.3)–(2.3.5)).

(ii) With initial capital x_2^*, solve Problem 2.1.5 (optimal strategies $\pi_2(\cdot)$ and $C_2(\cdot) \equiv 0$, optimal wealth $X_2(\cdot)$ as in (2.3.6)–(2.3.8)).

(iii) Superpose the optimal strategies for these two problems:

$$\pi_0(\cdot) = \pi_1(\cdot) + \pi_2(\cdot), \quad c_0(\cdot) = c_1(\cdot).$$

The result of this superposition is the optimal pair of Theorem 2.2.2 *for* Problem 2.1.6, *and the corresponding optimal wealth process in also given by superposition:* $X_0(\cdot) = X_1(\cdot) + X_2(\cdot)$.

Notice that the initial division of capital at $t = 0$ is done according to the recipe $V_1'(x_1^*) = V_2'(x_2^*)$, which "equates marginal utilities" from the two problems.

2.3.4. EXAMPLE. Consider the Problem 2.1.5 with $U_2(x) = \log x$. We have $I_2(y) = \mathcal{X}_2(y) = \frac{1}{y}$, $\mathcal{Y}_2(x) = \frac{1}{x}$,

$$G(y) = \mathbb{E}\int_0^T \Big(r(t) + \frac{1}{2}\|\theta(t)\|^2\Big)\, dt - \log y$$

and Theorem 2.3.2 gives the optimal wealth and portfolio processes as

$$(2.3.13) \quad X_2(t) = \frac{x}{H_0(t)}, \quad \pi_2(t) = \big(\sigma(t)\sigma'(t)\big)^{-1}\big[b(t) - r(t)\mathbf{1}_d\big]X_2(t);$$

$$0 \le t \le T.$$

Note that *these expressions do not depend on the time-horizon $T > 0$.*

2.3.5. PROPOSITION. *The portfolio $\pi_2(\cdot)$ of (2.3.13) maximizes the* long-term growth rate from investment *over an infinite horizon: i.e., for any $\mathbb{F}$-progressively measurable $\pi \colon [0,\infty) \times \Omega \to \mathbb{R}^d$ with $\mathbb{P}\big[\int_0^T \|\pi'(t)\sigma(t)\|^2\, dt + \int_0^T |\pi'(t)\big(b(t) - r(t)\mathbf{1}_d\big)|\, dt$*

$< \infty, \ \forall \ 0 < T < \infty] = 1$ *and corresponding wealth-process*

(2.3.14) $\qquad X^{\pi}(t) \equiv X^{x,\pi,0}(t)$

$$\triangleq \frac{1}{\gamma(t)} \left\{ x + \int_0^t \gamma(u)\pi'(u)\sigma(u)\big(dW(u) + \theta(u)\,du\big) \right\} > 0,$$

$$\forall \ 0 \le t < \infty$$

(by analogy with (0.2.16)–(0.2.17)), we have

(2.3.15) $\qquad \overline{\lim}_{T\to\infty} \frac{1}{T} \log X^{\pi}(T) \le \overline{\lim}_{T\to\infty} \frac{1}{T} \log X_2(T)$

almost surely, for any $x \in (0,\infty)$, provided that

(2.3.16) $\quad \mathbb{P}\left[\int_0^T \big(r(t) + \|\theta(t)\|^2\big)\,dt < \infty, \quad \inf_{0 \le t \le T} r(t) \ge -\eta\right] = 1, \ \forall \ 0 < T < \infty$

holds for some $\eta = \eta_T \ge 0$.

PROOF. For any $\pi(\cdot)$ as in (2.3.14), the ratio $R^{\pi}(t) \triangleq (X^{\pi}(t))/(X_2(t)) = H_0(t)X^{\pi}(t) \,/\, x$ satisfies (2.1.6) in the form

$$dR^{\pi}(t) = \frac{H_0(t)}{x}\big(\sigma'(t)\pi(t) - X^{\pi}(t)\theta(t)\big)'dW(t), \quad R^{\pi}(0) = 1$$

and is thus a positive local martingale and supermartingale. As such, $R^{\pi}(\cdot)$ has a last element $R^{\pi}(\infty) \triangleq \lim_{t\to\infty} R^{\pi}(t)$ a.s., and satisfies the inequality

$$e^{\delta n}\,\mathbb{P}\left[\sup_{n \le t < \infty} R^{\pi}(t) > e^{\delta n}\right] \le \mathbb{E}\,R^{\pi}(n) \le 1, \qquad \forall\,n \in \mathbb{N}, \quad 0 < \delta < 1$$

(cf. Karatzas & Shreve (1991), Problem 1.3.16 and Theorem 1.3.8). Consequently,

$$\sum_{n=1}^{\infty} \mathbb{P}\left[\sup_{n \le t < \infty}\big(\log R^{\pi}(t)\big) > \delta n\right] \le \sum_{n=1}^{\infty} e^{-\delta n} < \infty;$$

and from the Borel-Cantelli lemma, there exists a random variable $N_{\delta} : \Omega \to \mathbb{N}$ such that

$$\log R^{\pi}(t,w) \le \delta n \le \delta t; \qquad \forall\,n \ge N_{\delta}(w), \quad t \ge n$$

holds for $\mathbb{P} -$ a.e. $w \in \Omega$. In particular, for every such w we have

$$\sup_{n \le t < \infty} \frac{1}{t} \log X^{\pi}(t,w) \le \sup_{n \le t < \infty} \frac{1}{t} \log X_2(t,w) + \delta, \qquad \forall\,n \ge N_{\delta}(w),$$

whence

$$\overline{\lim}_{t\to\infty} \frac{1}{t} \log X^{\pi}(t,w) \le \overline{\lim}_{t\to\infty} \frac{1}{t} X_2(t,w) + \delta,$$

and (2.3.15) follows from the arbitrariness of $\delta \in (0,1)$. $\qquad \square$

2.3.6. EXERCISE. Under the conditions of (2.3.16), and assuming that

(2.3.17)

$$r_* \triangleq \lim_{T\to\infty} \frac{1}{T} \int_0^T r(t)\,dt,$$

$$\|\theta_*\|^2 \triangleq \lim_{T\to\infty} \frac{1}{T} \int_0^T \|\theta(t)\|^2\,dt$$

exist in $(0, \infty)$, a.s., show that the limit on the right-hand side of (2.3.15) exists and equals

$$(2.3.18) \qquad \lim_{T \to \infty} \frac{1}{T} \log X_2(T) = \lim_{T \to \infty} \frac{1}{T} \log \frac{1}{H_0(T)} = r_* + \frac{\|\theta_*\|^2}{2}.$$

2.4. Constant coefficients

The martingale methodology that we developed in Section 2, culminating with Theorem 2.2.2, provides very explicit results about the value function $V_0(\cdot)$, the optimal consumption-rate process $c_0(\cdot)$ and the optimal wealth-process $X_0(\cdot)$ of the stochastic control Problem 2.1.6. However, it fails to shed much light on the nature of the optimal portfolio process $\pi_0(\cdot)$, apart from guaranteeing its existence. For some special utility functions, such as those of Examples 2.2.4 and 2.2.5, one can in fact compute the optimal portfolio explicitly. Our objective in this section will be to do the same for fairly general utility functions and *constant coefficients*

$$(2.4.1) \quad r(t) \equiv r \in \mathbb{R}^+, \quad b(t) \equiv b \in \mathbb{R}^d \quad \text{and} \quad \sigma(t) \equiv \sigma \in L(\mathbb{R}^d; \mathbb{R}^d), \quad 0 \le t \le T$$

where the matrix σ is non-singular and $\theta = \sigma^{-1}(b - r\mathbf{1}_d) \neq \mathbf{0}$. This will enable us to obtain both $\pi_0(\cdot)$ and $c_0(\cdot)$ very explicitly *in feedback form* as functions of the current level $X_0(t)$ of wealth, i.e.,

$$(2.4.2) \qquad \pi_0(t) = \Pi\big(t, X_0(t)\big), \quad c_0(t) = \mathcal{C}\big(t, X_0(t)\big), \quad 0 \le t \le T$$

for suitable mappings $\Pi \colon [0, T] \times (0, \infty) \to \mathbb{R}^d$ and $\mathcal{C} \colon [0, T] \times (0, \infty) \to [0, \infty)$, and to compute very explicitly the convex dual $\tilde{V}_0(\cdot)$ of the value function $V_0(\cdot)$ as in (2.2.15). Our main tools will be the Feynman-Kac representation of solutions to parabolic partial differential equations, and the Hamilton-Jacobi-Bellman (HJB) equation of Dynamic Programming.

We shall need now a temporal, as well as spatial, parametrization: that is, for arbitrary $t \in [0, T]$, $x \in (0, \infty)$ we shall consider the analogue

$$(2.4.3) \quad V(t, x) \triangleq \sup_{(\pi, C) \in \mathcal{A}(t, x)} \mathbb{E}\left[\int_t^T e^{-\beta(s-t)} u_1\big(c(s)\big)\, ds + e^{-\beta(T-t)} u_2\big(X(T)\big) \right]$$

of the value function $V_0(\cdot) \equiv V(0, \cdot)$ of (2.2.10), for the Problem 2.1.6 on the finite horizon $[t, T]$, subject to the dynamics

$$(2.4.4) \quad X(s) = x + \int_t^s \big(rX(u) - c(u)\big)\, du + \int_t^s \pi'(u)\sigma\big[dW(u) + \theta\, du\big],$$

$$t \le s \le T$$

and the non-negativity constraint $X(s) \equiv X^{(t,x), \pi, C}(s) \ge 0$, $\forall\, s \in [t, T]$ a.s. for the wealth-process.

Finally, as is clear from (2.4.3), we are taking "separable" utility functions of the form

$$(2.4.5) \quad U_1(t, x) = e^{-\beta t} u_1(x), \quad U_2(x) = e^{-\beta T} u_2(x); \quad (t, x) \in [0, T] \times (0, \infty)$$

where $\beta > 0$ is a given real constant, and $u_1(\cdot)$, $u_2(\cdot)$ are utility functions (Definition 2.1.2) of class $C^3(0, \infty)$ satisfying the technical assumptions

(2.4.6)
$$u_k(0+) > -\infty, \quad \lim_{x \downarrow 0} \frac{(u_k'(x))^2}{u_k''(x)} \text{ exists,}$$

$$\lim_{x \to \infty} \frac{(u_k'(x))^\alpha}{u_k''(x)} = 0; \quad k = 1, 2$$

for some $\alpha > 2$. These conditions will allow our analysis to go through conveniently, as in Karatzas, Lechoczky & Shreve (1987); they are satisfied in the case of utility functions of the type $u(x) = (x^\delta/\delta)$ for $0 < \delta < 1$, but are far from the weakest possible under which our results hold. We shall use again the notation $i_k(\cdot) \triangleq (u_k'(\cdot))^{-1}$ and $\tilde{u}_k(y) \triangleq \max_{x>0}[u_k(x) - xy] = u_k(i_k(y)) - yi_k(y)$, $k = 1, 2$.

Let us start by recalling the exponential martingale $Z_0(t) = \exp(-\theta'W(t) - \frac{1}{2}\|\theta\|^2 t)$, $0 \le t \le T$ and introducing the processes $Z(t, s) \triangleq (Z_0(s)/Z_0(t))$, $H(t, s) \triangleq (H_0(s)/H_0(t)) = e^{-r(s-t)}Z(t, s)$, as well as

(2.4.7) $$Y^{(t,y)}(s) \triangleq ye^{\beta(s-t)}H(t, s), \quad t \le s \le T$$

for given $(t, y) \in [0, T] \times (0, \infty)$. This last process is a linear diffusion, with dynamics

(2.4.8) $$dY^{(t,y)}(s) = Y^{(t,y)}(s)[(\beta - r)\,ds - \theta'dW(s)], \quad Y^{(t,y)}(s) = y.$$

Consider also the analogues

(2.4.9) $$\mathcal{X}(t, y) \triangleq \mathbb{E}\left[\int_t^T H(t, s)i_1\big(yH(t, s)e^{\beta(s-t)}\big)\,ds \right.$$
$$\left. + H(t, T)i_2\big(yH(t, T)e^{\beta(T-t)}\big)\right]$$
$$= S(t, y)/y,$$

(2.4.10) $$G(t, y) \triangleq \mathbb{E}\left[\int_t^T e^{-\beta(s-t)}(u_1 \circ i_1)\big(Y^{(t,y)}(s)\big)\,ds \right.$$
$$\left. + e^{-\beta(T-t)}(u_2 \circ i_2)\big(Y^{(t,y)}(T)\big)\right],$$
$$(t, y) \in [0, T] \times (0, \infty)$$

of the functions $\mathcal{X}_0(\cdot) \equiv \mathcal{X}(0, \cdot)$, $G_0(\cdot) \equiv G(0, \cdot)$ in (2.2.10), (2.2.14), where

(2.4.11) $$S(t, y) \triangleq \mathbb{E}\left[\int_t^T e^{-\beta(s-t)}Y^{(t,y)}(s)i_1\big(Y^{(t,y)}(s)\big)\,ds \right.$$
$$\left. + e^{-\beta(T-t)}Y^{(t,y)}(T)i_2\big(Y^{(t,y)}(T)\big)\right].$$

For every $t \in [0, T]$, the function $\mathcal{X}(t, \cdot)$ is continuous, strictly decreasing and maps $(0, \infty)$ onto itself with $\mathcal{X}(t, 0+) = \infty$, $\mathcal{X}(t, \infty) = 0$; we denote its inverse by $\mathcal{Y}(t, \cdot)$.

Just as in Theorem 2.2.2, the value function of (2.4.3) is given by

(2.4.12) $$V(t, x) = G\big(t, \mathcal{Y}(t, x)\big),$$

and its convex dual as

(2.4.13) $\tilde{V}(t,y) \triangleq \sup_{x>0}\big[V(t,x) - xy\big] = G(t,y) - S(t,y)$

$$= \mathbb{E}\left[\int_t^T e^{-\beta(s-t)}\tilde{u}_1\big(Y^{(t,y)}(s)\big)\,ds + e^{-\beta(s-t)}\tilde{u}_2\big(Y^{(t,y)}(T)\big)\right].$$

Furthermore, we have the analogue of (2.2.21):

$$\tilde{V}_y(t,y) = -\mathcal{X}(t,y), \quad V_x(t,x) = \mathcal{Y}(t,x).$$

Consider now the infinitesimal generator

(2.4.14) $L\varphi \triangleq \dfrac{1}{2}\|\theta\|^2 y^2 \varphi_{yy} + (\beta - r)y\varphi_y - \beta\varphi$

of the diffusion process in (2.4.8), "killed" at the constant rate $\beta > 0$. It can be shown, using (2.4.6), that the functions G, S of (2.4.10), (2.4.11) are of class $C^{1,2}\big((0,T) \times (0,\infty)\big)$ and satisfy a growth condition of the type

$$\max_{0 \leq t \leq T}|\varphi(t,y)| \leq K(1 + y^\alpha + y^{-\alpha}), \quad 0 < y < \infty$$

for some positive real constants α and K. On the other hand, a Feynman-Kac-type result (Lemma 7.1 in Karatzas, Lehoczky & Shreve (1987)) guarantees that G and S are the unique solutions, with these properties, of the Cauchy problems

(2.4.15)
$$\left(\frac{\partial}{\partial t} + L\right)G(t,y) + u_1\big(i_1(y)\big) = 0; \quad (t,y) \in [0,T) \times (0,\infty)$$
$$G(T,y) = u_2\big(i_2(y)\big); \quad y \in (0,\infty)$$

and

(2.4.16)
$$\left(\frac{\partial}{\partial t} + L\right)S(t,y) + yi_1(y) = 0; \quad (t,y) \in [0,T) \times (0,\infty)$$
$$S(T,y) = yi_2(y); \quad y \in (0,\infty)$$

respectively. Since $S(t,y) = y\mathcal{X}(t,y)$, it follows from (2.4.16) that the function $\mathcal{X}$ of (2.4.9) solves the Cauchy problem

(2.4.17)
$$\mathcal{X}_t + \frac{\|\theta\|^2}{2}y^2\mathcal{X}_{yy} + \big(\beta - r + \|\theta\|^2\big)y\mathcal{X}_y - r\mathcal{X}$$
$$+ i_1(y) = 0; \quad (t,y) \in [0,T) \times (0,\infty)$$
$$\mathcal{X}(T,y) = i_2(y); \quad y \in (0,\infty).$$

Furthermore, by analogy with Theorem 2.2.2 and with $y = \mathcal{Y}(t,x)$, the optimal wealth-process for the Problem of (2.4.3) is given now by

(2.4.18) $X^{(t,x)}(s) = \dfrac{1}{H(t,s)}\mathbb{E}\left[\int_s^T H(t,\theta) \cdot i_1\big(yH(t,\theta)e^{\beta(\theta-t)}\big)\,d\theta \right.$

$$\left. + H(t,T) \cdot i_2\big(yH(t,T)e^{\beta(T-t)}\big)\,\Big|\,\mathcal{F}(s)\right]$$

$$= \frac{1}{Y^{(t,y)}(s)}\mathbb{E}\left[\int_s^T e^{-\beta(\theta-s)}Y^{(t,y)}(\theta)i_1\big(Y^{(t,y)}(\theta)\big)\,d\theta\right.$$

$$\left. + e^{-\beta(T-t)}Y^{(t,y)}(T)i_2\big(Y^{(t,y)}(T)\big)\,\Big|\,\mathcal{F}(s)\right]$$

$$= S\big(s,Y^{(t,y)}(s)\big)\Big/Y^{(t,y)}(s) = \mathcal{X}\big(s,Y^{(t,y)}(s)\big), \quad t \leq s \leq T$$

thanks to the Markov property of the process in (2.4.7), (2.4.8).

2.4.1. THEOREM. *The optimal wealth-process $X^{(t,x)}(\cdot)$ for the stochastic control Problem of (2.4.3) is given as*

$$(2.4.19) \qquad X^{(t,x)}(s) = \mathcal{X}\big(s, \eta^{(t,x)}(s)\big), \quad t \leq s \leq T$$

in terms of the function $\mathcal{X}$ of (2.4.9), (2.4.17) and with $\eta^{(t,x)}(\cdot) \triangleq Y^{(t,\mathcal{Y}(t,x))}(\cdot)$. In terms of $X^{(t,x)}(\cdot)$, the optimal portfolio and consumption/rate processes $\pi^{(t,x)}(\cdot)$, $c^{(t,x)}(\cdot)$ are given, in the feedback form of (2.4.2), by

$$(2.4.20) \qquad \pi(t,x)(s) = -(\sigma\sigma')^{-1}[b - r\mathbf{1}_d]\frac{\mathcal{Y}\big(s, X^{(t,x)}(s)\big)}{\mathcal{Y}_x\big(s, X^{(t,x)}(s)\big)}, \quad t \leq s \leq T$$

$$(2.4.21) \qquad c^{(t,x)}(s) = i_1\big(\mathcal{Y}\big(s, X^{(t,x)}(s)\big)\big), \quad t \leq s \leq T$$

respectively.

PROOF. The first claim has already been established, in (2.4.18). For the second, apply Itô's rule in (2.4.19); in conjunction with the equation (2.4.17) and the dynamics

$$d\eta^{(t,x)}(s) = \eta^{(t,x)}(s)\big[(\beta - r)\,ds - \theta'\,dW(s)\big], \quad \eta^{(t,x)}(t) = x$$

we obtain

$$dX^{(t,x)}(s) = \big(rX^{(t,x)}(s) - c^{(t,x)}(s)\big)\,ds + \big(\pi^{(t,x)}(s)\big)'\sigma\big[dW(s) + \theta\,ds\big]$$

in the notation of (2.4.20), (2.4.21). Comparing this equation with (2.4.4), we conclude that $X^{(t,x)}(\cdot)$ is the wealth-process corresponding to the pair $\big(\pi^{(t,x)}, C^{(t,x)}\big)$. $\square$

In particular, we have established the claim (2.4.2) with

$$(2.4.22) \quad C(t,x) = i_1\big(\mathcal{Y}(t,x)\big), \quad \Pi(t,x) = -(\sigma\sigma')^{-1}[b - r\mathbf{1}_d]\frac{\mathcal{Y}(t,x)}{\mathcal{Y}_x(t,x)};$$

$$(t,x) \in [0,T] \times (0,\infty).$$

Note from (2.4.22) that the relative proportions

$$\frac{\Pi_i(t,x)}{\Pi_j(t,x)} = \frac{((\sigma\sigma')^{-1}(b - r\mathbf{1}_d))_i}{((\sigma\sigma')^{-1}(b - r\mathbf{1}_d))_j}, \qquad 1 \leq i \neq j \leq d,$$

of investment in any two different stocks, are independent of the agent's level of wealth, and independent of his utility functions U_1, U_2 (this is true also in the context of general, time-dependent but deterministic, coefficients).

2.4.2. EXERCISE. Consider the value function $V(t,x)$ of (2.4.3), and its convex dual $\tilde{V}(t,y)$ as in (2.4.13). Show that:

(i) $V(\cdot, \cdot)$ satisfies the *nonlinear* second-order equation

$$(2.4.23) \quad \begin{aligned} V_t(t,x) + \max_{\substack{c \geq 0 \\ \pi \in \mathbb{R}^d}} &\left[\frac{1}{2}\|\sigma'\pi\|^2 V_{xx}(t,x)\right. \\ &\left. + \big(rx - c + \pi'(b - r\mathbf{1}_d)\big)V_x(t,x) + u_1(c)\right] \\ &- \beta V(t,x) = 0, \quad 0 \leq t < T, \quad x \in (0,\infty) \\ V(T,x) &= u_2(x); \quad x \in (0,\infty). \end{aligned}$$

This is the *Hamilton-Jacobi-Bellman* (HJB) *equation* associated with the stochastic control Problem of (2.4.3) and the dynamics of (2.4.4).

(i) The maximizing $\hat{\pi}$, $\hat{c}$ in (2.4.23) are given by $\hat{\pi} = \Pi(t,x)$, $\hat{c} = \mathcal{C}(t,x)$ as in (2.4.22).

(ii) The convex dual $\tilde{V}(\cdot,\cdot)$ satisfies the *linear* second-order equation

(2.4.24)
$$\left(\frac{\partial}{\partial t} + L\right)\tilde{V}(t,y) + \tilde{u}_1(y) = 0; \quad 0 \le t < T, \quad 0 < y < \infty$$

$$\tilde{V}(T,y) = \tilde{u}_2(y); \quad 0 < y < \infty.$$

Finally, let us turn to the question of *computing* the various functions that we have introduced. *Clearly, it suffices to compute the functions G, S of* (2.4.10), (2.4.11). For if these two are given, then so are $\mathcal{X}(t,y) = S(t,y)/y$ of (2.4.9), $\mathcal{Y}(t,\cdot) \triangleq \mathcal{X}^{-1}(t,\cdot)$, $\tilde{V} = G - S$ from (2.4.13), as well as the value function V of (2.4.3), either via the composition $V(t,x) = G\big(t, \mathcal{Y}(t,x)\big)$ or via the duality $V(t,x) = \inf_{y>0}\big[\tilde{V}(t,y) + xy\big]$ of (2.4.13). Consider the auxiliary Cauchy problem

(2.4.25)
$$\left(\frac{\partial v}{\partial t} + L\right)v(t,y;q) = 0, \quad (t,y) \in [0,T) \times (0,\infty)$$

$$v(T,y;q) = (q-y)^+, \quad y \in (0,\infty);$$

its unique solution is given by the following analogue of (1.3.15)

(2.4.26) $v(t,y;q) = \mathbb{E}\left[e^{-\beta(T-t)}\big(q - Y^{(t,y)}(T)\big)^+\right]$

$$= \begin{cases} qe^{-\beta(T-t)}\Phi\big(-\mu_-(T-t,y;q)\big) \\ \qquad -ye^{-r(T-t)}\Phi\big(-\mu_+(T-t,y;q)\big); & 0 \le t < T \\ (q-y)^+; & t = T \end{cases}$$

for the price of a European put-option, where now

$$\mu_\pm(s,p;q) \triangleq \frac{1}{\|\theta\|\sqrt{s}}\left[\log\left(\frac{p}{q}\right) + \left(\beta - r \pm \frac{\|\theta\|^2}{2}\right)\right]$$

is the analogue of (1.3.14). Let us also introduce the functions

(2.4.27) $g(y) \triangleq \dfrac{u_1(i_1(y))}{\beta} - \dfrac{2}{(\rho_+ - \rho_-)\|\theta\|^2}\left\{\dfrac{y^{1+\rho_+}}{1+\rho_+}J_+(y) - \dfrac{y^{1+\rho_-}}{1+\rho_-}J_-(y)\right\}$

(2.4.28) $s(y) \triangleq \dfrac{yi_1(y)}{r} - \dfrac{2}{(\rho_+ - \rho_-)\|\theta\|^2}\left\{\dfrac{y^{1+\rho_+}}{\rho_+}J_+(y) - \dfrac{y^{1+\rho_-}}{\rho_-}J_-(y)\right\},$

solutions of the ordinary differential equations $Lg(y) + u_1\big(i_1(y)\big) = 0$ and $Ls(y) + yi_1(y) = 0$, respectively, where $\rho_+ > 0$ and $\rho_- < 0$ are the roots of the quadratic equation $(\|\theta\|^2/2)\rho^2 + (\beta - r + \|\theta\|^2/2)\rho - r = 0$, and

$$J_+(y) \triangleq \int_0^{i_1(y)} \big(u_1'(c)\big)^{-\rho_+}\, dc, \quad J_-(y) \triangleq \int_0^{i_1(y)} \big(u_1'(c)\big)^{-\rho_-}\, dc.$$

2.4.3. EXERCISE. The functions G, S of (2.4.10), (2.4.11) admit the stochastic representations

(2.4.29) $G(t,y) = g(y) + \mathbb{E}\left[e^{-\beta(T-t)}\big\{u_2\big(i_2(Y^{(t,y)}(T))\big) - g(Y^{(t,y)}(T))\big\}\right]$

(2.4.30) $S(t,y) = s(y) + \mathbb{E}\left[e^{-\beta(T-t)}\big\{Y^{(t,y)}(T)i_2\big(Y^{(t,y)}(T)\big) - s(Y^{(t,y)}(T))\big\}\right],$

respectively, which lead to the explicit computations

$$(2.4.31) \quad G(t,y) = g(y) + \left(u_2(0) - \frac{u_1(0)}{\beta} \right) e^{-\beta(T-t)}$$

$$+ \int_0^\infty \left(u_2\big(i_2(q)\big) - g(q) \right)'' v(t,y;q)\, dq,$$

$$(2.4.32) \quad S(t,y) = s(y) + \int_0^\infty \left(q i_2(q) - s(q) \right)'' v(t,y;q)\, dq,$$

and thus with $h(y) \triangleq g(y) - s(y)$ we have also, from (2.4.13),

$$(2.4.33) \quad \tilde{V}(t,y) = h(y) + \left(u_2(0) - \frac{u_1(0)}{\beta} \right) e^{-\beta(T-t)}$$

$$+ \int_0^\infty \left(\tilde{u}_2(q) - h(q) \right)'' v(t,y;q)\, dq.$$

2.5. Drawdown constraints

Let us place ourselves again within the market model $\mathcal{M}$ of (2.1.1)–(2.1.3), but on the *infinite horizon* $[0,\infty)$, and assume that the conditions of (2.3.16) hold. Let us consider a small investor who employs a portfolio rule of the type

$$\pi_i(t) = \left(X^p(t) - \frac{\beta M^p(t)}{\gamma(t)} \right) p_i(t), \quad 0 \le t < \infty, \quad i = 1, \dots d$$

for a given fixed number $\beta \in (0,1)$, where $X^p(\cdot)$ is his wealth-process,

$$(2.5.1) \qquad M^p(t) \triangleq \max_{0 \le s \le t} \big(\gamma(s) X^p(s) \big), \quad 0 \le t < \infty$$

the maximum-to-date of his discounted wealth, and $p \colon [0,\infty) \times \Omega \to \mathbb{R}^d$ a progressively measurable process such that

$$(2.5.2) \qquad \mathbb{P}\left[X^p(t) > \frac{\beta M^p(t)}{\gamma(t)}, \ \forall\, 0 \le t \le T \right] = 1$$

holds for every $T \in (0,\infty)$. In other words, the investor does not allow the "drawdown" $1 - (\gamma(t)X^p(t))/(M^p(t))$ of his discounted wealth from its maximum-to-date" ever to exceed or equal the given constant $1 - \beta$, at any time $t \ge 0$. He invests a proportion $p_i(t)$ of the difference $X^p(t) - \beta M^p(t)/\gamma(t)$ in the ith stock, for every $i = 1, \dots d$, and the remainder

$$\left(1 - \sum_{i=1}^d p_i(t) \right) \left(X^p(t) - \beta \frac{M^p(t)}{\gamma(t)} \right) + \beta \frac{M^p(t)}{\gamma(t)}$$

he invests in the bond. Accordingly, his wealth process $X^p(\cdot)$ satisfies the *stochastic functional/differential equation*

$$(2.5.3) \quad dX^p(t) = \sum_{i=1}^{d} p_i(t) \left(X^p(t) - \beta \frac{M^p(t)}{\gamma(t)} \right) \cdot \left[b_i(t)\, dt + \sum_{j=1}^{d} \sigma_{ij}(t)\, dW_j(t) \right]$$

$$+ \left[\left(1 - \sum_{i=1}^{d} p_i(t) \right) \left(X^p(t) - \beta \frac{M^p(t)}{\gamma(t)} \right) + \beta \frac{M^p(t)}{\gamma(t)} \right] \cdot r(t)\, dt$$

$$= r(t) X^p(t)\, dt + \left(X^p(t) - \beta \frac{M^p(t)}{\gamma(t)} \right) p'(t) \sigma(t)\, dW^{(0)}(t),$$

$$X^p(0) = x \in (0, \infty).$$

2.5.1. DEFINITION. For a given initial capital $x \in (0, \infty)$, and a given time-horizon $T \in (0, \infty)$, let $\mathcal{A}_\beta(T, x)$ denote the class of $\mathbb{F}$-progressively measurable processes $p \colon [0, T] \times \Omega \to \mathbb{R}^d$ with $\int_0^T \|p'(t)\sigma(t)\|^2\, dt < \infty$ a.s., for which the equation (2.5.3) has a unique solution on $[0, T]$ that satisfies the "drawdown constraint" (2.5.2). We also let

$$(2.5.4) \qquad \mathcal{A}_\beta(x) \triangleq \bigcap_{T > 0} \mathcal{A}_\beta(T, x).$$

The following result shows that this class is not empty.

2.5.2. EXERCISE. For any given $x \in (0, \infty)$, $\beta \in (0, 1)$, and $\mathbb{F}$-progressively measurable $\rho \colon [0, \infty) \times \Omega \to \mathbb{R}^d$ with

$$\int_0^T \|\rho(t)\|^2\, dt < \infty \text{ a.s.,} \qquad \forall\ 0 < T < \infty,$$

the process $\hat{p}(\cdot) = \left(\rho'(\cdot)\sigma^{-1}(\cdot) \right)'$ is in the class $\mathcal{A}_\beta(x)$ of (2.5.4).

We are now in a position to formulate our basic portfolio optimization problem, subject to the "drawdown constraint" of (2.5.2).

2.5.3. PROBLEM. For some given $0 < \beta < 1$, $0 < \delta < 1$, maximize the long-run rate of growth

$$(2.5.5) \qquad G(p) \triangleq \overline{\lim}_{T \to \infty} \frac{1}{T} \log \mathbb{E} \left(X^p(T) \right)^\delta, \quad p \in \mathcal{A}_\beta(x)$$

of expected utility $\left(U(x) = x^\delta/\delta \right)$ from wealth, over portfolio-proportion processes $p(\cdot)$ in $\mathcal{A}_\beta(x)$. In particular, compute the value

$$(2.5.6) \qquad v(\beta) \triangleq \sup_{p \in \mathcal{A}_\beta(x)} G(p)$$

of this problem, and find an optimal $\hat{p} \in \mathcal{A}_\beta(x)$ for which $v(\beta) = G(\hat{p})$.

We shall solve this problem explicitly, by "reducing" it to *an auxiliary finite-horizon problem*. To this end, let us consider the process

$$(2.5.7) \qquad N^p(t) \triangleq \left(X^p(t) - \beta \frac{M^p(t)}{\gamma(t)} \right) \left(M^p(t) \right)^{\beta/(1-\beta)}, \quad 0 \leq t < \infty$$

for any given $p \in \mathcal{A}_\beta(x)$. Because $M^p(\cdot)$ is flat away from the set $\{t \geq 0/\gamma(t)X^p(t) = M^p(t)\}$, we see from (2.5.3) that this process satisfies

$$d\left(\gamma(t)N^p(t)\right) = \left(\gamma(t)N^p(t)\right)p'(t)\sigma(t)\, dW^{(0)}(t),$$

or equivalently

(2.5.8) $d\big(H_0(t)N^p(t)\big) = \big(H_0(t)N^p(t)\big)\big(\sigma'(t)p(t) - \theta(t)\big)'\,dW(t).$

As a consequence,

(2.5.9) $H_0(t)N^p(t) = (1 - \beta)x^{1/(1-\beta)}$

$$\times \exp\left\{\int_0^t \big(\sigma'(s)p(s) - \theta(s)\big)'\,dW(s) - \frac{1}{2}\int_0^T \big\|\sigma'(s)p(s) - \theta(s)\big\|^2\,ds\right\}$$

is a positive local martingale, hence also supermartingale:

(2.5.10) $\mathbb{E}\left(H_0(T)N^p(T)\right) \le (1 - \beta)x^{1/(1-\beta)}, \qquad \forall\, p \in \mathcal{A}_\beta(x), \quad \forall\, T \in (0, \infty).$

2.5.4. AUXILIARY PROBLEM ON $[0, T]$, $T < \infty$. For a given utility function U: $(0, \infty) \to \mathbb{R}$ as in Definition 2.1.2, and for given initial capital $x \in (0, \infty)$ and $0 < \beta < 1$, consider the stochastic control problem

(2.5.11) $V(\beta; T, x) \triangleq \sup_{p \in \mathcal{A}_\beta(T, x)} \mathbb{E}\, U\big(N^p(T)\big)$

in the notation of Definition 2.5.1 and of (2.5.7).

The martingale methods that we developed in Section 2.2, provide a complete solution to this problem as well; we leave the straightforward details as an exercise.

2.5.5. EXERCISE. There is a portfolio-proportion process $\hat{p} \in \mathcal{A}_\beta(T, x)$ with

(2.5.12) $N^{\hat{p}}(T) = I\big(\hat{y}H_0(T)\big),$

where $I = (U')^{-1}$ and $\hat{y} > 0$ is uniquely determined by the equation

(2.5.13) $\mathbb{E}\left[H_0(T)I\big(\hat{y}H_0(T)\big)\right] = (1 - \beta)x^{1/(1-\beta)}$

(this is just (2.5.10) for $p = \hat{p}$, valid as an equality). The process $\hat{p}(\cdot)$ is found by introducing the positive martingale $Q(\cdot)$ below, and representing it as a stochastic integral

(2.5.14) $Q(t) \triangleq \mathbb{E}\left[H_0(T)I\big(\hat{y}H_0(T)\big) \mid \mathcal{F}(t)\right]$

$$= (1 - \beta)x^{1/(1-\beta)} + \int_0^t Q(s)\varphi'(s)\,dW(s), \quad 0 \le t \le T,$$

by setting

(2.5.15) $\hat{p}(\cdot) = \big(\sigma^{-1}(\cdot)\big)'\left[\theta(\cdot) + \varphi(\cdot)\right], \quad H_0(\cdot)N^{\hat{p}}(\cdot) = Q(\cdot).$

This process attains the supremum in (2.5.11); in particular,

(2.5.16) $V(\beta; T, x) = \mathbb{E}\left[(U \circ I)(\hat{y}H_0(T))\right].$

For instance, consider Problem 2.5.3 with

(2.5.17) $U(x) = \dfrac{x^\alpha}{\alpha}, \quad 0 \le x < \infty \quad \text{for } \alpha = \delta(1 - \beta), \text{and let } \mu \triangleq \dfrac{\alpha}{1 - \alpha}.$

Then (2.5.13), (2.5.16) give $(\hat{y})^{-1/(1-\alpha)} = \big((1 - \beta)x^{1/(1-\beta)}\big)/\big(\mathbb{E}\,(H_0(T))^{-\mu}\big)$ and

(2.5.18) $V(\beta; T, x) = \dfrac{1}{\alpha}\left((1 - \beta)x^{1/(1-\beta)} \cdot \big(\mathbb{E}\,\big(H_0(T)\big)^{-\mu}\big)^{1/\mu}\right)^\alpha.$

If, in addition, *the coefficients $r(\cdot)$, $b(\cdot)$, $\sigma(\cdot)$ are deterministic*, then

$$\left(H_0(t)\right)^{-\mu} = \exp\left[\mu \int_0^t \theta'(s)\, dW(s) - \frac{\mu^2}{2} \int_0^t \|\theta(s)\|^2\, ds\right]$$

$$\times \exp\left\{\mu \int_0^t \left(r(s) + \frac{1+\mu}{2}\|\theta(s)\|^2\right) ds\right\}$$

and (2.5.18) becomes

(2.5.19) $V(\beta; T, x)$

$$= \frac{1}{\alpha}\left((1-\beta)x^{1/(1-\beta)} \cdot \exp\left\{\int_0^T \left(r(t) + \frac{1+\mu}{2}\|\theta(t)\|^2\right) dt\right\}\right)^\alpha;$$

on the other hand, from (2.5.14), (2.5.15) we obtain then

(2.5.20)
$$Q(t) = (1-\beta)x^{1/(1-\beta)} \exp\left\{\mu \int_0^t \theta'(s)\, dW(s) - \frac{\mu^2}{2} \int_0^t \|\theta(s)\|^2\, ds\right\},$$

$$\varphi(t) = \mu\theta(t)$$

and

(2.5.21) $\hat{p}(t) = (1+\mu)\left(\sigma^{-1}(t)\right)'\theta(t) = \dfrac{1}{1 - \delta(1-\beta)}\left(\sigma^{-1}(t)\right)'\theta(t), \quad 0 \le t < \infty.$

The optimal portfolio/proportion process $\hat{p}(\cdot)$ is thus well-defined by (2.5.21), for all $0 \le t < \infty$; from Exercise 2.5.2, it belongs to the class $\mathcal{A}_\beta(x)$ for every $x \in (0, \infty)$.

Here is the main result of this section.

2.5.6. THEOREM. *Suppose that the coefficients $r(\cdot)$, $b(\cdot)$, $\sigma(\cdot)$ of (2.1.1), (2.1.2) are deterministic, and that (2.3.17) holds. Then the portfolio/proportion process $\hat{p}(\cdot)$ of (2.5.21) is optimal for* Problem 2.5.3, *and we have*

(2.5.22) $v(\beta) = G(\hat{p}) = \displaystyle\lim_{T\to\infty} \frac{1}{T}\log \mathbb{E}\left(X^{\hat{p}}(T)\right)^\delta = V(\beta) + \beta\delta r_*,$

where

(2.5.23) $V(\beta) \triangleq \displaystyle\lim_{T\to\infty} \frac{1}{T}\log V(\beta; T, x) = \alpha r_* + \frac{\alpha}{2}(1+\mu)\|\theta_*\|^2$

$$= \delta(1-\beta)\left[r_* + \frac{\|\theta_*\|^2}{2}\frac{1}{1 - \delta(1-\beta)}\right].$$

PROOF. We shall consider the auxiliary problem

(2.5.24) $\bar{v}(\beta) \triangleq \displaystyle\sup_{p \in \mathcal{A}_\beta(x)} \bar{G}_\beta(p), \quad \bar{G}_\beta(p) \triangleq \overline{\lim}_{T\to\infty} \frac{1}{T}\log \mathbb{E}\left(N^p(T)\right)^{\delta(1-\beta)}.$

Since the process $\hat{p}(\cdot)$ of (2.5.21) does not depend on the horizon $T \in (0, \infty)$, we have from (2.5.17)–(2.5.21):

(2.5.25) $\bar{G}_\beta(\hat{p}) = \displaystyle\lim_{T\to\infty} \frac{1}{T}\log \mathbb{E}\left(N^{\hat{p}}(T)\right)^{\delta(1-\beta)}$

$$= \lim_{T\to\infty} \frac{1}{T}\log V(\beta; T, x) = V(\beta) = \bar{v}(\beta).$$

Notice also, from (2.5.7), that

(2.5.26) $\left(N^p(t)\right)^{\delta(1-\beta)} = \left(\gamma(t)\right)^{\beta\delta}\left(X^p(t)\right)^\delta \left(f_\beta\left(\dfrac{\beta M^p(t)}{\gamma(t)X^p(t)}\right)\right)^\delta,$

where

$$(2.5.27) \qquad f_\beta(x) \triangleq \left(\frac{x}{\beta}\right)^\beta (1-x)^{1-\beta}, \quad 0 \le x \le 1$$

is strictly increasing on $(0,\beta)$ and strictly decreasing on $(\beta,1)$. From (2.5.26) follows

$$(2.5.28) \qquad \mathbb{E}\left(N^p(T)\right)^{\delta(1-\beta)} \le \left(\gamma(T)\right)^{\beta\delta}(1-\beta)^{\delta(1-\beta)}\mathbb{E}\left(X^p(T)\right)^\delta,$$

and thus

$$(2.5.29) \qquad \bar{G}_\beta(p) \le G(p) - \beta\delta r_* \le v(\beta) - \beta\delta r_*, \qquad \forall\, p \in \mathcal{A}_\beta(x),$$

as well as $V(\beta) \le v(\beta) - \beta\delta r_*$ from (2.5.25), (2.5.24).

To obtain the inequality in the reverse direction, take $\eta \in (0,\beta)$ close enough to β, so that $f_\eta(\eta) \ge f_\eta(\eta/\beta)$, and observe from (2.5.27), (2.5.26) that

$$(2.5.30) \qquad \mathbb{E}\left(N^p(T)\right)^{\delta(1-\eta)} \ge \left(\gamma_0(T)\right)^{\delta\eta}\left(f_\eta\left(\frac{\eta}{\beta}\right)\right)^\delta \mathbb{E}\left(X^p(T)\right)^\delta$$

$$= \left(\gamma_0(T)\right)^{\eta\delta}\left(\beta^{-\eta}\left(1-\frac{\eta}{\beta}\right)^{(1-\eta)}\right)^\delta \mathbb{E}\left(X^p(T)\right)^\delta$$

holds for every $p \in \mathcal{A}_\beta(x) \subseteq \mathcal{A}_\eta(x)$. Therefore,

$$V(\eta) \ge \bar{G}_\eta(p) \ge G(p) - \delta\eta r_*, \qquad \forall\, p \in \mathcal{A}_\beta(x)$$

and thus $V(\eta) \ge v(\beta) - \delta\eta r_*$; now let $\eta \uparrow \beta$ and note that the function $V(\cdot)$ of (2.5.23) is continuous, to obtain $V(\beta) \ge v(\beta) - \delta\beta r_*$, and hence also

$$(2.5.31) \qquad v(\beta) = V(\beta) + \beta\delta r_* = \delta r_* + \frac{\|\theta_*\|^2}{2}\frac{\delta(1-\beta)}{1-\delta(1-\beta)}.$$

On the other hand, from (2.5.29), (2.5.25) and (2.5.31) we obtain $v(\beta) \ge G(\hat{p}) \ge \bar{G}_\beta(\hat{p}) + \delta\beta r_* = V(\beta) + \beta\delta r_* = v(\beta)$; in particular, this implies

$$(2.5.32) \qquad v(\beta) = G(\hat{p}).$$

It remains to verify the existence of the limit in (2.5.22); to this effect, observe from (2.5.28), (2.5.30) that we have the double inequality

$$-\frac{\delta(1-\beta)}{T}\log(1-\beta) + \frac{\beta\delta}{T}\int_0^T r(t)\,dt + \frac{1}{T}\log\mathbb{E}\left(N^{\hat{p}}(T)\right)^{(\delta(1-\beta))}$$

$$\le \frac{1}{T}\log\mathbb{E}\left(X^{\hat{p}}(T)\right)^\delta$$

$$\le -\frac{\delta}{T}\log\left(\frac{(1-\eta/\beta)^{(1-\eta)}}{\beta^\eta}\right) + \frac{\eta\delta}{T}\int_0^T r(t)\,dt$$

$$+ \frac{1}{T}\log\mathbb{E}\left(N^{\hat{p}}(T)\right)^{\delta(1-\eta)}.$$

Letting $T \to \infty$ and recalling (2.5.25), (2.3.17) we get

$$\beta\delta r_* + V(\beta) \le \varliminf_{T\to\infty}\frac{1}{T}\log\mathbb{E}\left(X^{\hat{p}}(T)\right)^\delta$$

$$\le \varlimsup_{T\to\infty}\frac{1}{T}\log\mathbb{E}\left(X^{\hat{p}}(T)\right)^\delta$$

$$\le \eta\delta r_* + V(\eta),$$

and letting $\eta \uparrow \beta$ we obtain

$$(2.5.33) \qquad \lim_{T \to \infty} \frac{1}{T} \log \mathbb{E}\left(X^{\hat{p}}(T)\right)^{\delta} = \beta \delta r_* + V(\beta).$$

All the claims of the Theorem (in particular, the equalities of (2.5.22)) follow now from (2.5.31)–(2.5.33). $\qquad\qquad\qquad\qquad\qquad\qquad\qquad\qquad\qquad\qquad\qquad\square$

2.5.7. REMARK. Setting formally $\beta = 0$ in (2.5.21), (2.5.2) we recover the optimal portfolio/proportion rule

$$(2.5.34) \qquad \hat{p}(t) \triangleq \frac{(\sigma^{-1}(t))'}{1 - \delta}\theta(t) = \frac{(\sigma(t)\sigma'(t))^{-1}}{1 - \delta}\left[b(t) - r(t)\mathbf{1}_d\right], \quad 0 \le t \le T$$

for the investment problem of Exercise 2.5.2, with utility function $U(x) = x^{\delta}/\delta$ from terminal wealth, and deterministic coefficients. It would be nice, to see whether the tools of this section could help treat Problem 2.1.5, on a finite-horizon $[0, T]$, but under the drawdown constraint (2.5.2) on portfolios.

2.5.8. EXERCISE. Show that the portfolio/proportion process $\hat{p}(\cdot) \in \mathcal{A}_{\beta}(x)$

$$(2.5.35) \qquad \hat{p}(t) \triangleq \left(\sigma^{-1}(t)\right)'\theta(t) = \left(\sigma(t)\sigma'(t)\right)^{-1}\left[b(t) - r(t)\mathbf{1}_d\right], \quad 0 \le t < \infty$$

maximizes the long-term growth rate from investment:

$$(2.5.36) \quad \overline{\lim}_{T \to \infty} \frac{1}{T} \log X^p(T) \le \lim_{T \to \infty} \frac{1}{T} \log X^{\hat{p}}(T) = r_* + (1 - \beta)\frac{\|\theta_*\|^2}{2}, \text{ a.s.}$$

over all $p(\cdot) \in \mathcal{A}_{\beta}(x)$, for any $x \in (0, \infty)$. (Note that, the process of (2.5.35) corresponds formally to that of (2.5.21) with $\delta = 0$. This result is the analogue of Proposition 2.3.5, in the case of the "drawdown constraint" (2.5.2). Just as in Proposition 2.3.5, the result is valid for general random, adapted coefficients, here under the additional condition (2.3.17).)

2.5.9. REMARK. Here is an argument for Exercise 2.5.2: clearly, it suffices to show that the equation

$$(2.5.37) \quad d\hat{X}(t) = \left(\hat{X}(t) - \beta \cdot \max_{0 \le s \le t} \hat{X}(s)\right)\rho'(t)\,dW^{(0)}(t), \quad \hat{X}(0) = x \in (0, \infty)$$

has a unique $\mathbb{F}$-adapted solution $\hat{X}(\cdot)$, which satisfies

$$(2.5.38) \qquad \mathbb{P}\left[\hat{X}(t) > \beta \hat{M}(t), \ \forall \ 0 \le t < \infty\right] = 1 \quad \text{with} \quad \hat{M}(t) \triangleq \max_{0 \le s \le t} \hat{X}(s).$$

Assume that such a solution exists; then, from (2.5.37),

$$d\log\left(\frac{\hat{X}(t)}{\hat{M}(t)} - \beta\right) = d\xi(t) - \frac{1}{1 - \beta}\frac{d\hat{M}(t)}{\hat{M}(t)},$$

where

$$\xi(t) \triangleq \int_0^t \rho'(s)\,dW^{(0)}(s) - \frac{1}{2}\int_0^t \|\rho(s)\|^2\,ds.$$

Consequently,

$$(2.5.39) \qquad 0 \le R(t) \triangleq \log\left(\frac{1 - \beta}{(\hat{X}(t)/\hat{M}(t)) - \beta}\right) = -\xi(t) + K(t), \quad 0 \le t < \infty$$

where the continuous, increasing process $K(t) \triangleq \log(\hat{M}(t)/x)/(1-\beta)$ is flat away from the set $\{t \geq 0/\hat{X}(t) = \hat{M}(t)\} = \{t \geq 0/R(t) = 0\}$. Now the theory of the Skorohod reflection problem gives

$$K(t) = \max_{0 \leq s \leq t} \xi(s)$$

(cf. Karatzas & Shreve (1991), §3.6) whence $\hat{M}(t) = x \cdot \exp\{(1-\beta)\max_{0 \leq s \leq t} \xi(s)\}$, and back in (2.5.39) this gives

$$(2.5.40) \quad \hat{X}(t) = x \cdot \exp\left\{(1-\beta) \cdot \max_{0 \leq s \leq t} \xi(s)\right\}$$
$$\times \left[\beta + (1-\beta) \cdot \exp\{\xi(t) - \max_{0 \leq s \leq t} \xi(s)\}\right], \quad 0 \leq t < \infty.$$

It is now relatively easy, to check that the right-hand side of (2.5.40) satisfies the equation (2.5.37) and the condition (2.5.38).

2.6. Goal problems

Let us consider now the model of (2.1.1), (2.1.2) with $r(\cdot) \equiv 0$, $\sigma(\cdot) \equiv 1$, and $b(\cdot) \equiv b \in (0, \infty)$ a given constant. Then for any given initial capital $x \in [0, 1]$, the wealth-process $X(\cdot) \equiv X^{x,\pi}(\cdot) \equiv X^{x,\pi,0}(\cdot)$ satisfies

$$(2.6.1) \qquad dX(t) = \pi(t)[dW(t) + b\,dt], \quad X(0) = x.$$

We shall denote by $\mathcal{H}(x)$ the class of (portfolio) processes $\pi \colon [0,T] \times \Omega \to \mathbb{R}$ which are $\mathbb{F}$-progressively measurable and satisfy

$$(2.6.2) \qquad \int_0^T \pi^2(t)\,dt < \infty \quad \text{and} \quad 0 \leq X^{x,\pi}(t) \leq 1, \qquad \forall\, 0 \leq t \leq T$$

almost surely.

2.6.1. REMARK. For an arbitrary $\mathbb{F}$-progressively measurable process $s \colon [0,T] \times \Omega \to \mathbb{R}$ with $\int_0^T s^2(t)\,dt < \infty$ a.s. and with

$$\chi(t) \triangleq x + \int_0^t s(u)[dW(u) + b\,du], \quad 0 \leq t \leq T,$$
$$\sigma \triangleq \inf\{t \in [0,T] \,/\, \chi(t) \notin (0,1)\} \wedge T$$

we have that

$$\pi(t) \triangleq \begin{cases} s(t); & 0 \leq t \leq \sigma \\ 0; & \sigma < t \leq T \end{cases} \quad \text{belongs to } \mathcal{H}(x),$$

and $X^{x,\pi}(\cdot) \equiv \chi(\cdot \wedge \sigma)$.

2.6.2. EXERCISE. For any $\pi(\cdot) \in \mathcal{H}(x)$ and with $\tau \triangleq \inf\{t \in [0,T]/X^{x,\pi}(t) \notin (0,1)\} \wedge T$, we have $X^{x,\pi}(\cdot) \equiv X^{x,\pi}(\cdot \wedge \tau)$.

In other words, the interval $S = [0,1]$ is now our state-space, and its endpoints $0, 1$ are *absorbing*. Our goal is to avoid getting absorbed at the origin, and to maximize the probability of reaching the wealth-level $x = 1$ by the time $t = T$.

2.6.3. PROBLEM. *Compute the value*

$$(2.6.3) \qquad G(x) \triangleq \sup_{\pi(\cdot) \in \mathcal{H}(x)} \mathbb{P}[X^{x,\pi}(T) = 1], \qquad 0 \leq x \leq 1,$$

and find a portfolio process $\hat{\pi}(\cdot) \in \mathcal{H}(x)$ that attains the supremum in (2.6.3).

Now let us observe from (0.2.11)–(0.2.13), (0.3.5) that we have here $\theta(t) \equiv b > 0$, $Z_0(t) = \exp\{-bW(t) - \frac{1}{2}b^2t\}$, $W^{(0)}(t) = W(t) + bt$ for $0 \le t \le T$ and $\mathbb{P}^0(A) = \mathbb{E}\left[Z_0(T)1_A\right]$, $A \in \mathcal{F}(T)$. Furthermore, for every $\pi(\cdot) \in \mathcal{H}(x)$ the process $X^{x,\pi}(\cdot)$ is a $\mathbb{P}^0$-local martingale with values in $[0,1]$, hence a $\mathbb{P}^0$-martingale; thus

$$(2.6.4) \qquad \mathbb{P}^0\left[X^{x,\pi}(T) = 1\right] = \mathbb{E}^0\left[X^{x,\pi}(T)1_{\{X^{x,\pi}(T)=1\}}\right] \le \mathbb{E}^0\left[X^{x,\pi}(T)\right] = x,$$

$$(2.6.5) \qquad \mathbb{P}\left[X^{x,\pi}(T) = 1\right] \le \sup_{\substack{B \in \mathcal{F}(T) \\ \mathbb{P}^0(B) \le x}} \mathbb{P}(B) =: G_*(x), \qquad \forall\, \pi(\cdot) \in \mathcal{H}(x).$$

Clearly from (2.6.3), (2.6.5): $G(x) \le G_*(x)$, and we shall see in Theorem 2.6.4 below that actually $G(x) = G_*(x)$. The point here is that $G_*(x)$ is *very easy to compute*, thanks to the celebrated Neyman-Pearson lemma (cf. Lehmann (1986), p. 74).

According to this result, if we can find a number $k = k(x) > 0$ such that the event

$$(2.6.6) \qquad B_k \triangleq \left\{ \frac{d\mathbb{P}}{d\mathbb{P}^0} \ge k \right\} \quad \text{has} \quad \mathbb{P}^0(B_k) = x, \quad \text{then} \quad G_*(x) = \mathbb{P}(B_k).$$

But $(d\mathbb{P}/d\mathbb{P}^0) = \exp\{bW(T) + \frac{1}{2}b^2T\} = \exp\{bW^{(0)}(T) - \frac{b^2}{2}T\}$, and thus

$$\mathbb{P}^0(B_k) = \mathbb{P}^0\left[\frac{W^{(0)}(T)}{\sqrt{T}} \ge \frac{\log k}{b\sqrt{T}} + \frac{b}{2}\sqrt{T}\right] = \Phi\left(-\frac{b}{2}\sqrt{T} - \frac{\log k}{b\sqrt{T}}\right),$$

with the notation

$$\Phi(x) \triangleq \int_{-\infty}^x \varphi(u)\, du, \qquad \varphi(x) \triangleq \frac{1}{\sqrt{2\pi}} e^{-x^2/2}.$$

In other words, the requirement $\mathbb{P}^0(B_k) = x$ of (2.6.6) is equivalent to

$$(2.6.7) \qquad \log k = -b\sqrt{T} \cdot \Phi^{-1}(x) - \frac{b^2}{2}T,$$

and from (2.6.6), (2.6.7) we deduce

$$(2.6.8) \qquad G_*(x) = \mathbb{P}(B_k) = \mathbb{P}\left[bW(T) + \frac{b^2}{2}T \ge \log k\right]$$

$$= \mathbb{P}\left[-\frac{W(T)}{\sqrt{T}} \le \Phi^{-1}(x) + b\sqrt{T}\right]$$

$$= \Phi\left(\Phi^{-1}(x) + b\sqrt{T}\right), \quad 0 \le x \le 1.$$

2.6.4. THEOREM (Kulldorff (1993), Heath (1993)). *The value function $G(\cdot)$ of Problem 2.6.3 is given as*

$$(2.6.9) \qquad G(x) = \Phi\left(\Phi^{-1}(x) + b\sqrt{T}\right), \quad 0 \le x \le 1.$$

An optimal portfolio process $\hat{\pi}(\cdot) \in \mathcal{H}(x)$, and its corresponding wealth process $\hat{X}(\cdot) = X^{x,\hat{\pi}}(\cdot)$, are given by

$$(2.6.10) \qquad \hat{X}(t) = Q\left(t, W(t) + bt; x\right), \quad \hat{\pi}(t) = \frac{1}{\sqrt{T-t}} \varphi\left(\Phi^{-1}(\hat{X}(t))\right)1_{[0,T)}(t)$$

where

$$(2.6.11) \qquad Q(t,y;x) \triangleq \left\{ \begin{array}{l} \Phi\left(\dfrac{y + \sqrt{T}\Phi^{-1}(x)}{\sqrt{T-t}}\right); \quad 0 \le t < T \\[2ex] 1_{[-\sqrt{T}\Phi^{-1}(x),\infty)}(y); \quad t = T \end{array} \right\}.$$

PROOF. We have already shown that $G(x) \le G_*(x)$; in order to establish the reverse inequality (and thus (2.6.9) are well), it suffices to exhibit a process $\hat{\pi}(\cdot) \in \mathcal{H}(x)$ such that

$$(2.6.12) \qquad \{X^{x,\hat{\pi}}(T) = 1\} = B_k, \qquad \text{mod } \mathbb{P}.$$

To this end, introduce the $\mathbb{P}^0$-martingale

$$(2.6.13) \qquad \hat{X}(t) \triangleq \mathbb{P}^0[B_k \mid \mathcal{F}(t)] = \mathbb{P}^0\left[bW^{(0)}(T) - \frac{b^2}{2}T \ge \log k \,\Big|\, \mathcal{F}(t)\right]$$

$$= \mathbb{P}^0\left[W^{(0)}(T) - W^{(0)}(t) \ge -W^{(0)}(t) - \sqrt{T}\Phi^{-1}(x) \mid \mathcal{F}(t)\right]$$

$$= Q(t, W^{(0)}(t); x), \quad 0 \le t \le T$$

in the notation of (2.6.11); clearly $\hat{X}(0) = x$, $\hat{X}(T) = 1_{B_k}$ a.s. and $\hat{X}(\cdot)$ takes values in the interval $[0,1]$. From the martingale representation result of Exercise 0.3.6, there exists an $\mathbb{F}$-progressively measurable process $\hat{\pi} \colon [0,T] \times \Omega \to \mathbb{R}$ with $\int_0^T (\hat{\pi}(t))^2 \, dt < \infty$ a.s. and

$$(2.6.14) \qquad \hat{X}(t) = x + \int_0^t \hat{\pi}(s)[dW(s) + b\,ds], \quad 0 \le t \le T.$$

Clearly then $\hat{X}(\cdot) = X^{x,\hat{\pi}}(\cdot)$, (2.6.12) is satisfied, and $\hat{\pi}(\cdot) \in \mathcal{H}(x)$.

In order now to *compute* this $\hat{\pi}(\cdot) \in \mathcal{H}(x)$, let us observe that the function Q of (2.6.11) satisfies the backwards heat equation

$$Q_t + \frac{1}{2}Q_{yy} = 0 \quad \text{on } [0,T) \times (0,1);$$

thus, an application of Itô's rule to $\hat{X}(t) = Q(t, W^{(0)}(t); x)$ of (2.6.13) gives

$$(2.6.15) \qquad \hat{X}(t) = x + \int_0^t Q_y(s, W^{(0)}(s); x)\, dW^{(0)}(s), \quad 0 \le t \le T,$$

and a comparison of (2.6.14), (2.6.15) leads to the portfolio

$$\hat{\pi}(t) = Q_y(t, W^{(0)}(t); x)$$

$$= \frac{1}{\sqrt{T-t}}\varphi\left(\frac{W^{(0)}(t) + \sqrt{T}\Phi^{-1}(x)}{\sqrt{T-t}}\right) = \frac{1}{\sqrt{T-t}}\varphi\big(\Phi^{-1}(\hat{X}(t))\big)$$

of (2.6.10). $\qquad\qquad\qquad\qquad\qquad\qquad\qquad\qquad\qquad\qquad\qquad\qquad\qquad\square$

2.6.5. EXERCISE. The portfolio $\hat{\pi}(\cdot)$ of Theorem 2.6.4 is tame, and attains also the supremum in

$$(2.6.16) \quad G_0(x) \triangleq \sup_{\substack{\pi(\cdot) \text{ tame} \\ X^{x,\pi}(T) \ge 0, \text{ a.s.}}} \mathbb{P}\big[X^{x,\pi}(T) \ge 1\big] = \Phi\big(\Phi^{-1}(x) + b\sqrt{T}\big),$$

$$0 \le x \le 1.$$

(*Hint*: Clearly $G_*(x) = G(x) \leq G_0(x)$ from Theorem 2.6.4 and (2.6.16); on the other hand, for any $\pi(\cdot)$ tame with $X^{x,\pi}(T) \geq 0$ a.s., we have the analogue $\mathbb{P}^0[X^{x,\pi}(T) \geq 1] \leq \mathbb{E}^0[X^{x,\pi}(T)1_{\{X^{x,\pi}(T) \geq 1\}}] \leq \mathbb{E}^0[X^{x,\pi}(T)] \leq x$ of (2.6.4) since $X^{x,\pi}(\cdot)$ is a $\mathbb{P}^0$-supermartingale, which gives $G_0(x) \leq G_*(x)$.)

2.6.6. REMARK (Maximizing probability of perfect hedge; Föllmer (1995)). Let us consider now a contingent claim Y which, in order to simplify ideas, will be assumed a.s. bounded: $\mathbb{P}[0 \leq Y \leq a] = 1$, for some $a \in (0, \infty)$. Then we have

$$(2.6.17) \qquad \mathbb{E}^0(Y \mid \mathcal{F}(t)) = u_0 + \int_0^t \pi^Y(s)\,dW^{(0)}(s), \quad 0 \leq t \leq T$$

where $\pi^Y(\cdot)$ is the tame hedging portfolio of Theorem 1.2.1, and $u_0 \triangleq \mathbb{E}^0(Y) \in (0, \infty)$ coincides with the (upper) hedging price

$$u_0 = h_{\mathrm{up}} = \inf\{x \geq 0 \;/\; \exists \xi(\cdot) \text{ tame s.t. } X^{x,\xi}(T) \geq Y, \text{ a.s. }\}$$

of Y. Suppose that *an agent starts out with initial capital* $x_0 \in (0, u_0)$ *strictly smaller than this hedging price.* Clearly, he cannot achieve a "perfect hedge" $X^{x_0,\xi}(T) \geq Y$ almost surely (recall Exercise 0.3.3); so he looks at the probability

$$(2.6.18) \qquad p(\xi) \triangleq \mathbb{P}[X^{x_0,\xi}(T) \geq Y], \quad \xi(\cdot) \text{ tame}, \quad X^{x_0+u_0,\xi}(T) \geq Y \text{ a.s.}$$

of a perfect hedge, and tries to maximize it over all tame portfolios $\xi(\cdot)$ that satisfy $X^{x_0+u_0,\xi}(T) \geq Y$ a.s. Now from (2.6.18), (2.6.17) and (2.6.1) we have

$$(2.6.19) \qquad p(\xi) = \mathbb{P}\left[x_0 + \int_0^T \xi(t)\,dW^{(0)}(t) \geq u_0 + \int_0^T \pi^Y(t)\,dW^{(0)}(t)\right]$$

$$= \mathbb{P}\left[x + \int_0^T \pi(t)\,dW^{(0)}(t) \geq 1\right],$$

where $x \triangleq (x_0/u_0) \in (0,1)$, and $\pi(\cdot) \triangleq (\xi(\cdot) - \pi^Y(\cdot))/u_0$ defines a tame portfolio with $X^{x,\pi}(T) \geq 0$ a.s. Thus (2.6.19) and (2.6.16) lead to

$$(2.6.20) \qquad p(\xi) \leq \mathbb{P}\left[x + \int_0^T \hat{\pi}(t)\,dW^{(0)}(t) \geq 1\right] = p(\hat{\xi}) = \Phi(\Phi^{-1}(x) + b\sqrt{T})$$

for any portfolio $\xi(\cdot)$ as in (2.6.18), where

$$(2.6.21) \qquad \hat{\xi}(\cdot) = u_0\hat{\pi}(\cdot) + \pi^Y(\cdot)$$

and $\hat{\pi}(\cdot)$ is the portfolio of Theorem 2.6.4.

The portfolio $\hat{\xi}(\cdot)$ of (2.6.21) satisfies the conditions in (2.6.18); and we know from (2.6.20) that, among such portfolios, $\hat{\xi}(\cdot)$ maximizes the probability of achieving a perfect hedge, this maximal probability being

$$(2.6.22) \qquad \Phi\left(\Phi^{-1}\left(\frac{x_0}{u_0}\right) + b\sqrt{T}\right).$$

For instance, if the agent can tolerate a risk of $100\varepsilon\%$ ($0 < \varepsilon < 1$) of missing the perfect hedge, then he can determine the "right" initial capital $x_0 \in (0, u_0)$ by setting the expression of (2.6.22) equal to $1 - \varepsilon$, namely

$$(2.6.23) \qquad x_0 = u_0 \cdot \Phi(\Phi^{-1}(1 - \varepsilon) - b\sqrt{T}).$$

For example, if $b = T = 1$ and $\varepsilon = 1\%$, then $(x_0/u_0) = 90\%$; if $\varepsilon = 5\%$, then $(x_0/u_0) = 74\%$.

REMARKS. A very attractive feature of the feedback formula

$$\hat{\pi}(t) = \frac{1}{\sqrt{T-t}} \varphi \big(\Phi^{-1} \big(\hat{X}(t) \big) \big) 1_{[0,T)}(t)$$

of (2.6.10) for the optimal portfolio, is that it does not involve the stock appreciation rate b, as long as this rate is a known positive constant. This ceases to be the case even for deterministic, strictly positive but time-varying $b(\cdot)$, as the reader can verify easily by going through the computations once more. It would be interesting to study Problem 2.6.3 with random, adapted $b(\cdot)$, in some generality.

CHAPTER 3

Equilibrium

3.1. Introduction

We shall consider in this chapter an economy consisting of a finite number K of agents, who are endowed continuously in units of a single perishable commodity. Their (exogenous) *endowment-rate processes* $\varepsilon_k \colon [0,T] \times \Omega \to [0,\infty)$, $k = 1, \ldots, K$ will be assumed progressively measurable with respect to the augmentation $\mathbb{F}$ of the natural filtration generated by an $\mathbb{R}^d$-valued Brownian motion $W = (W_1, \ldots, W_d)'$, as in (0.1.3). The *aggregate endowment*

$$(3.1.1) \qquad \varepsilon(t) \triangleq \sum_{k=1}^{K} \varepsilon_k(t), \qquad 0 \le t \le T$$

will be taken as a continuous, positive semimartingale

$$(3.1.2) \qquad d\varepsilon(t) = \varepsilon(t)\big[\nu(t)\,dt + \rho'(t)dW(t)\big], \quad \varepsilon(0) > 0;$$

here $\nu(\cdot)$, $\rho(\cdot)$ are bounded, $\mathbb{F}$-progressively measurable processes with values in $\mathbb{R}$ and $\mathbb{R}^d$, respectively. It will be assumed throughout that for suitable constants δ and Δ we have

$$(3.1.3) \qquad 0 < \delta \le \varepsilon(t) \le \Delta < \infty, \qquad \forall\, 0 \le t \le T$$

almost surely, and

$$(3.1.4) \qquad (\lambda \otimes \mathbb{P})\{\varepsilon_k > 0\} > 0, \qquad \forall\, k = 1, \ldots, K.$$

In addition to his endowment-rate process, each agent has a *utility function* $U_k \colon (0, \infty) \to \mathbb{R}$ of class $C^3(0, \infty)$, as in Definition 2.1.2. The collections of endowment-rate processes and utility functions $\big\{\varepsilon_k(\cdot), U_k(\cdot)\big\}_{k=1}^{K}$ constitute the *primitives* of the economy.

In order to hedge the uncertainty associated with their future endowments, and to smooth-out the nonuniformities in both their endowments and utilities, these agents find it useful to trade in a market $\mathcal{M}$ consisting of one bond and several stocks, as in (0.1.1)–(0.1.2). Let us suppose that each agent's goal is to maximize his expected utility from consumption of the commodity over the finite time-horizon $[0, T]$, by proper choice of portfolio/consumption rules. The *equilibrium problem* is to construct the market $\mathcal{M}$ based on the law of supply-and-demand; in other words, to describe bond- and stock-prices which, when accepted by the individual agents in the determination of their optimal strategies, ensure that the commodity is consumed in its entirety as it enters the economy (cf. condition (3.4.1) below) and that all assets are held in zero net-supply (cf. conditions (3.4.2)–(3.4.3) below).

We set up the market model $\mathcal{M}$, and solve within it the individual agents' optimization problems using the martingale methodologies of Chapter 2, in Sections 3.2 and 3.3, respectively. Equilibrium is defined formally in Section 3.4, and the search for it is reduced to finding a vector $\Lambda^* = (\lambda_1^*, \ldots, \lambda_K^*)'$ of positive numbers, representing the "weights" that a fictitious "representative agent" attaches to the various agents according to each one's relative importance in the economy; cf. Section 3.5 and equation (3.4.9). Under appropriate conditions existence and uniqueness of equilibrium are established in Section 3.6; some simple examples, which admit explicit computations, are presented in Section 3.8; and the determination of equilibrium asset prices, the famous *Capital Asset Pricing Model*, is developed in Section 3.7.

3.2. The market model

Consider a *standard, complete* market model $\mathcal{M}$, with asset prices

$$(3.2.1) \qquad\qquad\qquad dB(t) = B(t)r(t)\,dt$$

$$(3.2.2) \qquad dP_i(t) = P_i(t)\left[b_i(t)\,dt + \sum_{j=1}^{d} \sigma_{ij}(t)dW_j(t) \right], \quad P_i(0) = p_i \in (0, \infty),$$

$$i = 1, \ldots, d$$

denominated in units of the commodity (recall Definition 0.2.5 and Theorem 0.3.5). It will be assumed that the volatility matrix $\sigma(\cdot) = \{\sigma_{ij}(\cdot)\}_{1 \leq i,j \leq d}$ is *invertible* a.e. on $[0, T] \times \Omega$, and we shall impose the a.s. conditions

$$(3.2.3) \qquad \kappa \geq r(t) \geq -\eta, \quad \delta_0 \leq H_0(t) \leq \Delta_0; \qquad \forall\, 0 \leq t \leq T$$

on the interest rate $r(\cdot)$ and on the "state-price-density" process $H_0(\cdot)$ of (2.1.5), for some real numbers $\eta \geq 0$, $\kappa > 0$, $\Delta_0 > \delta_0 > 0$.

Each agent $k = 1, \ldots, K$ can choose a *portfolio process* $\pi_k \colon [0, T] \times \Omega \to \mathbb{R}^d$ and a *consumption-rate process* $c_k \colon [0, T] \times \Omega \to [0, \infty)$. These are both $\mathbb{F}$-progressively measurable, and satisfy

$$\int_0^T c_k(t)\,dt < \infty, \quad \int_0^T \left\| \sigma'(t)\pi_k(t) \right\|^2 dt < \infty$$

almost surely. Then the *wealth process* $X_k(\cdot) \equiv X^{0, \pi_k, C_k - E_k}(\cdot)$ corresponding to the cumulative consumption process $C_k(t) = \int_0^t c_k(s)\,ds$ and the cumulative endowment process $E_k(t) = \int_0^t \varepsilon_k(s)\,ds$, $0 \leq t \leq T$ as in Remark 0.2.8, is given by

$$(3.2.4) \quad \gamma(t)X_k(t) = \int_0^t \gamma(u)\left[\varepsilon_k(u) - c_k(u) \right]du + \int_0^t \gamma(u)\pi_k'(u)\sigma(u)\,dW^{(0)}(u),$$

$$0 \leq t \leq T$$

by analogy with (0.2.21), or equivalently as

$$(3.2.5) \quad H_0(t)X_k(t) + \int_0^t H_0(s)\left[c_k(s) - \varepsilon_k(s) \right]ds$$

$$= \int_0^t H_0(s)\left(\sigma'(s)\pi_k(s) - X_k(s)\theta(s) \right)' dW(s), \qquad 0 \leq t \leq T$$

(by analogy with (2.1.6)).

3.2.1. DEFINITION. A portfolio/consumption process pair (π_k, C_k) is said to be *admissible for the kth agent*, if the corresponding wealth process $X_k(\cdot)$ of (3.2.5) satisfies

$$(3.2.6) \qquad H_0(t)X_k(t) + \mathbb{E}\left(\int_t^T H_0(s)\varepsilon_k(s)\,ds \;\Big|\; \mathcal{F}(t)\right) \geq 0, \qquad \forall\, 0 \leq t \leq T$$

almost surely. The resulting class of pairs (π_k, C_k) will be denoted by $\mathcal{A}_k$.

The condition (3.2.6) is a weakening of the requirement $X_k(t) \geq 0$ of (2.1.4). In the presence of a positive random endowment stream, the wealth is allowed to become negative, provided that the "present value of future endowments" process $\mathbb{E}\left[\int_t^T H_0(s)\varepsilon_k(s)\,ds \mid \mathcal{F}(t)\right] / H_0(t)$, evaluated according to the state-price-density process $H_0(\cdot)$ of (2.1.5), is large enough to offset such a negative value in the manner of (3.2.6). On the other hand, using the conditions (3.1.3), (3.2.3) and the nonnegativity of $c_k(\cdot)$, it is not hard to see that (3.2.6) *implies the tameness of the portfolio* $\pi_k(\cdot)$. Similar reasoning shows that, for every pair $(\pi_k, C_k) \in \mathcal{A}_k$, the process of (3.2.5) is a local martingale and is bounded from below, hence a supermartingale, and this implies

$$(3.2.7) \qquad \mathbb{E}\int_0^T H_0(t)c_k(t)\,dt \leq \mathbb{E}\left[H_0(T)X_k(T) + \int_0^T H_0(t)c_k(t)\,dt\right]$$

$$\leq \mathbb{E}\int_0^T H_0(t)\varepsilon_k(t)\,dt$$

in conjunction with (3.2.6). We also have the following analogue of Proposition 2.2.1.

3.2.2. PROPOSITION. *Let $C_k(\cdot) = \int_0^{\cdot} c_k(s)\,ds$ be a consumption process which satisfies (3.2.7) as an equality, i.e.*

$$(3.2.8) \qquad \mathbb{E}\int_0^T H_0(t)c_k(t)\,dt = \mathbb{E}\int_0^T H_0(t)\varepsilon_k(t)\,dt.$$

There exists then a portfolio process $\pi_k(\cdot)$ such that $(\pi_k, C_k) \in \mathcal{A}_k$, and the corresponding wealth-process $X_k(\cdot) \equiv X^{0,\pi_k, C_k - E_k}(\cdot)$ is given by

$$(3.2.9) \qquad X_k(t) = \frac{1}{H_0(t)}\mathbb{E}\left[\int_t^T H_0(s)\big(c_k(s) - \varepsilon_k(s)\big)\,ds \;\Big|\; \mathcal{F}(t)\right], \qquad 0 \leq t \leq T.$$

3.3. Individual optimization problem

Each agent, say the kth, is faced with the following problem: *to maximize the expected total discounted utility from consumption*

$$(3.3.1) \qquad \mathbb{E}\int_0^T e^{-\int_0^t \beta(s)\,ds} U_k\big(c_k(t)\big)\,dt$$

over portfolio/consumption process pairs in the class

$$(3.3.2) \qquad \mathcal{A}_k^* \triangleq \left\{(\pi_k, C_k) \in \mathcal{A}_k \;\Big/\; \mathbb{E}\int_0^T e^{-\int_0^t \beta(s)\,ds} U_k^-\big(c_k(t)\big)\,dt < \infty\right\}.$$

Here $\beta \colon [0, T] \to \mathbb{R}$ is a given bounded measurable function, that plays the role of a "discount rate" in the economy.

By analogy with Theorem 2.3.1, the optimal pair $(\hat{\pi}_k, \hat{C}_k)$ for this problem, and the corresponding wealth process $\hat{X}_k(\cdot) \equiv X^{0,\hat{\pi}_k,\hat{C}_k - E_k}(\cdot)$, are given by

$$(3.3.3) \qquad \hat{c}_k(t) = I_k\left(y_k H_0(t) e^{\int_0^t \beta(s)\,ds}\right)$$

$$(3.3.4) \qquad \sigma'(t)\hat{\pi}_k(t) = \frac{1}{H_0(t)}\psi_k(t) + \hat{X}_k(t)\theta(t)$$

$$(3.3.5) \qquad \hat{X}_k(t) = \frac{1}{H_0(t)}\mathbb{E}\left[\int_t^T H_0(s)\bigl(\hat{c}_k(s) - \varepsilon_k(s)\bigr)\,ds \,\Big|\, \mathcal{F}(t)\right], \qquad 0 \le t \le T.$$

Here $\psi_k(\cdot)$ is the integrand in the representation of the martingale

$$(3.3.6) \qquad \hat{M}_k(t) \triangleq \mathbb{E}\left[\int_0^T H_0(s)\bigl(\hat{c}_k(s) - \varepsilon_k(s)\bigr)\,ds \,\Big|\, \mathcal{F}(t)\right]$$

$$= \int_0^t \psi_k'(s)\,dW(s), \qquad 0 \le t \le T$$

as a stochastic integral with respect to the Brownian motion W; the function $I_k(\cdot) = \left(U_k'(\cdot)\right)^{-1}$ is as in Section 2.1; and the number $y_k > 0$ is uniquely determined by the equation

$$(3.3.7) \quad \mathbb{E}\int_0^T H_0(t)I_k\left(y_k H_0(t)e^{\int_0^t \beta(s)\,ds}\right)dt = \mathbb{E}\int_0^T H_0(t)\varepsilon_k(t)\,dt,$$

$$k = 1, \ldots, K.$$

3.3.1. EXERCISE. Show that the function

$$\mathcal{X}_k(y) \triangleq \mathbb{E}\int_0^T H_0(t)I_k\left(yH_0(t)e^{\int_0^t \beta(s)\,ds}\right)dt, \quad 0 < y < \infty$$

maps $(0, \infty)$ onto itself, and is continuous and strictly increasing with $\mathcal{X}_k(0+) = \infty$, $\mathcal{X}_k(\infty) = 0$. In particular, $y_k > 0$ is uniquely determined by (3.3.7).

3.3.2. EXERCISE. Show that the pair $(\hat{\pi}_k, \hat{C}_k)$ is the unique pair in the class $\mathcal{A}_k^*$ of (3.3.2), that attains the supremum of the expression (3.3.1) over this class (i.e., is optimal in $\mathcal{A}_k^*$ for the problem of this section).

3.4. Equilibrium

We shall say that the financial market $\mathcal{M}$ of (3.2.1)–(3.2.3) results in *equilibrium* if the following conditions hold, almost surely.

(i) *Clearing of the commodity market:*

$$(3.4.1) \qquad \sum_{k=1}^K \hat{c}_k(t) = \varepsilon(t), \qquad 0 \le t \le T.$$

(ii) *Clearing of the stock markets:* For every $j = 1, \ldots, d$, we have

$$(3.4.2) \qquad \sum_{k=1}^K \hat{\pi}_{kj}(t) = 0, \qquad 0 \le t \le T.$$

(iii) *Clearing of the bond market:*

$$(3.4.3) \qquad \sum_{k=1}^K \hat{X}_k(t) = 0, \qquad 0 \le t \le T.$$

Here, $\hat{c}_k(\cdot)$, $\hat{\pi}_k(\cdot)$, $\hat{X}_k(\cdot)$ are the optimal processes in (3.3.3)–(3.3.5) of the previous section.

For the remainder of this chapter, our efforts will focus on characterizing, and then constructing, such an equilibrium market $\mathcal{M}$.

3.4.1. PROPOSITION. *The conditions (3.4.1)–(3.4.3) lead to the* a.s. *equality*

$$(3.4.4) \qquad \varepsilon(t) = \sum_{k=1}^{K} I_k\big(y_k H_0(t) e^{\int_0^t \beta(s)\,ds}\big), \qquad 0 \le t \le T$$

where $y_1,\ldots,y_K$ are given by (3.3.7). Conversely, suppose that there exists a standard financial market $\mathcal{M}$ as in (3.2.1)–(3.2.3), for which the process $H_0(\cdot)$ of (2.1.5) satisfies (3.3.7) and (3.4.4), for suitable $(y_1,\ldots,y_K) \in (0,\infty)^K$. Then this market results in equilibrium.

PROOF. For the first claim, just observe that (3.4.4) follows from (3.4.1), (3.3.3). To see the converse, note that for the market $\mathcal{M}$ in question the optimal consumption-rate and wealth processes $\hat{c}_k(\cdot)$, $\hat{X}_k(\cdot)$, $k = 1,\ldots,K$ are still given by (3.3.3), (3.3.5) respectively. The condition (3.4.1) follows then directly from (3.4.4), (3.3.3); it leads in turn to both (3.4.3) and (3.4.2) because, by summing up over $k = 1,\ldots,K$ in (3.3.3)–(3.3.6), one obtains successively $\sum_{k=1}^{K} \hat{X}_k(t) \equiv 0$ (i.e., (3.4.3)), as well as $\sum_{k=1}^{K} \hat{M}_k(t) \equiv 0$, $\sum_{k=1}^{K} \psi_k(t) \equiv 0$, and $\sigma'(t)\sum_{k=1}^{K} \hat{\pi}_k(t) \equiv 0$, almost surely. From this last expression, and from our assumptions on $\sigma(\cdot)$, follows (3.4.2). □

We can rewrite (3.4.4) as

$$(3.4.5) \qquad \varepsilon(t) = I\big(H_0(t) e^{\int_0^t \beta(s)\,ds}; \Lambda^*\big) \quad \text{with} \quad \Lambda^* = \left(\frac{1}{y_1},\ldots,\frac{1}{y_K}\right),$$

where we have set

$$(3.4.6) \qquad I(y;\Lambda) \triangleq \sum_{k=1}^{K} I_k\left(\frac{y}{\lambda_k}\right), \quad 0 < y < \infty$$

for any given $\Lambda = (\lambda_1 \ldots, \lambda_K) \in (0,\infty)^K$. The function $I(\cdot;\Lambda)$ is continuous and strictly decreasing, and maps $(0,\infty)$ onto itself with $I(0+;\Lambda) = \infty$ and $I(\infty;\Lambda) = 0$; therefore, it has a continuous, strictly decreasing inverse $\mathcal{H}(\cdot;\Lambda): (0,\infty) \overset{\text{onto}}{\to} (0,\infty)$ with $\mathcal{H}(0+;\Lambda) = \infty$, $\mathcal{H}(\infty;\Lambda) = 0$, namely

$$(3.4.7) \qquad I\big(\mathcal{H}(x;\Lambda);\Lambda\big) = x, \qquad \forall\, 0 < x < \infty.$$

In terms of this function, the equation (3.4.5) is written as

$$(3.4.8) \qquad H_0(t) = e^{-\int_0^t \beta(s)\,ds}\mathcal{H}\big(\varepsilon(t);\Lambda^*\big), \qquad 0 \le t \le T,$$

and substituting this expression back into (3.3.7) we obtain

$$(3.4.9) \quad \mathbb{E}\int_0^T e^{-\int_0^t \beta(s)\,ds}\mathcal{H}\big(\varepsilon(t);\Lambda^*\big) I_k\left(\frac{\mathcal{H}(\varepsilon(t);\Lambda^*)}{\lambda_k^*}\right) dt$$

$$= \mathbb{E}\int_0^T e^{-\int_0^t \beta(s)\,ds}\mathcal{H}\big(\varepsilon(t);\Lambda^*\big)\varepsilon_k(t)\,dt, \quad \text{for every} \quad k = 1,\ldots,K.$$

In other words, *the search for an equilibrium market $\mathcal{M}$ has been reduced to the search for a vector $\Lambda^* \in (0,\infty)^K$ which satisfies (3.4.9).* Because then, the positive numbers $y_k = 1/(\lambda_k^*)$ $k = 1, \ldots, K$, and the process $H_0(\cdot)$ of (3.4.8), solve the equations of (3.3.7) and (3.4.4); the conditions for equilibrium are guaranteed by Proposition 3.4.1, and the optimal consumption-rate processes are given by (3.3.3), (3.4.8) as

$$(3.4.10) \quad \hat{c}_k(t) \equiv \hat{c}_k(t; \Lambda^*) \triangleq I_k\left(\frac{1}{\lambda_k^*}\mathcal{H}(\varepsilon(t); \Lambda^*)\right); \qquad 0 \leq t \leq T, \quad k = 1, \ldots, K.$$

3.5. Representative agent

It turns out that the function $\mathcal{H}(\cdot; \Lambda)$ of (3.4.7) is closely related to the utility function of a so-called *representative agent*. To introduce this notion, consider for any vector $\Lambda = (\lambda_1, \ldots, \lambda_K) \in (0, \infty)^K$ the function

$$(3.5.1) \qquad U(x; \Lambda) \triangleq \max_{\substack{x_1 > 0, \ldots, x_K > 0 \\ x_1 + \cdots + x_K = x}} \sum_{k=1}^{K} \lambda_k U_k(x_k), \quad 0 < x < \infty.$$

As we show in the next result, this function inherits many properties of the utility functions $U_1, \ldots, U_K$; it can be thought of as the "utility function of a representative agent, who assigns the weights $\lambda_1, \ldots \lambda_K$ to the corresponding individual agents in the economy".

3.5.1. PROPOSITION. *For fixed* $\Lambda \in (0, \infty)^K$, *the function* $U(\cdot; \Lambda): (0, \infty) \to \mathbb{R}$ *of (3.5.1) is of class* $C^3(0, \infty)$, *strictly increasing and strictly concave, with*

$$(3.5.2) \qquad U'(x; \Lambda) = \mathcal{H}(x; \Lambda), \quad 0 < x < \infty.$$

PROOF. For given $x \in (0, \infty)$, define

$$(3.5.3) \qquad c_k \triangleq I_k\left(\frac{1}{\lambda_k}\mathcal{H}(x; \Lambda)\right), \quad k = 1, \ldots, K.$$

Observe that $\sum_{k=1}^{K} c_k = I\big(\mathcal{H}(x; \Lambda); \Lambda\big) = x$ from (3.4.6), (3.4.7) and

$$(3.5.4) \qquad \lambda_k U_k'(c_k) = \mathcal{H}(x; \Lambda), \quad k = 1, \ldots, K.$$

For any other $(x_1, \ldots, x_K) \in (0, \infty)^K$ with $\sum_{k=1}^{K} x_k = x$, we have from the strict concavity of $U_k(\cdot)$, $k = 1, \ldots, K$ and (3.5.4):

$$\sum_{k=1}^{K} \lambda_k U_k(x_k) < \sum_{k=1}^{K} \lambda_k \big\{U_k(c_k) + (x_k - c_k)U_k'(c_k)\big\}$$

$$= \sum_{k=1}^{K} \lambda_k U_k(c_k) + \mathcal{H}(x; \Lambda) \cdot \sum_{k=1}^{K} (x_k - c_k)$$

$$= \sum_{k=1}^{K} \lambda_k U_k(c_k).$$

We have just shown that the maximum in (3.5.1) is attained uniquely at the vector $(c_1, \ldots c_K)' \in (0, \infty)^K$ of (3.5.3), and thus

$$(3.5.5) \qquad U(x; \Lambda) = \sum_{k=1}^{K} \lambda_k \cdot (U_k \circ I_k)\left(\frac{1}{\lambda_k}\mathcal{H}(x; \Lambda)\right).$$

Now let us differentiate this expression with respect to x:

(3.5.6)
$$\frac{d}{dx}\left[\lambda_k \cdot (U_k \circ I_k)\left(\frac{1}{\lambda_k}\mathcal{H}(x;\Lambda)\right)\right]$$

$$= \left((U_k' \circ I_k)\cdot I_k'\right)\left(\frac{1}{\lambda_k}\mathcal{H}(x;\Lambda)\right)\cdot\mathcal{H}'(x;\Lambda)$$

$$= \frac{\mathcal{H}(x;\Lambda)}{\lambda_k}\mathcal{H}'(x;\Lambda)I_k'\left(\frac{\mathcal{H}(x;\Lambda)}{\lambda_k}\right).$$

Notice here that, since each $U_k(\cdot)$ is of class $C^3(0,\infty)$, the corresponding $I_k(\cdot) = \left(U_k'(\cdot)\right)^{-1}$ is of class $C^2(0,\infty)$, and thus so are both functions $I(\cdot;\Lambda)$ and $\mathcal{H}(\cdot;\Lambda)$. In particular, from (3.4.6) and (3.4.7):

$$\frac{d}{dx}I\bigl(\mathcal{H}(x;\Lambda);\Lambda\bigr) = \mathcal{H}'(x;\Lambda)\cdot\sum_{k=1}^{K}\frac{1}{\lambda_k}I_k'\left(\frac{\mathcal{H}(x;\Lambda)}{\lambda_k}\right) = 1.$$

Back into (3.5.6) and (3.5.5), this yields (3.5.2). The other claims follow readily. □

From the remark at the end of the last section, and from Proposition 3.5.1, it follows that the search for equilibrium can be cast equivalently as the search for a vector $\Lambda = (\lambda_1,\ldots,\lambda_K) \in (0,\infty)^K$ of "appropriate weights" for the "representative agent". Finally, we should point out the *positive homogeneity* property $U(x;\eta\Lambda) = \eta U(x;\Lambda)$, $\eta > 0$ of the utility function in (3.5.1), which implies

(3.5.7) $\qquad \mathcal{H}(x;\eta\Lambda) = \eta\mathcal{H}(x;\Lambda); \qquad \forall\, \eta > 0, \quad x > 0, \quad \Lambda \in (0,\infty)^K$

in conjunction with (3.5.2).

3.6. Existence and uniqueness of equilibrium

It follows from (3.5.7) that, if a vector $\Lambda^* \in (0,\infty)^K$ satisfies the equations of (3.4.9), then so does every other vector $\eta\Lambda^*$, $\eta \in (0,\infty)$ on the same ray through the origin; and for all such vectors, the optimal consumption-rates of (3.4.10) are the same:

(3.6.1) $\qquad \hat{c}_k(\cdot;\eta\Lambda^*) = \hat{c}_k(\cdot;\Lambda^*); \qquad \forall\, \eta \in (0,\infty), \quad k = 1,\ldots,K.$

Our next result guarantees that such a ray of solutions to (3.4.9) indeed exists, and spells out conditions under which it is unique.

3.6.1. THEOREM. *There exists a vector $\Lambda^* \in (0,\infty)^K$ which satisfies the equations of (3.4.9). Furthermore, suppose that the agents' utility functions $U_k(\cdot)$, $k = 1,\ldots,K$, satisfy the condition*

(3.6.2) $\qquad\qquad\qquad x \mapsto xU'(x)$ *is increasing;*

then this vector is unique, up to a multiplicative constant.

PROOF OF EXISTENCE. Let $\mathbf{e}_1,\ldots,\mathbf{e}_K$ be basis vectors in $\mathbb{R}^K$, and let $\mathbb{K} = \{1,\ldots,K\}$. For any $\mathbb{B} \subseteq \mathbb{K}$, denote by

$$\mathcal{S}_{\mathbb{B}} \triangleq \left\{\sum_{k\in\mathbb{B}}\lambda_k\mathbf{e}_k \,\Big/\, \lambda_k \geq 0, \ \forall\, k\in\mathbb{B} \ \text{ and } \ \sum_{k\in\mathbb{B}}\lambda_k = 1\right\}$$

the convex hull (simplex) of $\{\mathbf{e}_k\}_{k\in\mathbb{B}}$, and let

$$\mathcal{S}_{\mathbb{B}}^+ \triangleq \left\{ \sum_{k\in\mathbb{B}} \lambda_k \mathbf{e}_k \Big/ \lambda_k > 0, \ \forall \, k \in \mathbb{B} \ \text{ and } \ \sum_{k\in\mathbb{B}} \lambda_k = 1 \right\}.$$

Now for every $k \in \mathbb{K}$, define the function $R_k \colon \mathcal{S}_{\mathbb{K}} \to \mathbb{R}$ by

$$(3.6.3) \quad R_k(\Lambda) \triangleq \left\{ \begin{array}{l} \mathbb{E} \displaystyle\int_0^T e^{-\int_0^t \beta(s)\,ds} \mathcal{H}\big(\varepsilon(t); \Lambda\big) \left[I_k\left(\dfrac{\mathcal{H}(\varepsilon(t); \Lambda)}{\lambda_k} \right) - \varepsilon_k(t) \right] dt; \\ \qquad\qquad\qquad\qquad\qquad \text{if } \lambda_k > 0 \\[2ex] -\mathbb{E} \displaystyle\int_0^T e^{-\int_0^t \beta(s)\,ds} \mathcal{H}\big(\varepsilon(t); \Lambda\big)\varepsilon_k(t)\,dt; \quad \text{if } \lambda_k = 0. \end{array} \right\}$$

This function is continuous, and so the set

$$F_k \triangleq \big\{ \Lambda \in \mathcal{S}_{\mathbb{K}} \, / \, R_k(\Lambda) \ge 0 \big\}$$

is closed; on the other hand,

$$(3.6.4) \qquad\qquad \sum_{k\in\mathbb{K}} R_k(\Lambda) = 0, \qquad \forall\,\Lambda \in \mathcal{S}_{\mathbb{K}}$$

from (3.4.6)–(3.4.7). We claim that

$$(3.6.5) \qquad\qquad \mathcal{S}_{\mathbb{K}} = \bigcup_{k\in\mathbb{K}} F_k$$

holds; for if there existed $\hat{\Lambda} \in \mathcal{S}_{\mathbb{K}}$ with $\hat{\Lambda} \notin \bigcup_{k\in\mathbb{K}} F_k$, then we should have $R_k(\hat{\Lambda}) < 0$ for every $k \in \mathbb{K}$, contradicting (3.6.4). Similarly, we have

$$(3.6.6) \qquad\qquad \mathcal{S}_{\mathbb{B}} \subseteq \bigcup_{k\in\mathbb{B}} F_k, \qquad \forall\,\mathbb{B} \subseteq \mathbb{K};$$

for if there existed $\hat{\Lambda} \in \mathcal{S}_{\mathbb{B}}$ with $\hat{\Lambda} \notin \bigcup_{k\in\mathbb{B}} F_k$, then we should have $R_k(\hat{\Lambda}) < 0$, $\forall\,k \in \mathbb{B}$ and therefore $\sum_{k\in\mathbb{K}} R_k(\hat{\Lambda}) < 0$ (again contradicting (3.6.4)), since (3.6.3) and (3.1.4) give $R_j(\hat{\Lambda}) < 0$ for every $j \in \mathbb{K}$ such that $\lambda_j = 0$, $\hat{\Lambda} \in \mathcal{S}_{\mathbb{K}}$.

Now from (3.6.6) and the Knaster-Kuratowski-Mazurkiewicz (1929) Theorem (cf. Border (1985), p. 26), *the set* $\bigcap_{k\in\mathbb{K}} F_k$ *is nonempty.* For any $\Lambda^* \in \bigcap_{k\in\mathbb{K}} F_k$, we have

$$(3.6.7) \qquad\qquad R_k(\Lambda^*) = 0, \qquad \forall\,k \in \mathbb{K}$$

(for otherwise we would have $\sum_{k\in\mathbb{K}} R_k(\Lambda^*) > 0$, contradicting (3.6.4)) and $\Lambda^* \in \mathcal{S}_{\mathbb{K}}^+$ (for if we had $\lambda_k^* = 0$ for some $k \in \mathbb{K}$, we would also obtain $R_k(\Lambda^*) < 0$ from (3.6.3), contradicting (3.6.7)).

From (3.6.7), (3.6.3) it develops that such $\Lambda^* \in \bigcap_{k\in\mathbb{K}} F_k$ belongs to $(0,\infty)^K$, and satisfies the system of equations (3.4.9). $\qquad\Box$

PROOF OF UNIQUENESS UNDER (3.6.2). From (3.6.2), the functions

$$(3.6.8) \qquad\qquad y \mapsto \varphi_k(y) \triangleq yI_k(y), \quad k = 1, \dots, K$$

are all decreasing on $(0,\infty)$. We introduce the usual partial ordering

$$\Lambda \le \mathbf{M} \iff \lambda_k \le \mu_k, \qquad \forall\,k = 1, \dots, K$$

on $(0, \infty)^K$, and write $\Lambda < \mathbf{M}$, iff $\Lambda \leq \mathbf{M}$ and $\Lambda \neq \mathbf{M}$. From (3.4.5)–(3.4.7) we have

$$(3.6.9) \quad \Lambda \underset{(<)}{\leq} \mathbf{M} \implies I(y; \Lambda) \underset{(<)}{\leq} I(y; \mathbf{M}), \qquad \forall\, y \in (0, \infty)$$

$$\implies \mathcal{H}\big(\varepsilon(t, w); \Lambda\big) \underset{(<)}{\leq} \mathcal{H}\big(\varepsilon(t, w); \mathbf{M}\big), \qquad \forall\, (t, w) \in [0, T] \times \Omega.$$

Now let Λ, $\hat{\Lambda}$ be two solutions of (3.4.9), and define $\eta \triangleq \max_{1 \leq k \leq K}(\lambda_k / \hat{\lambda}_k)$, $\mathbf{M} \triangleq \eta \hat{\Lambda}$. Then $\mathbf{M}$ is also a solution of (3.4.9) (recall the remark at the beginning of this section) and $\Lambda \leq \mathbf{M}$. If $\Lambda = \mathbf{M}$, then Λ is a positive multiple of $\hat{\Lambda}$; consequently, it suffices to rule out the case $\Lambda < \mathbf{M}$.

Suppose that $\Lambda < \mathbf{M}$ were true; then for any integer $k \in \mathbb{K}$ satisfying $\lambda_k = \eta \hat{\lambda}_k$ ($= \mu_k$), we would have

$$\mathbb{E} \int_0^T e^{-\int_0^t \beta(s)\,ds} \frac{1}{\lambda_k} \mathcal{H}\big(\varepsilon(t); \Lambda\big) \varepsilon_k(t)\,dt < \mathbb{E} \int_0^T e^{-\int_0^t \beta(s)\,ds} \frac{1}{\mu_k} \mathcal{H}\big(\varepsilon(t); \mathbf{M}\big) \varepsilon_k(t)\,dt$$

and

$$\mathbb{E} \int_0^T e^{-\int_0^t \beta(s)\,ds} \varphi_k\left(\frac{\mathcal{H}(\varepsilon(t); \Lambda)}{\lambda_k}\right) dt \geq \mathbb{E} \int_0^T e^{-\int_0^t \beta(s)\,ds} \varphi_k\left(\frac{\mathcal{H}(\varepsilon(t); \mathbf{M})}{\mu_k}\right) dt$$

from (3.6.9), (3.6.8), and by subtracting

$$\frac{1}{\lambda_k} R_k(\Lambda) > \frac{1}{\mu_k} R_k(\mathbf{M}),$$

in the notation of (3.6.3) — a contradiction, since $\lambda_k = \mu_k$ by assumption and $R_k(\Lambda) = R_k(\mathbf{M}) = 0$. $\qquad\qquad\qquad\qquad\qquad\qquad\qquad\qquad\qquad\qquad \Box$

3.7. Equilibrium prices

We shall assume in this section that *the conditions of* Theorem 3.6.1 *are satisfied*. Then we know that there exists a unique ray $\mathcal{L} = \{\eta \Lambda\}_{\eta > 0}$ of solutions to the system of equations (3.4.9); and from Section 4 we know that if we can find a market model $\mathcal{M}$ as in (3.2.1)–(3.2.3) for which (3.4.8) holds as well, then this market results in equilibrium. Our purpose in this section is to characterize such an equilibrium market $\mathcal{M}$.

To this end, let us consider a vector Λ on the ray $\mathcal{L}$ of solutions to the equations of (3.4.9), as well as the process

$$(3.7.1) \qquad h(t) \triangleq \mathcal{H}\big(\varepsilon(t); \Lambda\big) = U'\big(\varepsilon(t); \Lambda\big), \qquad 0 \leq t \leq T.$$

An application of Itô's rule gives

$$(3.7.2) \quad h(t) = U'\big(\varepsilon(0); \Lambda\big)$$

$$+ \int_0^t \left\{ U''\big(\varepsilon(s); \Lambda\big) \varepsilon(s) \nu(s) + \frac{1}{2} U'''\big(\varepsilon(s); \Lambda\big) \varepsilon^2(s) \|\rho(s)\|^2 \right\} ds$$

$$+ \int_0^t U''\big(\varepsilon(s); \Lambda\big) \varepsilon(s) \rho'(s)\, dW(s), \qquad 0 \leq t \leq T$$

in conjunction with Proposition 3.4.1 and the equation (3.1.3). On the other hand, the process

$$(3.7.3) \qquad \zeta(t) \triangleq H_0(t) e^{\int_0^t \beta(s)\,ds} = Z_0(t) e^{\int_0^t (\beta(s) - r(s))\,ds}, \qquad 0 \leq t \leq T$$

satisfies the equation

$$(3.7.4) \quad \zeta(t) = 1 + \int_0^t \zeta(s)\big(\beta(s) - r(s)\big)\, ds - \int_0^t \zeta(s)\theta'(s)\, dW(s), \qquad 0 \le t \le T.$$

Now (3.4.8) holds if and only if $\zeta(\cdot) \equiv h(\cdot)$, or equivalently

$$(3.7.5) \qquad\qquad\qquad U'\big(\varepsilon(0); \Lambda\big) = 1$$

$(3.7.6)\quad r(t) = \beta(t)$

$$- \frac{1}{U'(\varepsilon(t); \Lambda)}\left[U''\big(\varepsilon(t); \Lambda\big)\varepsilon(t)\nu(t) + \frac{1}{2}U'''\big(\varepsilon(t); \Lambda\big)\varepsilon^2(t)\|\rho(t)\|^2 \right]$$

$$(3.7.7) \qquad \theta(t) = J\big(\varepsilon(t); \Lambda\big)\rho(t), \quad \text{where } J(x; \Lambda) \triangleq -\frac{xU''(x; \Lambda)}{U'(x; \Lambda)},$$

upon comparing (3.7.2) with (3.7.4). The function $J(\cdot; \Lambda)$ of (3.7.7) is the "index of relative risk-aversion" for the representative agent's utility function (3.5.1).

3.7.1. THEOREM. *Assume the conditions of* Theorem 3.6.1. *Then there exists a unique vector* $\Lambda \in (0, \infty)^K$ *that satisfies the equations of* (3.4.9) *and* (3.7.5). *With this vector, with an arbitrary bounded,* $\mathbb{F}$*-progressively measurable and nonsingular matrix-valued process* $\sigma(\cdot) = \{\sigma_{ij}(\cdot)\}_{1 \le i,j \le d}$, *with* $r(\cdot)$ *and* $\theta(\cdot)$ *given by* (3.7.6) *and* (3.7.7), *and with the vector-process*

$$(3.7.8) \qquad\qquad b(t) = r(t)\mathbf{1}_d + \sigma(t)\theta(t), \qquad 0 \le t \le T,$$

the market $\mathcal{M}$ *of* (3.2.1), (3.2.2) *results in equilibrium.*

PROOF. The only things that have to be checked, are the martingale property of the exponential process $Z_0(\cdot)$ in (0.2.11) and the conditions of (3.2.3). Now from the boundedness of the function $\beta(\cdot)$ and of the processes $\nu(\cdot)$, $\rho(\cdot)$ in (3.1.2), from condition (3.1.3), and from the continuity of the function $U(\cdot)$ in (3.5.1) and its derivatives up to order three (Proposition 3.5.1), it follows that

(i) the vector-process $\theta(\cdot)$ in (3.7.7), and the scalar-process $r(\cdot)$ in (3.7.6), are bounded (uniformly in (t, w));

(ii) the process $H_0(t) = e^{-\int_0^t \beta(s)\, ds} U'\big(\varepsilon(t); \Lambda\big)$ of (3.4.8), (2.1.5) is bounded, both from above and away from zero; and

(iii) the exponential local martingale

$$(3.7.9) \qquad Z_0(t) = e^{\int_0^t r(s)\, ds} H_0(t) = e^{\int_0^t \left(r(s) - \beta(s)\right) ds} U'\big(\varepsilon(t); \Lambda\big), \qquad 0 \le t \le T$$

of (0.2.11) is bounded (again, both from above and away from zero), and is thus a martingale. $\qquad\Box$

3.7.2. REMARK. The representative agent's "marginal utility from consumption" process of (3.7.1),

$$h(t) = U'\big(\varepsilon(t); \Lambda\big) = U'\left(\sum_{j=1}^d \hat{c}_j(t; \Lambda); \Lambda\right), \qquad 0 \le t \le T,$$

satisfies, from (3.7.2)-(3.7.7), the dynamics

$$(3.7.10) \qquad dh(t) = h(t)\big[\big(\beta(t) - r(t)\big)\, dt - \theta'(t)\, dW(t)\big], \quad h(0) = 1.$$

3.7.3. REMARK (The Capital Asset Pricing Model (CAPM)). Let us observe, from (3.7.10) and (3.7.6), that

(3.7.11)
$$\left\{ \begin{array}{l} \text{the rate of growth } r(t) = \frac{dB(t)}{B(t)\,dt} \text{ of a riskless asset, should be equal} \\ \text{to the discount rate } \beta(t), \text{ minus the growth rate of the representa-} \\ \text{tive agent's marginal utility from consumption.} \end{array} \right\}$$

On the other hand, from (3.7.8), (3.7.7) and (3.2.2), (3.1.2) we have

$$(3.7.12) \qquad b_i(t) - r(t) = J\big(\varepsilon(t); \Lambda\big) \sum_{j=1}^{d} \sigma_{ij}(t)\rho_j(t)$$

$$= J\big(\varepsilon(t); \Lambda\big) \frac{d\langle P_i, \varepsilon\rangle(t)}{P_i(t)\varepsilon(t)\,dt}, \quad i = 1, \ldots, d.$$

In other words:

(3.7.13)
$$\left\{ \begin{array}{l} \text{The excess (above the risk-free) rate of return from a risky} \\ \text{asset, is proportional to the relative covariance between} \\ \text{the price } P_i(\cdot) \text{ of that asset and the aggregate consump-} \\ \text{tion } \varepsilon(\cdot) = \sum_{j=1}^{d} \hat{c}_j(\cdot; \Lambda); \text{ the proprotionality constant is} \\ \text{independent of the particular asset, and is given by the} \\ \text{``index of relative risk-aversion'' of a representative agent.} \end{array} \right\}$$

The conclusions (3.7.11), (3.7.13) constitute the basic tenets of the consumption-based *Capital Asset Pricing Model* (Breeden (1979), Merton (1973)).

3.7.4. REMARK. Observe that the equilibrium state-price-density $H_0(t)$ of (3.4.8), and the optimal consumption-rates $\hat{c}_k(t)$, $k = 1, \ldots, K$ of (3.4.10), are deterministic functions of the aggregate-endowment $\varepsilon(t)$, $\forall\ 0 \le t \le T$. In particular, $H_0(\cdot)$ and $\hat{c}_k(\cdot)$ are *adapted to the* (augmented) *filtration* $\mathbb{F}^{\varepsilon}$ *generated by the aggregate-endowment process* $\varepsilon(\cdot)$. The equilibrium interest-rate $r(\cdot)$, relative risk $\theta(\cdot)$, and exponential martingale $Z_0(\cdot)$ processes of (3.7.6)–(3.7.9) are also adapted to $\mathbb{F}^{\varepsilon}$, if the processes $\nu(t)$, $\rho_j(t)$, $j = 1, \ldots, d$ take the form $\Gamma\big(t, \varepsilon(\cdot)\big)$ of progressively measurable (nonanticipative) functionals of $\varepsilon(\cdot)$, as in Exercise 0.3.8, and the resulting Stochastic (Functional-) Differential Equation (3.1.2) has a pathwise unique, strong solution.

3.8. Examples

We conclude this chapter with a discussion of a few special cases, in which explicit computations are possible.

3.8.1. EXAMPLE. $U_k(x) = \gamma_k \log x$, $0 < x < \infty$ with $\gamma_k > 0$, $k = 1, \ldots K$. We compute then from (3.4.9), (3.7.5)

$$(3.8.1) \qquad \lambda_k^* = \frac{\varepsilon(0)}{\gamma_k} \frac{\mathbb{E} \int_0^T e^{-\int_0^t \beta(s)\,ds} \big(\varepsilon_k(t)/\varepsilon(t)\big)\,dt}{\int_0^T e^{-\int_0^t \beta(s)\,ds}\,dt}, \quad k = 1, \ldots K,$$

and from (3.5.1), (3.5.3):

$$(3.8.2) \quad U(x; \Lambda^*) = \varepsilon(0) \log\left(\frac{x}{\varepsilon(0)}\right) + \sum_{k=1}^{K} \gamma_k \lambda_k^* \cdot \log(\gamma_k \lambda_k^*),$$

$$\hat{c}_k(t) = \gamma_k \lambda_k^*\left(\frac{\varepsilon(t)}{\varepsilon(0)}\right) \quad \text{for } 0 \le t \le T.$$

The equilibrium market coefficients of (3.7.6), (3.7.7) now become

$$(3.8.3) \qquad r(t) = \beta(t) + \nu(t) - \|\rho(t)\|^2, \quad \theta(t) = \rho(t).$$

3.8.2. EXAMPLE. $U_k(x) = (\gamma_k^{1-\alpha}/\alpha)x^\alpha$, $0 < x < \infty$ with $\gamma_k > 0$ for every $k = 1, \dots K$ and $\alpha \in (-\infty, 1)\backslash\{0\}$. In this case, the analogues of (3.8.1)–(3.8.3) are

$$(3.8.4) \qquad (\lambda_k^*)^{1/(1-\alpha)} = \frac{\varepsilon(0)}{\gamma_k} \frac{\mathbb{E} \int_0^T e^{-\int_0^t \beta(s)\,ds}(\varepsilon(t))^{\alpha-1}\varepsilon_k(t)\,dt}{\mathbb{E} \int_0^T e^{-\int_0^t \beta(s)\,ds}(\varepsilon(t))^\alpha\,dt}, \qquad k = 1, \dots K$$

$$(3.8.5) \quad U(x; \Lambda^*) = \frac{(\varepsilon(0))^{1-\alpha}}{\alpha} x^\alpha, \quad \hat{c}_k(t) = (\lambda_k^*)^{1/(1-\alpha)}\gamma_k\left(\frac{\varepsilon(t)}{\varepsilon(0)}\right), \qquad 0 \le t \le T$$

and

$$(3.8.6) \quad r(t) = \beta(t) + (1-\alpha)\left[\nu(t) - \left(1 - \frac{\alpha}{2}\right)\|\rho(t)\|^2\right], \quad \theta(t) = (1-\alpha)\rho(t).$$

Notice that the condition (3.6.2) is satisfied only for $0 < \alpha < 1$; yet we have existence and uniqueness of equilibrium even for $\alpha < 0$. This shows that condition (3.6.2) is far from necessary for the uniqueness part of Theorem 3.6.1

3.8.3. EXAMPLE (Constant aggregate endowment $\varepsilon(t) \equiv \varepsilon > 0$). Now (3.4.9), (3.7.5) yield $\Lambda^* = \left(1/U'(\hat{c}_1), \dots 1/U'(\hat{c}_K)\right)$, where

$$\hat{c}_k = \frac{\mathbb{E} \int_0^T e^{-\int_0^t \beta(s)\,ds}\varepsilon_k(t)\,dt}{\int_0^T e^{-\int_0^t \beta(s)\,ds}\,dt}, \qquad k = 1, \dots, K$$

are the optimal consumption rates of (3.4.10). In order to finance these consumption rates, the agents may still have to trade with one another (since, despite the constancy of $\varepsilon(\cdot) = \sum_{k=1}^K \varepsilon_k(\cdot) \equiv \varepsilon$, the individual endowment rates $\varepsilon_k(\cdot)$ may still be random and time-varying). Finally, we have $\nu(\cdot) \equiv 0$, $\rho(\cdot) \equiv 0$ in (3.1.2), so that

$$r(t) = \beta(t), \quad \theta(t) = 0; \qquad 0 \le t \le T.$$

Part 2

Incomplete markets

CHAPTER 4

Hedging

4.1. The model

Throughout this chapter and the next, we shall deal with the market model

$$(4.1.1) \qquad\qquad dB(t) = B(t)r(t)\,dt$$

$$(4.1.2) \qquad dP_i(t) = P_i(t)\left[b_i(t)\,dt + \sum_{j=1}^{d}\sigma_{ij}(t)\,dW_j(t)\right],$$

$$P_i(0) = p_i \in (0,\infty), \qquad i = 1,\dots,d$$

of Section 2.1, under some additional conditions. Namely, we shall assume again that the volatility matrix $\sigma(\cdot) = \{\sigma_{ij}(\cdot)\}_{1\le i,j\le d}$ is *invertible*, but also that both matrices

$$(4.1.3) \qquad \sigma(\cdot), \quad \sigma^{-1}(\cdot) \text{ are bounded uniformly on } [0,T] \times \Omega.$$

And just as in Section 2.1, we shall impose that the interest-rate $r(\cdot)$ and relative-risk $\theta(\cdot) = \sigma^{-1}(\cdot)[b(\cdot) - r(\cdot)\mathbf{1}_d]$ processes satisfy the conditions of (2.1.3):

$$(4.1.4) \qquad \mathbb{E}\int_0^T \left(\|\theta(t)\|^2 + r(t)\right)dt < \infty,$$

$$\mathbb{P}[r(t) \ge -\eta, \ \forall\, 0 \le t \le T] = 1 \quad \text{for some real } \eta \ge 0.$$

Let us consider now a given *closed, convex cone* $K \subseteq \mathbb{R}^d$, centered at the origin, and denote by

$$(4.1.5) \qquad \tilde{K} \triangleq \{x \in \mathbb{R}^d \ / \ \pi'x \ge 0, \forall\, \pi \in K\}$$

the *polar cone* of $-K$. The set K will quantify, in this chapter and the next, our constraints on portfolio choice: *only those portfolio processes $\pi(\cdot)$ will be admitted, which take values in the cone K.*

More precisely, by analogy with the class $\mathcal{A}(x)$ of Definition 2.1.1, we shall consider, for any given initial capital $x \ge 0$, the set

$$(4.1.6) \quad \mathcal{A}(x;K) \triangleq \{(\pi,C) \in \mathcal{A}(x) \ / \ \pi(\cdot) \in K, \ (\lambda \otimes \mathbb{P}) - \text{ a.e. on } [0,T] \times \Omega\}$$

of *K-admissible* portfolio/consumption strategies.

The market model of (4.1.1)–(4.1.4), thus constrained in the choice of portfolio processes available to agents, will be denoted by $\mathcal{M}(K)$; clearly, $\mathcal{M} \equiv \mathcal{M}(\mathbb{R}^d)$ and $\mathcal{A}(x) \equiv \mathcal{A}(x;\mathbb{R}^d)$. Here are some examples of constraint sets.

4.1.1. EXAMPLE (Prohibition of short-selling of stocks). $K \triangleq [0,\infty)^d$, and so $\tilde{K} = K$.

4.1.2. EXAMPLE (Incomplete market). $K \triangleq \{\pi \in \mathbb{R}^d \ / \ \pi_{n+1} = \cdots = \pi_d = 0\}$ for some $n = 1,\dots,d-1$; then $\tilde{K} = \{x \in \mathbb{R}^d \ / \ x_1 = \cdots = x_n = 0\}$.

4.1.3. EXAMPLE (Incomplete market, no short-selling of stocks). In this case, we have $K \triangleq \{\pi \in \mathbb{R}^d \ / \ \pi_1 \geq 0, \ldots, \pi_n \geq 0, \pi_{n+1} = \cdots = \pi_d = 0\}$ and thus $\tilde{K} = \{x \in \mathbb{R}^d \ / \ x_1 \geq 0, \ldots, x_n \geq 0\}$, with n as in Example 4.1.2.

In the context of such a constrained market $\mathcal{M}(K)$, we discuss in this Chapter the question of *hedging contingent claims* Y; we introduce analogues $h_{\mathrm{up}}(K)$, $h_{\mathrm{low}}(K)$ of the upper- and lower- hedging prices as in (0.4.2), (0.4.4), but now with portfolios constrained to take values in K. We provide characterizations of these hedging prices in terms of *auxiliary stochastic control problems*. More precisely, in contrast to the situation $h_{\mathrm{up}}(\mathbb{R}^d) = h_{\mathrm{low}}(\mathbb{R}^d) = u_0 = \mathbb{E}^0[\gamma(T)Y]$ of Theorem 1.2.1 for a complete, unconstrained market where u_0 is the only arbitrage-free price, here the singleton $\{u_0\}$ is replaced by an entire interval $[h_{\mathrm{low}}(K), h_{\mathrm{up}}(K)]$: every price p outside this interval leads to arbitrage, while no price in the interior of the interval does (cf. Section 4.3).

To characterize the endpoints of this "arbitrage-free interval", we embed our constrained-market model $\mathcal{M}(K)$ into a family $\{\mathcal{M}_\nu\}_{\nu \in \mathcal{D}_b}$ of auxiliary models, suitably constructed in Section 4.2 to reflect the constraint-set K, and containing $\mathcal{M} = \mathcal{M}(\mathbb{R}^d)$ as a member. With $u_\nu = \mathbb{E}^\nu[\gamma(T)Y]$ denoting the hedging price of Y using unconstrained portfolios in $\mathcal{M}_\nu$, we have then the characterizations

$$h_{\mathrm{up}}(K) = \sup_{\nu \in \mathcal{D}_b} u_\nu, \quad h_{\mathrm{low}}(K) = \inf_{\nu \in \mathcal{D}_b} u_\nu$$

(cf. (4.3.10) and Theorems 4.4.1, 4.6.1) for the upper- and lower- hedging price. We discuss also, in Section 4.5, the question of *attainability of contingent claims* with constrained portfolios, much in the spirit of Definition 0.3.1.

4.2. Embedding

We shall embed now the market model $\mathcal{M}(K)$ into a family $\{\mathcal{M}_\nu\}_{\nu \in \mathcal{D}}$ of *unconstrained* models, as follows. Consider the Hilbert space $\mathcal{H}$ of $\mathbb{F}$-progressively measurable processes $\nu \colon [0, T] \times \Omega \to \mathbb{R}^d$ with

$$(4.2.1) \qquad [\![\nu]\!]^2 \triangleq \mathbb{E} \int_0^T \|\nu(t)\|^2 \, dt < \infty, \quad \langle \nu_1, \nu_2 \rangle \triangleq \mathbb{E} \int_0^T \nu_1'(t)\nu_2(t) \, dt,$$

and denote

$$(4.2.2) \qquad \mathcal{D} \triangleq \{\nu \in \mathcal{H} \ / \ \nu(t, w) \in \tilde{K}, \ (\lambda \otimes \mathbb{P}) - \text{a.e.} \, (t, w) \in [0, T] \times \Omega\}.$$

Corresponding now to any given process $\nu \in \mathcal{D}$, let us consider the *market model* $\mathcal{M}_\nu$ governed by the equations

$$(4.2.3) \qquad\qquad dB(t) = B(t)r(t) \, dt$$

$$(4.2.4) \qquad dP_i^{(\nu)}(t) = P_i^{(\nu)}(t)\left[(b_i(t) + \nu_i(t)) \, dt + \sum_{j=1}^d \sigma_{ij}(t) \, dW_j(t) \right],$$

$$P_i(0) = p_i \in (0, \infty), \qquad i = 1, \ldots, d.$$

This has the same interest rate $r(\cdot)$ and volatility matrix $\sigma(\cdot)$ as $\mathcal{M}$, but appreciation rate vector $b^{(\nu)}(\cdot) \triangleq b(\cdot) + \nu(\cdot)$. For this model, the analogues of the processes $\theta(\cdot)$, $Z_0(\cdot)$, $W^{(0)}(\cdot)$ and $H_0(\cdot)$ of (0.3.5), (0.2.11), (0.2.13) and (2.1.5) are given, respectively, by

$$(4.2.5) \qquad \theta^{(\nu)}(t) \triangleq \sigma^{-1}(t)\big[b(t) + \nu(t) - r(t)\mathbf{1}_d\big] = \theta(t) + \sigma^{-1}(t)\nu(t),$$

$$(4.2.6) \qquad W^{(\nu)}(t) \triangleq W(t) + \int_0^t \theta^{(\nu)}(s)\,ds = W^{(0)}(t) + \int_0^t \sigma^{-1}(s)\nu(s)\,ds,$$

$$0 \le t \le T$$

$$(4.2.7) \qquad Z_\nu(t) \triangleq \exp\left[-\int_0^t \big(\theta^{(\nu)}(s)\big)'\,dW(s) - \frac{1}{2}\int_0^t \big\|\theta^{(\nu)}(s)\big\|^2\,ds\right],$$

and

$$(4.2.8) \qquad H_\nu(t) \triangleq \gamma(t)Z_\nu(t), \qquad 0 \le t \le T.$$

Clearly, with $\nu(\cdot) \equiv 0$ we recover the model $\mathcal{M} \equiv \mathcal{M}_0$ of (4.1.1), (4.1.2); on the other hand, the boundedness of $\sigma^{-1}(\cdot)$ and the definition of the space $\mathcal{D}$ in (4.1.3), (4.2.2), respectively, imply $\mathbb{E}\int_0^T \big\|\theta^{(\nu)}(t)\big\|^2\,dt < \infty$, $\nu \in \mathcal{D}$. In other words, the conditions imposed on $\mathcal{M} = \mathcal{M}_0$ are also satisfied by every member $\mathcal{M}_\nu$ of this auxiliary family.

4.2.1. REMARK. The wealth process $X^{(\nu)}(\cdot) \equiv X_\nu^{x,\pi,C}(\cdot)$ in $\mathcal{M}_\nu$, corresponding to an (unconstrained) portfolio/cumulative consumption process pair (π, C), is given by analogy with (0.2.17), (2.1.6) as

$$(4.2.9) \quad \gamma(t)X^{(\nu)}(t) + \int_{(0,t]} \gamma(u)\,dC(u) = x + \int_0^t \gamma(u)\pi'(u)\sigma(u)\,dW^{(\nu)}(u)$$

$$= x + M_\nu^\pi(t)$$

$$= x + \int_0^t \gamma(u)\pi'(u)\sigma(u)\,dW^{(0)}(u)$$

$$+ \int_0^t \gamma(u)\pi'(u)\nu(u)\,du, \qquad 0 \le t \le T$$

or equivalently

$$(4.2.10) \quad H_\nu(t)X^{(\nu)}(t) + \int_{(0,t]} H_\nu(u)\,dC(u)$$

$$= x + \int_0^t H_\nu(u)\big(\sigma'(u)\pi(u) - X^{(\nu)}(u)\theta^{(\nu)}(u)\big)'\,dW(u), \qquad 0 \le t \le T.$$

4.2.2. REMARK. If $\pi(\cdot) \in K$ $(\lambda \otimes \mathbb{P} - \text{a.e.})$, then from (4.2.9), (0.2.17) and the definitions of $\tilde{K}$, $\mathcal{D}$ in (4.1.5), (4.2.2) we deduce

$$(4.2.11) \qquad \left\{ \begin{array}{l} X_\nu^{x,\pi,C}(t) \ge X^{x,\pi,C}(t), \quad \forall\, 0 \le t \le T \text{ almost surely,} \\ \text{with equality iff } \pi'(\cdot)\nu(u) = 0, \ (\lambda \otimes \mathbb{P}) - \text{ a.e.} \end{array} \right\}$$

It was with this comparison in mind, that we constructed the auxiliary market model $\mathcal{M}_\nu$ in (4.2.3), (4.2.4).

4.2.3. DEFINITION. For any given initial capital $x \ge 0$, we denote by $\mathcal{A}^{(\nu)}(x)$ the class of portfolio/cumulative consumption process pairs (π, C) for which we have the analogue of (2.1.4):

$$(4.2.12) \qquad X^{(\nu)}(t) \equiv X_\nu^{x,\pi,C}(t) \ge 0, \qquad \forall\, 0 \le t \le T$$

almost surely, for every $\nu \in \mathcal{D}$.

4.2.4. REMARK. Clearly, from (4.1.6), (4.2.11) and (4.2.12) we obtain

$$(4.2.13) \qquad \mathcal{A}(x;K) \subseteq \mathcal{A}^{(\nu)}(x), \qquad \forall \, \nu \in \mathcal{D}$$

and from (4.2.10) we have the analogue

$$(4.2.14) \qquad \mathbb{E}\left[H_\nu(T) X_\nu^{x,\pi,C}(T) + \int_{(0,T]} H_\nu(t)\, dC(t) \right] \le x$$

of (2.1.7), for every $(\pi, C) \in \mathcal{A}^{(\nu)}(x), \forall \, \nu \in \mathcal{D}$.

4.3. Contingent claims

Suppose now that, in addition to the conditions of (4.1.1)–(4.1.4), we impose also that the relative-risk process

$$(4.3.1) \qquad \theta(\cdot) \text{ is bounded, uniformly in } (t,w) \in [0,T] \times \Omega,$$

and consider the subsets

$$(4.3.2) \qquad \begin{aligned} \mathcal{D}_m &\triangleq \left\{ \nu \in \mathcal{D} \,/\, Z_\nu(\cdot) \text{ of (4.2.7) is martingale} \right\} \\ \mathcal{D}_b &\triangleq \bigcup_{n=1}^{\infty} \left\{ \nu \in \mathcal{D} \,/\, \|\nu(t,w)\| \le n, \, (\lambda \otimes \mathbb{P}) - \text{ a.e. on } [0,T] \times \Omega \right\} \end{aligned}$$

of the class $\mathcal{D}$ in (4.2.2). We have $\mathcal{D}_b \subseteq \mathcal{D}_m$, because the conditions (4.3.1) and (4.1.3) imply that the exponential process $Z_\nu(\cdot)$ in (4.2.7) is a martingale for every $\nu \in \mathcal{D}_b$ (in particular, for $\nu(\cdot) \equiv 0$). For every $\nu \in \mathcal{D}_m$,

$$(4.3.3) \qquad \mathbb{P}^\nu(A) \triangleq \mathbb{E}\left[Z_\nu(T) 1_A \right], \quad A \in \mathcal{F}(T)$$

defines a probability measure on $\mathcal{F}(T)$, by analogy with (0.2.12). Under this measure, the process $W^{(\nu)}(\cdot)$ of (4.2.6) is Brownian, by Girsanov's theorem (e.g. Karatzas & Shreve (1991), pp. 191–195), and we may re-write (4.1.2) as

$$(4.3.4) \qquad \begin{aligned} dP_i(t) &= P_i(t)\left[(r(t) - \nu_i(t))\, dt + \sum_{j=1}^{d} \sigma_{ij}(t)\, dW_j^{(\nu)}(t) \right]; \\ P_i(0) &= p_i \in (0,\infty), \qquad i = 1,\dots,d. \end{aligned}$$

4.3.1. REMARK (Incomplete market). In the special case of Example 4.1.2, the equations (4.3.4) and the condition (4.1.3) show that the discounted stock-prices

$$\gamma(t) P_i(t) = p_i \exp\left\{ \sum_{j=1}^{d} \int_0^t \sigma_{ij}(u)\, dW_j^{(\nu)}(u) - \frac{1}{2} \sum_{j=1}^{d} \int_0^t \sigma_{ij}^2(u)\, du \right\}; \qquad i = 1,\dots,n$$

are martingales under $\mathbb{P}^\nu$, for every $\nu \in \mathcal{D}_m$. Thus, the whole *family* of probability measures $\{\mathbb{P}^\nu\}_{\nu \in \mathcal{D}_m}$ constitute "equivalent martingale measures" in this setup, in the sense of Section 0.2.

Consider now a European contingent claim as in Section 1.2, that is, an $\mathcal{F}(T)$-measurable random variable $Y : \Omega \to [0,\infty)$ with

$$(4.3.5) \qquad u_0 \triangleq \mathbb{E}^0\left[\gamma(T) Y \right] \in (0,\infty).$$

By analogy with (0.4.2) and (0.4.4), we define the *upper- and lower- hedging prices* of this contingent claim in $\mathcal{M}(K)$, as

$$(4.3.6) \qquad h_{\mathrm{up}}(K) \triangleq \inf \left\{ x \ge 0 \,\left/\, \begin{array}{l} \exists (\hat{\pi}, \hat{C}) \text{ with } \hat{\pi}(\cdot) \text{ tame, } \hat{\pi}(\cdot) \in K \text{ a.e.,} \\ \text{and } X^{x,\hat{\pi},\hat{C}}(T) \ge Y \text{ a.s.} \end{array} \right. \right\}$$

and, in the notation of (4.2.9), (4.3.2),

(4.3.7) $h_{\text{low}}(K)$

$$\triangleq \sup \left\{ x \geq 0 \;\middle/\; \begin{array}{l} \exists (\tilde{\pi}, \check{C}) \text{ with } M_\nu^{\tilde{\pi}}(\cdot) \text{ a } \mathbb{P}^\nu\text{-supermartingale } \forall\, \nu \in \\ \mathcal{D}_b,\, \tilde{\pi}(\cdot) \in K \text{ a.e., and } X^{-x,\tilde{\pi},\check{C}}(T) \geq -Y \text{ a.s.} \end{array} \right\}$$

respectively. Just as in Proposition 0.4.1, we have

(4.3.8) $$0 \leq h_{\text{low}}(K) \leq u_0 \leq h_{\text{up}}(K) \leq \infty;$$

whereas from Theorem 1.2.1,

(4.3.9) $$h_{\text{low}}(\mathbb{R}^d) = h_{\text{up}}(\mathbb{R}^d) = u_0 = \mathbb{E}^0\big[\gamma(T)Y\big].$$

How can we compute $h_{\text{up}}(K)$, $h_{\text{low}}(K)$ for a general convex cone constraint set K? We shall show in this chapter that the answer to this question is provided in terms of the following *stochastic control problems*:

(4.3.10) $$h_{\text{up}}(K) = \sup_{\nu \in \mathcal{D}_b} u_\nu, \qquad h_{\text{low}}(K) = \inf_{\nu \in \mathcal{D}_b} u_\nu.$$

Here

(4.3.11) $$u_\nu \triangleq \mathbb{E}^\nu\big[\gamma(T)Y\big], \quad \nu \in \mathcal{D}_m$$

is the analogue of u_0 in (4.3.5), namely the "hedging price of Y with unconstrained portfolios in $\mathcal{M}_\nu$", in the auxiliary market model of (4.2.3), (4.2.4).

We have the following analogue of the notion in Definition 0.3.1.

4.3.2. DEFINITION. A contingent claim Y is called *K-attainable*, if $h_{\text{up}}(K) < \infty$ and if there exists a tame portfolio $\pi: [0,T] \times \Omega \to K$ such that

(4.3.12) $$X^{x,\pi,0}(T) = Y \text{ a.s.}, \text{ with } x = h_{\text{up}}(K).$$

Characterizations of K-attainable contingent claims will be provided in Section 4.5; and the represetions of $h_{\text{up}}(K)$, $h_{\text{low}}(K)$ in (4.3.10) will be established in Sections 4.4 and 4.6, respectively.

Suppose now that the contingent claim Y is priced at $p > 0$ in the market $\mathcal{M}(K)$, at time $t = 0$. We say that the triple $\big(\mathcal{M}(K), p, Y\big)$ *admits an arbitrage opportunity*, if there exists either

(i) a pair $(\hat{\pi}, \hat{C})$ with $\hat{\pi}(\cdot)$ tame, $\hat{\pi}(\cdot) \in K$ a.e. and

(4.3.13) $$X^{x,\hat{\pi},\hat{C}}(T) \geq Y \text{ a.s.}, \quad \text{for some } 0 < x < p,$$

or

(ii) a pair $(\tilde{\pi}, \check{C})$ with $\tilde{\pi}(\cdot) \in K$ a.e., $M^{\tilde{\pi}}(\cdot)$ a $\mathbb{P}^\nu$-supermartingale for every $\nu \in \mathcal{D}_b$, and

(4.3.14) $$X^{-x,\tilde{\pi},\check{C}}(T) \geq -Y \text{ a.s.}, \quad \text{for some } x > p.$$

The meaning of this Definition should be clear. In the first case, an agent can *sell* the contingent claim at time $t = 0$ for $p > x$ (i.e., for more than is required in order to hedge it perfectly at time $t = T$). In the second case, the agent can *buy* the contingent claim for $p < x$ (i.e., for less than the amount which allows him to cover, at time $t = T$, his initial debt without risk). Clearly, any price $p > 0$ that leads to such an opportunity should be excluded.

4.3.3. EXERCISE. Every $p > 0$ outside the interval $\big[h_{\mathrm{low}}(K), h_{\mathrm{up}}(K)\big]$ leads to an arbitrage opportunity in $\big(\mathcal{M}(K), p, Y\big)$, while no $p > 0$ in the interior of this interval does. Thus, we call $\big[h_{\mathrm{low}}(K), h_{\mathrm{up}}(K)\big]$ the *arbitrage-free interval*.

(*Hint*: It is not hard to see that the sets $\mathcal{U}$, $\mathcal{L}$ in (4.3.6), (4.3.7), respectively, are intervals: $(x \in \mathcal{L}, 0 \le y \le x)$ imply $y \in \mathcal{L}$, and $(x \in \mathcal{U}, y \ge x)$ imply $y \in \mathcal{U}$. Suppose $p > h_{\mathrm{up}}(K)$; then for any $x \in \big(h_{\mathrm{up}}(K), p\big)$ the above property gives $x \in \mathcal{U}$, that is (4.3.13). Similarly for $p < h_{\mathrm{low}}(K)$. On the other hand, suppose $h_{\mathrm{low}}(K) < p < h_{\mathrm{up}}(K)$, and that the conditions (i) are satisfied; then from the definition of $h_{\mathrm{up}}(K)$ in (4.3.6) we get $h_{\mathrm{up}}(K) \le x < p$, a contradiction. Similarly if (ii) is satisfied.)

4.4. Upper hedging price

Let $Y: \Omega \to [0, \infty)$ be a European contingent claim in the constrained market model $\mathcal{M}(K)$ of Section 4.1, *under the condition* (4.3.1). For any $\nu \in \mathcal{D}_m$ with $u_\nu = \mathbb{E}^\nu\big[\gamma(T)Y\big] \in (0, \infty)$, we know from Theorem 1.2.1 that u_ν is equal to the upper- (and lower-) *hedging price of Y in the market* $\mathcal{M}_\nu$ of (4.2.3), (4.2.4) *using unconstrained portfolios*; and that there exists a tame portfolio $\hat{\pi}_\nu : [0, T] \times \Omega \to \mathbb{R}^d$ with corresponding wealth process

$$(4.4.1) \qquad X^{u_\nu, \hat{\pi}_\nu, 0}(t) \equiv \hat{X}_\nu(t) \triangleq \frac{1}{\gamma(t)} \mathbb{E}^\nu\big[\gamma(T)Y \mid \mathcal{F}(t)\big], \qquad 0 \le t \le T.$$

We shall show in this section that the upper-hedging price $h_{\mathrm{up}}(K)$ of (4.3.6), for the contingent claim Y in the constraint market $\mathcal{M}(K)$, is given by the supremum of the numbers u_ν in (4.3.11) over the class $\mathcal{D}_b$ of (4.3.2), as promised in (4.3.10).

4.4.1. THEOREM. *For any European Contingent claim Y, we have*

$$(4.4.2) \qquad h_{\mathrm{up}}(K) = \sup_{\nu \in \mathcal{D}_b} u_\nu =: h \qquad \left(= \sup_{\nu \in \mathcal{D}_m} u_\nu =: g \right).$$

If $h < \infty$, there exists a pair $(\hat{\pi}, \hat{C}) \in \mathcal{A}(h; K)$ with corresponding wealth process given by

$$(4.4.3) \qquad X^{h, \hat{\pi}, \hat{C}}(t) \equiv X(t) \triangleq \operatorname*{ess\,sup}_{\nu \in \mathcal{D}_b} \frac{1}{\gamma(t)} \mathbb{E}^\nu\big[\gamma(T)Y \mid \mathcal{F}(t)\big], \qquad 0 \le t \le T$$

and in particular,

$$(4.4.4) \qquad X^{h, \hat{\pi}, \hat{C}}(T) = Y, \quad \text{a.s.}$$

The inequality $g \le h_{\mathrm{up}}(K)$ is obvious if $h_{\mathrm{up}}(K) = \infty$; if not, let $x \ge 0$ be an arbitrary element of the set in (4.3.6), and let (π, C) be a portfolio/consumption process pair with $X^{x, \pi, C}(T) \ge Y$ a.s. and with $\pi(\cdot)$ tame, $\pi(\cdot) \in K$ a.e. These two properties mean, in particular, that the process of (4.2.9) is then bounded from below and a $\mathbb{P}^\nu$-local martingale, hence also a $\mathbb{P}^\nu$-supermartingale, for every $\nu \in \mathcal{D}_m$. Thus, in conjunction with (4.2.11), we have

$$u_\nu = \mathbb{E}^\nu\big[\gamma(T)Y\big] \le \mathbb{E}^\nu\big[\gamma(T)X^{x, \pi, C}(T)\big]$$

$$\le \mathbb{E}\left[\gamma(T)X_\nu^{x, \pi, C}(T) + \int_{(0, T]} \gamma(t)\, dC(t)\right] \le x, \qquad \forall\, \nu \in \mathcal{D}_m,$$

whence $g \le x$, and $g \le h_{\mathrm{up}}(K)$ from the arbitrariness of x.

In order to prove the reverse inequality $h \geq h_{\text{up}}(K)$, and the remaining claims of the theorem, it suffices to *assume that $h < \infty$* (for otherwise the inequality is obvious) *and construct a pair*

(4.4.5) $(\hat{\pi}, \hat{C}) \in \mathcal{A}(h; K)$ *such that* $X^{h, \hat{\pi}, \hat{C}}(\cdot) \equiv X(\cdot),$

where $X(\cdot)$ is the nonnegative process in (4.4.3) with $X(0) = h$, $X(T) = Y$ a.s. This process has the following properties; their proof is fairly technical, so we send the interested reader to the Appendix in Cvitanić & Karatzas (1993) for the complete arguments.

4.4.2. PROPOSITION. *The process $X(\cdot)$ of (4.4.3) can be considered in its right-continuous, left-limited* (RCLL) *modification; it satisfies the* equation

(4.4.6) $$X(s) = \operatorname*{ess\,sup}_{\nu \in \mathcal{D}_b} \frac{1}{\gamma(s)} \mathbb{E}^{\nu}\big[\gamma(t)X(t) \mid \mathcal{F}(s)\big], \quad \text{a.s.}$$

of Dynamic Programming, for every $0 \leq s \leq t \leq T$; in particular, for every $\nu \in \mathcal{D}_b$, the process

(4.4.7) $\gamma(\cdot)X(\cdot)$ *is a $\mathbb{P}^{\nu}$-supermartingale with RCLL paths.*

From (4.4.7), the Doob-Meyer decomposition (Protter (1992), Theorem 7 of p. 94; Karatzas & Shreve (1991), pp. 24–28), and the martingale representation result of Exercise 0.3.6, *for every $\nu \in \mathcal{D}_b$* there exist a natural increasing process $A_{\nu}(\cdot)$ with right-continuous paths and $A_{\nu}(0) = 0$, $\mathbb{E}^{\nu}A_{\nu}(T) < \infty$, and a progressively measurable process $\psi_{\nu} : [0, T] \times \Omega \to \mathbb{R}^d$ with $\int_0^T \|\psi_{\nu}(t)\|^2 \, dt < \infty$ a.s., such that

(4.4.8) $$\gamma(t)X(t) = h + \int_0^t \psi_{\nu}'(s) \, dW^{(\nu)}(s) - A_{\nu}(t), \qquad 0 \leq t \leq T$$

holds almost surely. It should be stressed that (4.4.8) is a *simultaneous Doob-Meyer decomposition*, valid for all $\nu \in \mathcal{D}_b$. In particular, for any two $\mu \in \mathcal{D}_b$, $\nu \in \mathcal{D}_b$ it develops from (4.4.8) and (4.2.6):

$$\gamma(t)X(t) = h + \int_0^t \psi_{\nu}'(s) \, dW^{(\mu)}(s) - \left[A_{\nu}(t) + \int_0^t \psi_{\nu}'(s)\sigma^{-1}(s)\big(\mu(s) - \nu(s)\big) \, ds\right]$$

$$= h + \int_0^t \psi_{\mu}'(s) \, dW^{(\mu)}(s) - A_{\mu}(t), \qquad 0 \leq t \leq T$$

almost surely. But the $\mathbb{P}^{\mu}$-semimartingale decomposition of $\gamma(\cdot)X(\cdot)$ is unique, and thus $\psi_{\nu}(\cdot) = \psi_{\mu}(\cdot)$, $A_{\nu}(\cdot) + \int_0^{\cdot} \psi_{\nu}'(s)\sigma^{-1}(s)\big(\mu(s) - \nu(s)\big) \, ds = A_{\mu}(\cdot)$. In other words, we have

(4.4.9) $$\psi_{\nu}(\cdot) \equiv \psi_0(\cdot), \quad A_{\nu}(\cdot) - \int_0^{\cdot} \psi_0'(s)\sigma^{-1}(s)\nu(s) \, ds \equiv A_0(\cdot)$$

for all $\nu \in \mathcal{D}_b$.

PROOF OF (4.4.5). We define now a portfolio process $\hat{\pi} : [0, T] \times \Omega \to \mathbb{R}^d$ and a cumulative consumption process $\hat{C} : [0, T] \times \Omega \to [0, \infty)$ via

(4.4.10) $$\hat{\pi}'(t) \triangleq \frac{1}{\gamma(t)} \psi_0'(t)\sigma^{-1}(t), \quad \hat{C}(t) \triangleq \int_{(0,t]} \frac{1}{\gamma(s)} dA_0(s); \qquad 0 \leq t \leq T.$$

Indeed, it is clear from the properties of $\psi_0(\cdot)$, $A_0(\cdot)$ and (4.1.3), (4.3.1) that the requirements of Definition 0.2.1 are satisfied. It also follows, from (4.4.8) with $\nu(\cdot) \equiv 0$, that

(4.4.11) $\gamma(t)X(t)$

$$= h + \int_0^t \gamma(s)\hat{\pi}'(s)\sigma(s)\, dW^{(0)}(s) - \int_{(0,t]} \gamma(s)\, d\hat{C}(s), \qquad 0 \le t \le T,$$

which implies that $X(\cdot)$ is the wealth process corresponding to initial capital $h \in (0,\infty)$ and portfolio/cumulative consumption processes $(\hat{\pi}, \hat{C})$ as in (4.4.10):

$$X^{h,\hat{\pi},\hat{C}}(\cdot) \equiv X(\cdot) \ge 0.$$

In particular, the pair $(\hat{\pi}, \hat{C})$ belongs to the class $\mathcal{A}(h)$ of Definition 2.1.1, and thus $\hat{\pi}(\cdot)$ is tame. *It remains to show that*

(4.4.12) $\hat{\pi}(t,w) \in K, \quad \text{for} \quad (\lambda \otimes \mathbb{P}) - \text{a.e.}\ (t,w) \in [0,T] \times \Omega.$

We claim that

(4.4.13) $(\lambda \otimes \mathbb{P})(F_r) = 0, \quad \forall\, r \in \tilde{K},$

$$\text{where } F_r \triangleq \big\{ (t,w) \in [0,T] \times \Omega\ /\ r'\hat{\pi}(t,w) < 0 \big\}.$$

Indeed, suppose $(\lambda \otimes \mathbb{P})(F_r) > 0$ for some $r \in \tilde{K}$, and consider the process

$$\nu(t,w) \triangleq r \cdot 1_{F_r^c}(t,w) + \ell r \cdot 1_{F_r}(t,w)$$

for suitable $\ell \in \mathbb{N}$; this process belongs to the class $\mathcal{D}_b$ of (4.3.2), and we obtain from (4.4.9) that

$$\mathbb{E}^0 A_\nu(T) = \mathbb{E}^0 \left[A_0(T) + \int_0^T \gamma(t)\nu'(t)\hat{\pi}(t)\, dt \right]$$

$$= \mathbb{E}^0 A_0(T) + \iint_{F_r^c} \gamma(t,w) \cdot r'\hat{\pi}(t,w)\, dt\, \mathbb{P}^0(dw)$$

$$+ \ell \iint_{F_r} \gamma(t,w) r'\hat{\pi}(t,w)\, dt\, \mathbb{P}^0(dw)$$

is negative for $\ell \in \mathbb{N}$ large enough, contradicting the a.s. non-negativity of $A_\nu(T)$. Clearly now, (4.4.13) implies

(4.4.14) $r'\hat{\pi}(t,w) \ge 0, \qquad \forall\, r \in \tilde{K}$

for $(\lambda \otimes \mathbb{P}) -$ a.e. $(t,w) \in [0,T] \times \Omega$; and this leads to (4.4.12), from Theorem 13.1, p. 112 in Rockafellar (1970). $\square$

The proof of Theorem 4.4.1 is now complete.

4.4.3. EXERCISE. Show that the process of (4.4.3) is also given, almost surely, as

(4.4.15) $X(t) = \operatorname*{ess\,sup}_{\nu \in \mathcal{D}_m} \dfrac{1}{\gamma(t)} \mathbb{E}^\nu \big[\gamma(T)Y \mid \mathcal{F}(t) \big], \qquad 0 \le t \le T.$

(*Hint*: This is clearly an extension of $X(0) = \sup_{\nu \in \mathcal{D}_b} u_\nu = \sup_{\nu \in \mathcal{D}_m} u_\nu$ in (4.4.2). We argue as follows: for every $\nu \in \mathcal{D}_m$, we deduce from (4.4.11), (4.2.6) and (4.1.5) that

$$\gamma(t)X(t) = h + \int_0^t \gamma(s)\hat{\pi}'(s)\sigma(s) \, dW^{(\nu)}(s) - \int_0^t \gamma(s)\nu'(s)\hat{\pi}(s) \, ds$$
$$- \int_{(0,t]} \gamma(s) \, d\hat{C}(s), \qquad 0 \le t \le T$$

is a $\mathbb{P}^\nu$-supermartingale, for every $\nu \in \mathcal{D}_m$. In particular

$$X(t) \ge \operatorname*{ess\,sup}_{\nu \in \mathcal{D}_m} \frac{1}{\gamma(t)} \mathbb{E}^\nu \big[\gamma(T)Y \mid \mathcal{F}(t) \big] \quad \text{a.s.}$$

holds for every $t \in [0, T]$, since $X(T) = Y$ a.s. The reverse inequality is obvious from the definition (4.4.3) of $X(\cdot)$, and (4.4.15) follows from the fact that both sides can be considered in their RCLL modification, as in Proposition 4.4.2.)

4.4.4. EXERCISE. For the contingent claim Y of Theorem 4.4.1, let $\hat{\pi}_\nu(\cdot)$ be the unconstrained hedging portfolio in the market $\mathcal{M}_\nu$, $\nu \in \mathcal{D}_m$ as in (4.4.1), (4.3.11). Suppose that for some $\mu \in \mathcal{D}_m$ with $u_\mu < \infty$, we have

(4.4.16) $\hat{\pi}_\mu(\cdot) \in K$ and $\mu'(\cdot)\hat{\pi}_\mu(\cdot) = 0$,   a.e. on $[0, T] \times \Omega$.

Show then that

(4.4.17) $h_{\mathrm{up}}(K) = g = u_\mu$, $X(\cdot) \equiv \hat{X}_\mu(\cdot)$.

(*Hint*: We have, by assumption, $(\pi_\mu, 0) \in \mathcal{A}(u_\mu; K)$ and $X^{u_\mu, \hat{\pi}_\mu, 0}(T) = Y$ a.s., and thus from (4.3.6): $h_{\mathrm{up}}(K) \le u_\mu < \infty$. On the other hand, Theorem 4.4.1 gives $u_\mu \le \sup_{\nu \in \mathcal{D}_m} u_\nu = g = h_{\mathrm{up}}(K)$, proving the first claim in (4.4.17). To prove $X(\cdot) = \hat{X}_\mu(\cdot)$, where $X(\cdot)$ is the process of (4.4.3) and $\hat{X}_\mu(\cdot) \triangleq X^{u_\mu, \hat{\pi}_\mu, 0}(\cdot)$, we argue as before: observe from (4.2.9) that

$$\gamma(t)\hat{X}_\mu(t) = u_\mu + \int_0^t \gamma(u)\hat{\pi}'_\mu(u)\sigma(u) \, dW^{(\mu)}(u)$$
$$= u_\mu + \int_0^t \gamma(u)\hat{\pi}'_\mu(u)\sigma(u) \big[dW^{(\nu)}(u) + \sigma^{-1}(u)\big(\mu(u) - \nu(u)\big) \, du \big]$$
$$= u_\mu + \int_0^t \gamma(u)\hat{\pi}'_\mu(u)\sigma(u) \, dW^{(\nu)}(u) - \int_0^t \gamma(u)\nu'(u)\hat{\pi}_\mu(u) \, du, \quad 0 \le t \le T$$

is a $\mathbb{P}^\nu$-supermartingale, for every $\nu \in \mathcal{D}_m$. Thus $\hat{X}_\mu(t) \ge (1/\gamma(t))\mathbb{E}^\nu\big[\gamma(T)\hat{X}_\mu(T) \mid \mathcal{F}(t)\big] = (1/\gamma(t))\mathbb{E}^\nu\big[\gamma(T)Y \mid \mathcal{F}(t)\big]$ a.s. for every $t \in [0, T]$ and $\nu \in \mathcal{D}_m$, yielding $\hat{X}_\mu(\cdot) \ge X(\cdot)$ in conjunction with (4.4.15); the reverse inequality is obvious.)

4.5. Attainability

Let us use now the results of the previous section, to decide the question of K-*attainability* (Definition 4.3.2) for a given contingent claim Y as in Theorem 4.4.1, and assume

(4.5.1) $g \triangleq \sup_{\nu \in \mathcal{D}_m} u_\nu < \infty.$

4.5.1. THEOREM. *For any given $\mu \in \mathcal{D}_m$, the conditions*

$$(4.5.2) \qquad\qquad \gamma(\cdot)X(\cdot) \text{ is a } \mathbb{P}^\mu - \text{martingale,}$$

$$(4.5.3) \qquad\qquad g = u_\mu$$

$$(4.5.4) \qquad \begin{cases} Y \text{ is } K\text{-attainable by a tame portfolio } \pi(\cdot) \\ \text{and } \gamma(\cdot)X^{g,\pi,0}(\cdot) \text{ is a } \mathbb{P}^\mu\text{-martingale} \end{cases}$$

are equivalent, and imply

$$(4.5.5) \qquad\qquad \mu'(\cdot)\hat{\pi}(\cdot) = 0 \text{ a.e.,} \quad \text{and} \quad \hat{C}(T) = 0 \text{ a.s.}$$

PROOF. In view of (4.4.7), the condition (4.5.2) is equivalent to the equality $X(0) = \mathbb{E}^\mu[\gamma(T)X(T)]$, that is $g = \mathbb{E}^\mu[\gamma(T)Y]$, i.e. (4.5.3).

On the other hand, (4.5.2) implies that the increasing process $A_\mu(\cdot)$, in the Doob-Meyer decomposition of (4.4.8), is identically equal to zero, and then (4.5.5) follows from

$$(4.5.6) \quad A_\nu(t) = \int_0^T \gamma(t)\nu'(t)\hat{\pi}(t)\,dt + \int_{(0,T]} \gamma(t)\,d\hat{C}(t); \qquad 0 \le t \le T, \quad \nu \in \mathcal{D}_m$$

(a consequence of (4.4.9), (4.4.10)).

Suppose now that (4.5.3) holds; then its consequences (4.5.2), (4.5.5) imply, in conjunction with (4.4.5), that $\gamma(\cdot)X^{g,\hat{\pi},0}(\cdot) \equiv \gamma(\cdot)X(\cdot)$ is a $\mathbb{P}^\mu$-martingale and that $X^{g,\hat{\pi},0}(T) = Y$, a.s. It develops that (4.5.4) is then valid, with $\pi(\cdot) \equiv \hat{\pi}(\cdot)$. Conversely, (4.5.4) implies

$$g = X^{g,\pi,0}(0) = \mathbb{E}^\mu[\gamma(T)X^{g,\pi,0}(T)] = \mathbb{E}^\mu[\gamma(T)Y] = u_\mu,$$

that is (4.5.3). $\square$

4.5.2. PROPOSITION. *Suppose that, for every process $\nu \in \mathcal{D}_m$ with $\nu'(\cdot)\hat{\pi}(\cdot) = 0(\lambda \otimes \mathbb{P}) -$ a.e. on $[0,T] \times \Omega$, we have that*

$$(4.5.7) \qquad \begin{cases} \text{the family of random variables } \{\gamma(\tau)X(\tau)\}_{\tau \in \mathcal{S}} \\ \text{is } \mathbb{P}^\nu\text{-uniformly integrable,} \end{cases}$$

in the notation of (0.2.19).

(i) *Then the conditions (4.5.2)–(4.5.5) are equivalent; and if they hold for some $\mu \in \mathcal{D}_m$, they also imply that*

$$(4.5.8) \qquad \begin{cases} Y \text{ is } K\text{-attainable by a tame portfolio } \pi(\cdot) \\ \text{and } \gamma(\cdot)X^{g,\pi,0}(\cdot) \text{ is a } \mathbb{P}^0\text{-martingale.} \end{cases}$$

(ii) *Conversely, if (4.5.8) holds, then (4.5.2)–(4.5.5) also hold for any $\mu \in \mathcal{D}_m$ with $\mu'(\cdot)\hat{\pi}(\cdot) = 0$, $(\lambda \otimes \mathbb{P}) -$ a.e. on $[0,T] \times \Omega$.*

PROOF.   (i) Suppose that (4.5.5) holds. Then from (4.5.6) we obtain $A_\mu(T) = 0$ a.s., so that $\gamma(\cdot)X(\cdot)$ is a $\mathbb{P}^\mu$-local martingale, hence also a $\mathbb{P}^\mu$-martingale (thanks to (4.4.8) and (4.5.7)); that is, (4.5.2) holds. In conjunction with Theorem 4.5.1, we deduce that (4.5.2)–(4.5.5) are now equivalent; and if they hold for some $\mu \in \mathcal{D}_m$ with the property of (4.5.5), then they also hold, clearly, for $\mu(\cdot) \equiv 0$, giving (4.5.8).

(ii) Now suppose that we have (4.5.8), that is, (4.5.4) with $\mu(\cdot) \equiv 0$. Then, from part (i), all of (4.5.2)–(4.5.5) hold for any $\mu \in \mathcal{D}_m$ as in (4.5.5).

$\square$

Sufficient conditions for (4.5.1), (4.5.7) are provided in Exercises 4.5.4, 4.5.5 below.

4.5.3. EXAMPLE (Incomplete markets). Recall the Example 4.1.2 with $K = \{\pi \in \mathbb{R}^d \,/\, \pi_{n+1} = \cdots = \pi_d = 0\}$, $\tilde{K} = \{x \in \mathbb{R}^d \,/\, x_1 = \cdots = x_n = 0\}$, where only n stocks are available for investment, and these are driven by the d-dimensional Brownian motion W with $d > n$. Clearly in this case,

$$(4.5.9) \qquad x'\pi = 0; \qquad \forall\, \pi \in K, \quad x \in \tilde{K}.$$

It follows from Theorem 4.5.1 and Proposition 4.5.2 that, *for any contingent claim* Y *satisfying* (4.5.1) *and* (4.5.7),

$$(4.5.10) \qquad \left\{ \begin{array}{l} \text{if the supremum } h_{\text{up}}(K) = g \triangleq \sup_{\nu \in \mathcal{D}_m} u_\nu \text{ is} \\ \text{attained by } \textit{some } \mu \in \mathcal{D}_m, \text{ then it is attained by} \\ \textit{every } \nu \in \mathcal{D}_m \colon g = u_\nu, \, \forall\, \nu \in \mathcal{D}_m. \end{array} \right\}$$

4.5.4. EXERCISE. If $\mathbb{P}[0 \leq Y \leq y] = 1$ for some $y \in (0, \infty)$, then both (4.5.1) and (4.5.7) are satisfied.

(*Hint*: It is not hard to see that (4.4.15) can be extended to read

$$(4.5.11) \qquad X(\tau) = \operatorname*{ess\,sup}_{\nu \in \mathcal{D}_m^{(\tau)}} \frac{1}{\gamma(\tau)} \mathbb{E}^\nu \big[\gamma(T) Y \mid \mathcal{F}(\tau)\big], \qquad \forall\, \tau \in \mathcal{S}$$

where $\mathcal{D}_m^{(\tau)}$ is the restriction of $\mathcal{D}_m$ to the stochastic interval $[\![\tau, T]\!]$. This gives (4.5.7) since $0 \leq \gamma(\tau) X(\tau) \leq y e^{\eta T} < \infty$ holds a.s. for every stopping time $\tau \in \mathcal{S}$, as well as (4.5.1) because we have $X(0) = g \leq y e^{\eta T} < \infty$.)

4.5.5. EXERCISE. Both (4.5.1), (4.5.7) are satisfied if $0 \leq Y \leq \alpha \cdot P_m(T)$ holds almost surely, for some $\alpha \in (0, \infty)$ and $m = 1, \ldots, d$, provided that the coordinate mapping

$$(4.5.12) \qquad x \mapsto x_m \text{ is bounded from below on } \tilde{K}.$$

This case covers the European call-option $Y = \big(P_m(T) - q\big)^+$, $q \geq 0$.

(*Hint*: Recall from (4.3.4), (4.1.3) that, for every $\mu \in \mathcal{D}_m$, the process

$$(4.5.13) \quad \gamma(t) e^{\int_0^t \mu_m(s)\, ds} P_m(t)$$

$$= p_m \exp\left\{ \sum_{j=1}^d \int_0^t \sigma_{mj}(s)\, dW_j^{(\mu)}(s) - \frac{1}{2} \sum_{j=1}^d \int_0^t \sigma_{mj}^2(s)\, ds \right\}, \qquad 0 \leq t \leq T$$

is a $\mathbb{P}^\mu$-martingale. Fix $\mu \in \mathcal{D}_m$ and assume, as you may, that the supremum in (4.5.11) is over processes $\nu(\cdot)$ that agree with $\mu(\cdot)$ on $[\![0, \tau]\!]$, to obtain

$$0 \leq \gamma(\tau) X(\tau) \leq \alpha \cdot \operatorname*{ess\,sup}_{\nu \in \mathcal{D}_m^{(\tau)}} \mathbb{E}^\nu \big[\gamma(T) P_m(T) \mid \mathcal{F}(\tau)\big]$$

$$\leq \text{constant} \cdot \operatorname*{ess\,sup}_{\nu \in \mathcal{D}_m^{(\tau)}} \mathbb{E}^\nu \big[\gamma(T) e^{\int_0^T \nu_m(s)\, ds} P_m(T) \mid \mathcal{F}(\tau)\big]$$

$$\leq \text{constant} \cdot \gamma(\tau) P_m(\tau) e^{\int_0^\tau \mu_m(s)\, ds}$$

$$= \text{constant} \cdot \mathbb{E}^\mu \big[\gamma(T) P_m(T) e^{\int_0^T \mu_m(s)\, ds} \mid \mathcal{F}(\tau)\big], \qquad \forall\, \tau \in \mathcal{S}.$$

This shows that the family $\{\gamma(\tau)X(\tau)\}_{\tau\in\mathcal{S}}$ is uniformly integrable under $\mathbb{P}^\mu$; and with $\mu(\cdot)\equiv 0$, $\tau=0$ it gives

$$X(0)=g\leq \text{constant}\cdot\mathbb{E}^0\big[\gamma(T)P_m(T)\big]=\text{constant}\cdot P_m(0)<\infty.)$$

4.5.6. EXERCISE. Show that in the case of a European call-option of the form $Y=\big(P_m(T)-q\big)^+$ with $q\geq 0$, we have $g\triangleq \sup_{\nu\in\mathcal{D}_m}u_\nu=\infty$ if (4.5.12) fails; that is, (4.5.12) *is then necessary as well as sufficient for the validity of* (4.5.1).
$\big($*Hint*: From (4.5.13) and Jensen's inequality, observe that

$$u_\nu=\mathbb{E}^\nu\big[\gamma(T)\big(P_m(T)-q\big)^+\big]\geq \big(\mathbb{E}^\nu\big[\gamma(T)P_m(T)\big]-q\cdot\mathbb{E}^\nu\gamma(T)\big)^+$$
$$\geq \bigg(P_m(0)\cdot\exp\bigg\{-\int_0^T\nu_m(t)\,dt\bigg\}-qe^{\eta T}\bigg)^+$$

holds for every *deterministic* $\nu(\cdot)\in\mathcal{D}_m$, i.e. for every L^2-function $\nu\colon[0,T]\to\tilde{K}$, by appropriate choice of which this last expression can be made arbitrarily large if (4.5.12) fails.$\big)$

4.5.7. EXERCISE. Consider the European call-option $Y=\big(P_1(T)-q\big)^+$ with $d=1$ and constant $r(\cdot)\equiv r$, $\sigma_{11}(\cdot)\equiv\sigma>0$, $q>0$, *under the no-short-selling constraint* $K=[0,\infty)$ of Example 4.1.1. Show that the upper hedging price is given by the Black-Scholes formula (1.3.13), (1.3.14):

$$h_{\text{up}}(K)=g=U\big(T,P_1(0);q\big).$$

(*Hint*: Recall the Remark 1.3.5).

4.6. Lower hedging price

Let $Y\colon\Omega\to[0,\infty)$ be a European contingent claim in the constrained market model $\mathcal{M}(K)$, as in Sections 4.3, 4.4 and under the additional condition

$$(4.6.1)\qquad\qquad \mathbb{E}\,(Y^{1+\varepsilon})<\infty\quad\text{for some }\varepsilon>0.$$

Our aim in this section will be to show that the *lower hedging price* $h_{\text{low}}(K)$ of Y in $\mathcal{M}(K)$ defined in (4.3.7), is given by the expression of (4.3.10), as the infimum of the numbers u_ν in (4.3.11) over the class $\mathcal{D}_b$.

4.6.1. THEOREM. *For any European Contingent claim Y as above, we have*

$$(4.6.2)\qquad\qquad h_{\text{low}}(K)=\inf_{\nu\in\mathcal{D}_b}u_\nu=:f.$$

If $f>0$, there exists a pair $(\check{\pi},\check{C})$ of portfolio/cumulative consumption processes with $\check{\pi}(\cdot)\in K$ a.e. in $[0,T]\times\Omega$ and corresponding wealth process $X^{-f,\check{\pi},\check{C}}(\cdot)$ given by

$$(4.6.3)\quad -X^{-f,\check{\pi},\check{C}}(t)\equiv Q(t)\triangleq \operatorname*{ess\,inf}_{\nu\in\mathcal{D}_b}\frac{1}{\gamma(t)}\mathbb{E}^\nu\big[\gamma(T)Y\mid\mathcal{F}(t)\big],\qquad 0\leq t\leq T$$

and in particular

$$(4.6.4)\qquad\qquad X^{-f,\check{\pi},\check{C}}(T)=-Y,\text{ almost surely.}$$

The proof proceeds by direct analogy with that of Theorem 4.4.1, so we only sketch the main arguments.

First, the inequality $h_{\text{low}}(K) \leq f$ is obvious if $h_{\text{low}}(K) = 0$; and if not, for an arbitrary $x \geq 0$ in the set of (4.3.7) and any pair $(\tilde{\pi}, \check{C})$ with the properties indicated there, we obtain from (4.2.9) and (4.2.11)

$$-x \geq \mathbb{E}^{\nu}\left[-x + M_{\nu}^{\tilde{\pi}}(T)\right] = \mathbb{E}^{\nu}\left[\gamma(T)X_{\nu}^{-x,\tilde{\pi},\check{C}}(T) + \int_{(0,T]} \gamma(t)\,d\check{C}(t)\right]$$

$$\geq \mathbb{E}^{\nu}\left[\gamma(T)X^{-x,\tilde{\pi},\check{C}}(T)\right] \geq -\mathbb{E}^{\nu}\left[\gamma(T)Y\right] = -u_{\nu}$$

for every $\nu \in \mathcal{D}_b$, whence $x \leq f$ and $h_{\text{low}}(K) \leq f$ from the arbitrariness of x.

Secondly, in order to prove the reverse inequality $h_{\text{low}}(K) \geq f$ and the remaining claims of the Theorem, it suffices to *assume $f > 0$* (for otherwise the inequality is obvious) *and construct a portfolio/cumulative consumption process pair*

(4.6.5)
$$\begin{cases} (\tilde{\pi}, \check{C}) \text{ with } \tilde{\pi}(\cdot) \in K \ (\lambda \otimes \mathbb{P} \text{ a.e.}), \ X^{-f,\tilde{\pi},\check{C}}(\cdot) \equiv -Q(\cdot), \\ \text{and } M_{\nu}^{\tilde{\pi}}(\cdot) \triangleq \int_0^{\cdot} \gamma(s)\tilde{\pi}'(s)\sigma(s)\,dW^{(\nu)}(s) = \mathbb{P}^{\nu}\text{-martingale}, \\ \forall \ \nu \in \mathcal{D}_b. \end{cases}$$

Here $Q(\cdot)$ is the nonnegative process of (4.6.3) with $Q(0) = f$ and $Q(T) = Y$ a.s. We have the following properties for this process; the first is analogous to Proposition 4.4.2, and the second is a consequence of the condition (4.6.1).

4.6.2. Proposition. *The process $Q(\cdot)$ of (4.6.3) can be taken in its* RCLL *modification; it satisfies the* equation of Dynamic Programming

(4.6.6)
$$Q(s) = \operatorname*{ess\,inf}_{\nu \in \mathcal{D}_b} \frac{1}{\gamma(s)} \mathbb{E}^{\nu}\left[\gamma(t)Q(t) \mid \mathcal{F}(s)\right], \quad \text{a.s.}$$

for $0 \leq s \leq t \leq T$, which implies that the process

(4.6.7)
$$\gamma(\cdot)Q(\cdot) \text{ is a RCLL } \mathbb{P}^{\nu}\text{-submartingale}, \quad \forall \ \nu \in \mathcal{D}_b.$$

4.6.3. Exercise. $\mathbb{E}^0\left[\sup_{0 \leq t \leq T}(Q(t))^p\right] < \infty$ and $\mathbb{E}^{\nu}\left[\sup_{0 \leq t \leq T}(\gamma(t)Q(t))^p\right] < \infty$ for any $p \in (1, 1+\varepsilon)$ and $\nu \in \mathcal{D}_b$; in particular, $u_{\nu} = \mathbb{E}^{\nu}\left[\gamma(T)Y\right] < \infty$, $\forall \ \nu \in \mathcal{D}_b$.

$\Big($ *Hint:* From (4.6.3), (4.1.4) we obtain

$$0 \leq Q(t) \leq \mathbb{E}^0\left[Ye^{-\int_t^T r(s)\,ds} \mid \mathcal{F}(t)\right] \leq e^{\eta T}Y(t), \text{ where } Y(t) \triangleq \mathbb{E}^0\left[Y \mid \mathcal{F}(t)\right].$$

Now for $r = (1+\varepsilon)/p > 1$ and $\frac{1}{r} + \frac{1}{s} = 1$, we obtain

$$\mathbb{E}^0\left(\sup_{0 \leq t \leq T}(Y(t))^p\right) \leq \text{constant } \mathbb{E}^0(Y(T))^p = \text{constant } \mathbb{E}\left[Z_0(T)Y^p\right]$$

$$\leq \text{constant } \left(\mathbb{E}(Y^{1+\varepsilon})\right)^{1/r}\left(\mathbb{E}(Z_0(T))^s\right)^{1/s} < \infty$$

from (4.6.1) and $\mathbb{E}(Z_0(T))^s \leq \exp(\frac{T}{2}s(s-1)c^2)$; we have used the Hölder inequality, Doob's maximal inequality, and the bound $\|\theta(\cdot)\| \leq c < \infty$ (condition (4.3.1)). This proves the first claim; for the second, observe that we have

$$\mathbb{E}^{\nu}\left(\sup_{0 \leq t \leq T} Y(t)\right) = \mathbb{E}^0\left[\frac{Z_{\nu}(T)}{Z_0(T)} \cdot \sup_{0 \leq t \leq T} Y(t)\right]$$

$$\leq \left(\mathbb{E}^0\left[\sup_{0 \leq t \leq T}(Y(t))^p\right]\right)^{1/p} \cdot \left(\mathbb{E}^0\left(\frac{Z_{\nu}(T)}{Z_0(T)}\right)^q\right)^{1/q} < \infty$$

for $\frac{1}{p} + \frac{1}{q} = 1$, using the uniform boundedness of $\sigma^{-1}(\cdot)\nu(\cdot)$, $\nu \in \mathcal{D}_b$ in

$$\frac{Z_\nu(T)}{Z_0(T)} = \exp\left[-\int_0^T \left(\sigma^{-1}(t)\nu(t)\right)' dW^{(0)}(t) - \frac{1}{2}\int_0^T \left\|\sigma^{-1}(t)\nu(t)\right\|^2 dt\right].\right)$$

It develops now, from (4.6.7) and Exercise 4.6.3, that $\gamma(\cdot)Q(\cdot)$ *is a submartingale of class* $D[0,T]$, *under each* $\mathbb{P}^\nu$, $\nu \in \mathcal{D}_b$. Thus, from the Doob-Meyer decomposition and the martingale representation property of the Brownian filtration (Exercise 0.3.6), we have

$$(4.6.8) \quad \gamma(t)Q(t) = f + M_\nu(t) + \Lambda_\nu(t), \quad M_\nu(t) = \int_0^t \varphi_\nu'(s)\, dW^{(\nu)}(s), \ 0 \le t \le T,$$

for every $\nu \in \mathcal{D}_b$. Here $M_\nu(\cdot)$ is a $\mathbb{P}^\nu$-martingale, and $\Lambda_\nu(\cdot)$ an adapted, right-continuous, natural increasing process with $\Lambda_\nu(0) = 0$, $\mathbb{E}^\nu \Lambda_\nu(T) < \infty$; and just as we saw in Theorem 4.4.1, here again

$$(4.6.9) \qquad \varphi_\nu(\cdot) \equiv \varphi_0(\cdot), \quad \Lambda_\nu(\cdot) + \int_0^\cdot \varphi_0'(s)\sigma^{-1}(s)\nu(s)\, ds \equiv \Lambda_0(\cdot)$$

for all $\nu \in \mathcal{D}_b$, and we have $\int_0^T \left\|\varphi_0(t)\right\|^2 dt < \infty$ a.s.

PROOF OF (4.6.5). Introduce

$$(4.6.10) \quad \check{\pi}'(t) \triangleq -\frac{1}{\gamma(t)}\varphi_0(t)\sigma^{-1}(t), \quad \check{C}(t) \triangleq \int_{(0,t]} \frac{1}{\gamma(s)} d\Lambda_0(s); \qquad 0 \le t \le T$$

and check that they define a portfolio/cumulative consumption process pair $(\check{\pi}, \check{C})$. Observe also, from (4.6.8) and (4.6.9), that: $M_\nu^{\check{\pi}}(\cdot) \equiv -M_\nu(\cdot)$ is a $\mathbb{P}^\nu$-martingale, $\forall \ \nu \in \mathcal{D}_b$ (notation of (4.6.5)),

$$-\gamma(t)Q(t) = -f + \int_0^t \gamma(s)\check{\pi}'(s)\sigma(s)\, dW^{(0)}(s) - \int_{(0,t]} \gamma(s)\, d\check{C}(s), \qquad 0 \le t \le T$$

as well as $Q(\cdot) = -X^{-f,\check{\pi},\check{C}}(\cdot)$, $\Lambda_\nu(\cdot) = \Lambda_0(\cdot) + \int_0^\cdot \gamma(s)\nu'(s)\check{\pi}(s)\, ds$.

It remains to check that $\check{\pi}(\cdot)$ takes values in the cone K; and this is done precisely as for (4.4.12). □

4.6.4. EXERCISE. If the contingent claim Y of Theorem 4.6.1 satisfies $0 \le Y \le \alpha P_m(T)$ a.s. for some $\alpha \in (0,\infty)$ and $m = 1,\ldots,d$, and the coordinate mapping

$$(4.6.11) \qquad\qquad x \mapsto x_m \text{ is unbounded from above on } \tilde{K},$$

then we have $f = 0$ in (4.6.2).

$\big($*Hint*: From (4.5.13) we obtain, for deterministic $\nu(\cdot)$ in $\mathcal{D}_b$,

$$u_\nu \le \alpha \cdot \mathbb{E}^\nu\left[\gamma(T)e^{\int_0^T \nu_m(t)\, dt} P_m(T)\right]e^{-\int_0^T \nu_m(t)\, dt} = \alpha P_m(0)e^{-\int_0^T \nu_m(t)\, dt},$$

and this last expression can be made arbitrarily close to zero, under condition (4.6.11).$\big)$

4.6.5. EXERCISE. For a European call-option $Y = \left(P_m(T) - q\right)^+$ with $0 \le q < p_m e^{-T(N+\eta)}$, where $m = 1,\ldots,d$, with η is as in (4.1.4) and with $N \triangleq \sup_{x \in \tilde{K}} x_m < \infty$, we have $f > 0$ in (4.6.2).

(*Hint*: For every $\nu \in \mathcal{D}_d$, we have from Jensen's inequality and (4.5.13):

$$u_\nu = \mathbb{E}^\nu \big[\gamma(T) \big(P_m(T) - q \big)^+ \big] \geq \big(\mathbb{E}^\nu \big[\gamma(T) P_m(T) e^{\int_0^T \nu_m(t)\, dt} \big] \cdot e^{-TN} - q e^{\eta T} \big)^+$$
$$= (p_m e^{-TN} - q e^{T\eta}) > 0.)$$

4.6.6. REMARK. From the proofs of Proposition 0.4.1 and Theorem 1.2.1, observe that we may replace the word "supermartingale" by "martingale", in the definition (0.4.4) of the lower-hedging price h_{low} in a complete market. Similarly, from the proof of Theorem 4.6.1, observe that we may do the same in the definition (4.3.7) of the lower-hedging price $h_{\text{low}}(K)$ with constrained portfolios.

It should also be clear from the proofs of Proposition 0.4.1 and Theorems 1.2.1, 4.4.1 that the requirement "$\hat{\pi}(\cdot)$ is tame" can be replaced in the definitions (0.4.2) of h_{up}, (4.3.6) of $h_{\text{up}}(K)$ by the requirements "$M^{\hat{\pi}}(\cdot)$ is a $\mathbb{P}^0$-(super)martingale" and "$M_\nu^{\hat{\pi}}(\cdot)$ is a $\mathbb{P}^\nu$-supermartingale, $\forall \nu \in \mathcal{D}$", respectively.

CHAPTER 5

Optimization

5.1. The problem

Throughout this chapter, we shall place ourselves again *within the market model* $\mathcal{M}(K)$ of (4.1.1)–(4.1.6), with the notation and assumptions of Section 4.1. We shall consider a utility function $U_2 \colon (0, \infty) \to \mathbb{R}$ and a time-dependent utility function $U_1 \colon [0, T] \times (0, \infty) \to \mathbb{R}$ as in Definitions 2.1.2, 2.1.3 respectively. The class of constrained portfolio/consumption process pairs (π, C) which are admissible for U_1, U_2, is given as

(5.1.1) $\mathcal{A}_*(x; K) \triangleq$

$$\left\{ (\pi, C) \in \mathcal{A}_0(x) \; / \; \pi(\cdot) \in K, \; (\lambda \otimes \mathbb{P}) - \text{a.e.} \; (t, w) \in [0, T] \times \Omega \right\}$$

in the notation of (2.1.16)–(2.1.18), or equivalently

(5.1.2) $\mathcal{A}_*(x; K) = \left\{ (\pi, C) \in \mathcal{A}(x; K) \; / \; C(\cdot) \text{ as in } (2.1.11), \right.$

$$\left. \mathbb{E}\, U_2^-\left(X^{x,\pi,C}(T)\right) < \infty \text{ and } \mathbb{E} \int_0^T U_1^-\big(t, c(t)\big)\, dt < \infty \right\}$$

in the notation of (4.1.6). Here again, K is the *closed convex cone* in which our portfolio processes $\pi(\cdot)$ are restricted to take values, just as in Section 4.1.

This chapter will be devoted to the analogue of Problem 2.1.6 with thus constrained portfolios.

5.1.1. PROBLEM (Utility maximization, constrained portfolios). With a pair $U_1(\cdot, \cdot)$ and $U_2(\cdot)$ of utility functions as above, maximize the expected utility from consumption and terminal wealth $\mathbb{E}[\int_0^T U_1(t, c(t))\, dt + U_2(X^{x,\pi,C}(T))]$, over the class $\mathcal{A}_*(x; K)$ of constrained portfolio and consumption process pairs (π, C) in (5.1.1) (or equivalently (5.1.2)). The *value function* of this problem will be denoted by

(5.1.3) $V(x) \triangleq \sup_{(\pi, C) \in \mathcal{A}_*(x; K)} \mathbb{E}\left[\int_0^T U_1\big(t, c(t)\big)\, dt + U_2\big(X^{x,\pi,C}(T)\big) \right], \quad 0 < x < \infty.$

Quite clearly, this function is dominated by the value of this same problem but with unconstrained portfolios, given by (2.1.20):

(5.1.4) $\qquad\qquad\qquad V(x) \le V_0(x), \qquad 0 < x < \infty.$

Our concerns will be similar to those that we addressed in Chapter 2: to compute the value $V(x)$ of the problem, and to single-out an optimal pair $(\hat{\pi}, \hat{C})$ that attains the supremum in (5.1.3), if such a pair exists. We shall approach these questions by looking instead at the unconstrained Problem 2.1.6 within each of the auxiliary random environments in the family $\{\mathcal{M}_\nu\}_{\nu \in \mathcal{D}}$ of Section 4.2, and denoting their values by $V_\nu(x)$ and their optimal strategies by (π_ν, C_ν); cf. *Section* 5.2. Then we shall try to select a member $\mathcal{M}_\mu$, $\mu \in \mathcal{D}$ of this family, for which $\pi_\mu(\cdot)$ takes values in K and satisfies the "complementary slackness" condition

$$\mu'(\cdot)\pi_\mu(\cdot) \equiv 0, \quad (\lambda \otimes \mathbb{P}) - \text{a.e.}$$

As we shall show in *Section* 5.3, these properties will guarantee that (π_μ, C_μ) is in fact optimal for Problem 5.1.1: $V(x) = V_\mu(x)$, $(\hat{\pi}, \hat{C}) = (\pi_\mu, C_\mu)$.

An important role in these developments will be played by the convex dual $\tilde{V}(y) \triangleq \sup_{x>0}[V(x) - xy]$ of the value function; the significance of this dual was already manifest in Chapter 2, where we were able actually to compute it explicitly (recall (2.2.16)). Here such an explicit computation is not possible in general; however, convex duality theory establishes, in *Section* 5.4, that $\tilde{V}(y) = \inf_{\nu \in \mathcal{D}} \tilde{V}_\nu(y)$ is the value of a "dual (minimization) problem". This dual problem is shown to admit an optimal solution, which in turn implies the existence of an optimal pair $(\hat{\pi}, \hat{C}) = (\pi_\mu, C_\mu)$ for Problem 5.1.1 (cf. *Section* 5.5). All this theory is illustrated in Example 5.3.2 with logarithmic utility functions, in *Section* 5.7 with constant coefficients for $\mathcal{M}$, and in *Section* 5.6 through its connections with relative entropy minimization.

5.2. Embedding

We shall approach the constrained optimization Problem 1.1 by *embedding it into a family of auxiliary unconstrained problems* with similar structure, but within the market models of the family $\{\mathcal{M}_\nu\}_{\nu \in \mathcal{D}}$ of auxiliary random environments in Section 4.2.

More precisely, for every process $\nu(\cdot)$ in the class $\mathcal{D}$ of (4.2.2), let us consider the following *unconstrained optimization problem* with value function

$$(5.2.1) \quad V_\nu(x) \triangleq \sup_{(\pi,C) \in \mathcal{A}_\nu(x)} \mathbb{E}\left[\int_0^T U_1(t, c(t))\, dt + U_2(X_\nu^{x,\pi,C}(T))\right], \quad 0 < x < \infty,$$

the analogue of Problem 2.1.6 for the market model $\mathcal{M}_\nu$ of (4.2.3)–(4.2.8). Here, $X_\nu^{x,\pi,C}(\cdot)$ is the wealth-process of Remark 4.2.1, corresponding to the initial wealth $x \in (0, \infty)$ and the portfolio/consumption process pair (π, C) as in (4.2.9), (4.2.10); and $\mathcal{A}_\nu(x)$ is the analogue of the class $\mathcal{A}_0(x)$ in (2.1.18), namely

$$(5.2.2) \quad \mathcal{A}_\nu(x) \triangleq \Big\{(\pi, C) \in \mathcal{A}^{(\nu)}(x) \,/\, C(\cdot) \text{ as in } (2.1.11),$$

$$\mathbb{E}\int_0^T U_1^-(t, c(t))\, dt + \mathbb{E}\, U_2^-(X_\nu^{x,\pi,C}(T)) < \infty\Big\}$$

in the notation of Definition 4.2.3.

The solution of this problem is quite straightforward to describe, by complete analogy with the solution of Problem 2.1.6 in Section 2.2. We consider the function

$$(5.2.3) \quad \mathcal{X}_\nu(y) \triangleq \mathbb{E}\left[\int_0^T H_\nu(t) I_1(t, y H_\nu(t))\, dt + H_\nu(T) I_2(y H_\nu(T))\right], \quad 0 < y < \infty$$

and define the subclass

$$(5.2.4) \quad \mathcal{D}_0 \triangleq \{\nu \in \mathcal{D} \,/\, \mathcal{X}_\nu(y) < \infty, \forall\, 0 < y < \infty\}$$

of the class $\mathcal{D}$ in (4.2.2). For every $\nu \in \mathcal{D}_0$, the function $\mathcal{X}_\nu(\cdot)$ is continuous, strictly decreasing, and maps $(0, \infty)$ *onto* itself with $\mathcal{X}_\nu(0+) = \infty$ and $\mathcal{X}_\nu(\infty) = 0$. We denote by $\mathcal{Y}_\nu(\cdot) \triangleq \mathcal{X}_\nu^{-1}(\cdot)$ the inverse of this mapping, and introduce the random variable

$$(5.2.5) \qquad \xi_\nu \triangleq I_2\big(\mathcal{Y}_\nu(x)H_\nu(T)\big)$$

(optimal level of terminal wealth), as well as the processes

$$(5.2.6) \qquad c_\nu(t) \triangleq I_1\big(t, \mathcal{Y}_\nu(x)H_\nu(t)\big), \qquad 0 \le t \le T$$

(optimal consumption rate) and

$$(5.2.7) \quad X_\nu(t) \triangleq \frac{1}{H_\nu(t)}\mathbb{E}\left[H_\nu(T)\xi_\nu + \int_t^T H_\nu(u)c_\nu(u)\,du \,\Big|\, \mathcal{F}(t)\right], \qquad 0 \le t \le T$$

(optimal wealth process) with $X_\nu(T) = \xi_\nu$ a.s. We introduce also the martingale

$$
\begin{aligned}
(5.2.8) \qquad M_\nu(t) &\triangleq H_\nu(t)X_\nu(t) + \int_0^t H_\nu(u)c_\nu(u)\,du \\
&= \mathbb{E}\left[H_\nu(T)\xi_\nu + \int_0^T H_\nu(u)c_\nu(u)\,du \,\Big|\, \mathcal{F}(t)\right], \qquad 0 \le t \le T
\end{aligned}
$$

with expectation $M_\nu(0) = \mathbb{E}\,M_\nu(T) = \mathcal{X}_\nu\big(\mathcal{Y}_\nu(x)\big) = x$. From the martingale representation theorem,

$$(5.2.9) \qquad M_\nu(t) = x + \int_0^t \psi_\nu'(u)\,dW(u), \qquad 0 \le t \le T$$

for an appropriate progressively measurable process $\psi_\nu : [0,T] \times \Omega \to \mathbb{R}^d$ with $\int_0^T \|\psi_\nu(t)\|^2\,dt < \infty$, a.s. By analogy now with Theorem 2.2.2 and Proposition 2.2.1 *the pair* (π_ν, C_ν) *defined as*

$$
\begin{aligned}
(5.2.10) \qquad \pi_\nu(t) &\triangleq \big(\sigma^{-1}(t)\big)'\left[X_\nu(t)\theta^{(\nu)}(t) + \frac{\psi_\nu(t)}{H_\nu(t)}\right], \\
C_\nu(t) &\triangleq \int_0^t c_\nu(u)\,du; \; 0 \le t \le T
\end{aligned}
$$

attains the supremum in (5.2.1), *and we have* $X^{x,\pi_\nu,C_\nu}(\cdot) \equiv X_\nu(\cdot)$. Furthermore, the value function $V_\nu(\cdot)$ of (5.2.1) and its convex dual $\tilde{V}_\nu(y) \triangleq \sup_{x>0}\big[V_\nu(x) - xy\big]$, $0 < y < \infty$ are given respectively by

$$
\begin{aligned}
(5.2.11) \qquad & V_\nu(x) = G_\nu\big(\mathcal{Y}_\nu(x)\big) \quad \text{and} \\
& \tilde{V}_\nu(y) \equiv G_\nu(y) - y\mathcal{X}_\nu(y) = \mathbb{E}\left[\int_0^T \tilde{U}_1\big(t, yH_\nu(t)\big)\,dt + \tilde{U}_2\big(yH_\nu(T)\big)\right]
\end{aligned}
$$

where

$$(5.2.12) \quad G_\nu(y) \triangleq \mathbb{E}\left[\int_0^T U_1\big(t, I_1\big(t, yH_\nu(t)\big)\big)\,dt + U_2\big(I_2\big(yH_\nu(T)\big)\big)\right], \; 0 < y < \infty.$$

5.2.1. REMARK. From Remarks 4.2.2 and 4.2.4, we deduce the inclusion

$$\mathcal{A}_*(x; K) \subseteq \mathcal{A}_\nu(x), \qquad \forall\, \nu \in \mathcal{D}$$

in the notation of (5.1.1), (5.1.2), as well as the comparison

$$(5.2.13) \qquad V(x) \le V_\nu(x), \qquad \forall\, \nu \in \mathcal{D}$$

which extends (5.1.4).

5.2.2. EXERCISE.   (i) Establish the analogues of (2.2.21)

$$(5.2.14) \qquad\qquad V_\nu'(\cdot) = \mathcal{Y}_\nu(\cdot), \quad \tilde{V}_\nu'(\cdot) = -\mathcal{X}_\nu(\cdot).$$

(ii) For any $x \in (0, \infty)$, $y \in (0, \infty)$, $\nu \in \mathcal{D}$ and $(\pi, C) \in \mathcal{A}_\nu(x)$ we have

$$(5.2.15) \qquad \mathbb{E}\left[\int_0^T U_1(t, c(t))\, dt + U_2\big(X_\nu^{x,\pi,C}(T)\big)\right] \le V_\nu(x) \le \tilde{V}_\nu(y) + xy;$$

show that equality holds in (5.2.15), if and only if

$$(5.2.16) \qquad y = \mathcal{Y}_\nu(x), \quad c(\cdot) \equiv c_\nu(\cdot) \quad \text{and} \quad X_\nu^{x,\pi,C}(T) = \xi_\nu \text{ a.s.}$$

Our approach to the constrained optimization Problem 5.1.1 with value $V(\cdot)$, will take the form of an *embedding into the family of unconstrained problems in* (5.2.1) with value functions $\{V_\nu(\cdot)\}_{\nu \in \mathcal{D}}$, in the following manner: we shall try to *find a process $\mu(\cdot)$ in the class $\mathcal{D}_0$ of* (5.2.4), *for which the optimal pair (π_μ, C_μ) in* (5.2.10) *is also optimal for* Problem 5.1.1. In other words,

$$(5.2.17) \quad V(x) = \mathbb{E}\left[\int_0^T U_1(t, c_\mu(t))\, dt + U_2(\xi_\mu)\right] = V_\mu(x) \le V_\nu(x), \qquad \forall\, \nu \in \mathcal{D}$$

in (5.2.13). Such a process $\mu(\cdot)$ should satisfy

$$(5.2.18) \qquad\qquad \pi_\mu(\cdot) \in K, \quad (\lambda \otimes \mathbb{P}) - \text{a.e. on } [0, T] \times \Omega,$$

as well as

$$(5.2.19) \qquad\qquad \mu'(\cdot)\pi_\mu(\cdot) \equiv 0, \quad (\lambda \otimes \mathbb{P}) - \text{a.e. on } [0, T] \times \Omega$$

from Remark 4.2.2.

5.2.3. EXERCISE. Suppose that (5.2.18), (5.2.19) are satisfied for some $\mu \in \mathcal{D}_0$. Show that the corresponding pair (π_μ, C_μ) in (5.2.10) is then optimal for the optimization Problem 5.1.1 with constrained portfolios, and (5.2.17) holds.

(*Hint*: From (4.2.9) and (5.2.18), (5.2.19) the equation for the process $X_\mu(\cdot)$ of (5.2.7) becomes

$$(5.2.20) \quad \gamma(t)X_\mu(t) + \int_{(0,t]} \gamma(u)c_\mu(u)\, du \;=\; x + \int_0^t \gamma(u)\pi_\mu'(u)\sigma(u)\, dW^{(0)}(u).$$

This means that $X_\mu(\cdot)$ coincides with the wealth-process corresponding to the pair (π_μ, C_μ) in the constrained market $\mathcal{M}(K)$ of Section 4.1; but then $V_\mu(x) = \mathbb{E}\left[\int_0^T U_1(t, c_\mu(t))\, dt + U_2\big(X^{x,\pi_\mu,C_\mu}(T)\big)\right] \le V(x)$, whereas the reverse inequality is valid from (5.2.13).)

5.2.4. EXERCISE. For any $x \in (0, \infty)$, $y \in (0, \infty)$, $(\pi, C) \in \mathcal{A}_*(x; K)$ and $\nu \in \mathcal{D}$, show that we have

$$(5.2.21) \quad \mathbb{E}\left[\int_0^T U_1(t, c(t))\, dt + U_2\big(X^{x,\pi,C}(T)\big)\right] \le V(x) \le V_\nu(x) \le \tilde{V}_\nu(y) + xy,$$

and that (5.2.21) is valid with equalities if and only if $y = \mathcal{Y}_\nu(x)$, $c(\cdot) \equiv c_\nu(\cdot)$, $X^{x,\pi,C}(T) = \xi_\nu$ and $\nu'(\cdot)\pi(\cdot) \equiv 0$ hold.

(*Hint:* Observe, by applying the product rule to $\gamma(\cdot)X^{x,\pi,C}(\cdot)$ and $Z_\nu(\cdot)$ in conjunction with (4.2.7), (4.2.8) and (0.2.17), that

$$(5.2.22) \quad H_\nu(t)X^{x,\pi,C}(t) + \int_0^t H_\nu(u)\big(c(u) + \pi'(u)\nu(u)\big)\, du$$

$$= x + \int_0^t H_\nu(u)\big(\sigma'(u)\pi(u) - X^{x,\pi,C}(u)\theta^{(\nu)}(u)\big)'\, dW(u)$$

is a nonnegative local martingale, for every $(\pi, C) \in \mathcal{A}_*(x; K)$ and $\nu \in \mathcal{D}$. Proceed then as in the proof of Theorem 2.2.2, to obtain

$$\mathbb{E}\left[\int_0^T U_1\big(t, c(t)\big)\, dt + U_2\big(X^{x,\pi,C}(T)\big)\right]$$

$$\leq \mathbb{E}\left[\int_0^T \tilde{U}_1\big(t, yH_\nu(t)\big)\, dt + \tilde{U}_2\big(yH_\nu(T)\big)\right]$$

$$+ y \cdot \mathbb{E}\left[\int_0^T H_\nu(t)c(t)\, dt + H_\nu(T)X^{x,\pi,C}(T)\right]$$

$$\leq \tilde{V}_\nu(y) + xy - y \cdot \mathbb{E}\int_0^T H_\nu(t)\nu'(t)\pi(t)\, dt \leq \tilde{V}_\nu(y) + xy.$$

All claims follow now readily, in conjunction with Exercise 5.2.2 (ii) and (5.2.13).)

5.3. Optimality conditions

Let us fix now an initial capital $x \in (0, \infty)$; for a given pair $(\hat{\pi}, \hat{C})$ in the class $\mathcal{A}_*(x; K)$ of (5.1.2), let $\hat{X}(\cdot) \equiv X^{x,\hat{\pi},\hat{C}}(\cdot)$ be the corresponding wealth process, and consider the statement that this pair is optimal for the constrained Problem 5.1.1:

5.3.1. Optimality of $(\hat{\pi}, \hat{C})$. The pair $(\hat{\pi}, \hat{C})$ satisfies

$$(5.3.1a) \quad \mathbb{E}\left[\int_0^T U_1\big(t, \hat{c}(t)\big)\, dt + U_2\big(\hat{X}(T)\big)\right]$$

$$\geq \mathbb{E}\left[\int_0^T U_1\big(t, c(t)\big)\, dt + U_2\big(X^{x,\pi,C}(T)\big)\right], \qquad \forall (\pi, C) \in \mathcal{A}_*(x; K)$$

as well as

$$(5.3.1b) \qquad \mathbb{E}\left[\int_0^T \hat{c}(t)U_1'\big(t, \hat{c}(t)\big)\, dt + \hat{X}(T)U_2'\big(\hat{X}(T)\big)\right] < \infty.$$

We shall characterize now the optimality property (5.3.1), in terms of the following conditions (5.3.2)–(5.3.4); *these concern a given process $\mu(\cdot)$ in the class $\mathcal{D}_0$ of (5.2.4).* The notation of (5.2.3)–(5.2.11) will be used frequently in what follows.

5.3.2. Financibility of $\big(C_\mu(\cdot), \xi_\mu\big)$. There exists a portfolio process $\pi_\mu(\cdot)$, such that

$$(5.3.2) \qquad \begin{aligned} (\pi_\mu, C_\mu) &\in \mathcal{A}_*(x; K), \quad \mu'(\cdot)\pi_\mu(\cdot) = 0 \text{ a.e. on } [0, T] \times \Omega, \\ X^{x,\pi_\mu,C_\mu}(t) &\equiv X_\mu(t) \qquad \forall\, t \in [0, T], \text{ a.s.} \end{aligned}$$

5.3.3. Minimality of $\mu(\cdot)$. For every $\nu \in \mathcal{D}$, we have

$$(5.3.3) \qquad V_\mu(x) \le V_\nu(x) = \mathbb{E}\left[\int_0^T U_1\big(t, c_\nu(t)\big)\,dt + U_2(\xi_\nu)\right].$$

5.3.4. Dual optimality of $\mu(\cdot)$. With $y = \mathcal{Y}_\mu(x)$, we have

$$(5.3.4) \quad \tilde{V}_\mu(y) \le \tilde{V}_\nu(y) = \mathbb{E}\left[\int_0^T \tilde{U}_1\big(t, yH_\nu(t)\big)\,dt + \tilde{U}_2\big(yH_\nu(T)\big)\right], \qquad \forall\,\nu \in \mathcal{D}.$$

The following result is the centerpiece of this chapter, as it provides necessary and sufficient conditions for optimality in Problem 5.1.1. Its condition (5.3.4) is the most useful, since it will lead us, via a *convex duality approach* (Section 5.4), to our basic existence and characterization results for this problem (Section 5.5).

5.3.1. THEOREM. *The conditions* (5.3.2)–(5.3.4) *are equivalent, and imply the properties* (5.3.1) *with* $(\hat{\pi}, \hat{C}) = (\pi_\mu, C_\mu)$.

Conversely, the conditions (5.3.1) *imply the existence of a process* $\mu(\cdot)$ *in the class* $\mathcal{D}_0$ *of* (5.2.4), *which satisfies* (5.3.2)–(5.3.4) *with* $\pi_\lambda(\cdot) \equiv \hat{\pi}(\cdot)$, *provided that the utility functions* $U_1(t, \cdot)$, $U_2(\cdot)$ *satisfy the conditions of* Exercise 2.2.8, (3.6.2) *as well as*

$$(5.3.5) \qquad \forall\,y \in (0, \infty), \qquad \exists\,\nu \in \mathcal{D} \quad with \quad \tilde{V}_\nu(y) < \infty.$$

The implications (5.3.2) $\Longrightarrow$ (5.3.1), (5.3.2) $\Longrightarrow$ (5.3.3), follow directly from Exercise 5.2.3 and the observation

$$\mathbb{E}\left[\int_0^T c_\mu(t)U_1'\big(t, c_\mu(t)\big)\,dt + \xi_\mu U_2'(\xi_\mu)\right] = \mathcal{Y}_\mu(x) \cdot \mathcal{X}_\mu\big(\mathcal{Y}_\mu(x)\big) = x\mathcal{Y}_\mu(x) < \infty.$$

On the other hand, with $y = \mathcal{Y}_\mu(x)$ we have the implication (5.3.3) $\Longrightarrow$ (5.3.4) from (5.2.11) and

$$\tilde{V}_\mu(y) = V_\mu\big(\mathcal{X}_\mu(y)\big) - y\mathcal{X}_\mu(y) = V_\mu(x) - xy \le V_\nu(x) - xy \le \sup_\xi\big[V_\nu(\xi) - y\xi\big] = \tilde{V}_\nu(y).$$

The implication (5.3.4) $\Longrightarrow$ (5.3.2) is established below. Finally, we send the reader to the Appendix A of Cvitanić & Karatzas (1992) for the (difficult) proof of (5.3.2) $\Longrightarrow$ (5.3.1); this implication will not be used or invoked in these lectures.

PROOF OF (5.3.4) $\Longrightarrow$ (5.3.2). We have to show that the portfolio process $\pi_\mu(\cdot)$ of (5.2.10) satisfies both conditions (5.2.18) and (5.2.19).

For suitable process $\nu(\cdot)$ in $\mathcal{D}$, and a suitable sequence $\{\tau_n\}$ of stopping times with $\tau_n \uparrow T$ a.s. (to be specified in (5.3.11) below), consider the *small random perturbation*

$$(5.3.6) \qquad \mu_*(t) \equiv \mu_{\varepsilon,n}^{(\nu)}(t)$$

$$\triangleq \begin{cases} (1 - \varepsilon)\mu(t) + \varepsilon\nu(t); & 0 \le t \le \tau_n \\ \mu(t); & \tau_n < t \le T \end{cases}$$

$$= \mu(t) + \varepsilon\big(\nu(t) - \mu(t)\big)1_{\{t \le \tau_n\}}, \qquad 0 \le t \le T$$

of the process $\mu(\cdot)$ *in* $\mathcal{D}_0$, *for* $n \in \mathbb{N}$ *and* $0 < \varepsilon < 1$. Clearly $\mu_*(\cdot)$ belongs to $\mathcal{D}$, and therefore

$$(5.3.7) \qquad 0 \le \frac{1}{\varepsilon y}\big[\tilde{V}_{\mu_*}(y) - \tilde{V}(y)\big] = \mathbb{E}\,(Y_n^\varepsilon)$$

where

$$(5.3.8) \quad \varepsilon y \cdot Y_n^\varepsilon \triangleq \int_0^T \left[\tilde{U}_1\big(t, yH_{\mu_*}(t)\big) - \tilde{U}_1\big(t, yH_\mu(t)\big) \right] dt$$
$$+ \left[\tilde{U}_2\big(yH_{\mu_*}(T)\big) - \tilde{U}_2\big(yH_\mu(T)\big) \right].$$

STEP 1. Introduce the ratio

$$(5.3.9) \quad R^\varepsilon(t) \triangleq \frac{H_{\mu_*}(t)}{H_\mu(t)} = \exp\left[-\varepsilon N(t \wedge \tau_n) - \frac{\varepsilon^2}{2}\langle N\rangle(t \wedge \tau_n) \right], \quad 0 \le t \le T,$$

where we have denoted

$$(5.3.10)$$
$$N(t) \triangleq \int_0^t \big(\sigma^{-1}(s)\big(\nu(s) - \mu(s)\big)\big)' \, dW^{(\mu)}(s),$$
$$\langle N\rangle(t) \triangleq \int_0^t \big\|\sigma^{-1}(s)\big(\nu(s) - \mu(s)\big)\big\|^2 \, ds,$$

and define the stopping times

$$(5.3.11) \quad \tau_n \triangleq \inf\left\{ t \in [0, T] \; \Big/ \; |N(t)| + \langle N\rangle(t) + \int_0^t \|\theta_\mu(s)\|^2 \, ds \right.$$
$$+ \int_0^t \gamma^2(s)\big[X_\mu^2(s)\big\|\sigma^{-1}(s)\big(\nu(s) - \mu(s)\big)\big\|^2$$
$$\left. + N^2(s)\big\|\pi_\mu'(s)\sigma(s)\big\|^2 \big] \, ds \ge n \right\} \wedge T, \qquad n \in \mathbb{N}$$

in (5.3.6). We have then $R^\varepsilon(\cdot) \ge e^{-2\varepsilon n}$ in (5.3.9), as well as the upper bounds for the random variable Y_n^ε in (5.3.7):

$$(5.3.12) \quad Y_n^\varepsilon \lesseqgtr Y_n \triangleq K_n\left[\int_0^T H_\mu(t)I_1\big(t, ye^{-2n}H_\mu(t)\big) \, dt \right.$$
$$\left. + H_\mu(T)I_2\big(ye^{-2n}H_\mu(T)\big) \right]$$

$$(5.3.13) \quad Y_n^\varepsilon \le Q_n^\varepsilon \triangleq \int_0^T H_\mu(t)\frac{1 - R^\varepsilon(t)}{\varepsilon}I_1\big(t, ye^{-2\varepsilon n}H_\mu(t)\big) \, dt$$
$$+ H_\mu(T)\frac{1 - R^\varepsilon(T)}{\varepsilon}I_2\big(ye^{-2\varepsilon n}H_\mu(T)\big).$$

We have set $K_n \triangleq \sup_{0 < \varepsilon < 1}(1 - e^{-2\varepsilon n})/\varepsilon$ and used (5.3.8), the mean-value theorem, and the decrease of $I(\cdot) = -\tilde{U}'(\cdot)$ in (2.1.13).

STEP 2. The random variable Y_n of (5.3.12) is integrable: $\mathbb{E}(Y_n) \le K_n \cdot \mathcal{X}_\mu(ye^{-2n}) < \infty$, since $\mu \in \mathcal{D}_0$. Therefore, from Fatou's lemma, (5.3.13), and (5.2.16), (5.2.15) (which now read $c_\mu(t) = I_1(t, yH_\mu(t))$, $\xi_\mu = I_2(yH_\mu(T))$), we obtain

$$(5.3.14) \quad \overline{\lim}_{\varepsilon\downarrow0}\mathbb{E}(Y_n^\varepsilon) \le \mathbb{E}\left(\overline{\lim}_{\varepsilon\downarrow0}Y_n^\varepsilon\right) \lesseqgtr \mathbb{E}\left(\overline{\lim}_{\varepsilon\downarrow0}Q_n^\varepsilon\right)$$
$$= \mathbb{E}\left[\int_0^T H_\mu(t)N(t \wedge \tau_n)c_\mu(t) \, dt + H_\mu(T)N(\tau_n)\xi_\mu \right].$$

It develops from (5.3.7), (5.3.14) that

$$(5.3.15) \qquad \mathbb{E}\left[\int_0^T H_\mu(t) N(t \wedge \tau_n) c_\mu(t)\, dt + H_\mu(T) N(\tau_n)\xi_\mu\right] \geq 0, \qquad \forall\, n \in \mathbb{N}.$$

Observe also, from the Girsanov and Novikov theorems (e.g. Karatzas & Shreve (1991), §3.5) that the stopped process $\left\{W^{(\mu)}(t \wedge \tau_n), 0 \leq t \leq T\right\}$ is Brownian motion under the probability measure

$$(5.3.16) \qquad \tilde{\mathbb{P}}_n(A) \triangleq \mathbb{E}\left[Z_\mu(\tau_n) \cdot 1_A\right], \quad A \in \mathcal{F}(T) \quad \text{for every } n \in \mathbb{N}.$$

STEP 3. The inequality (5.3.15) can be re-written as

$$(5.3.17) \qquad \mathbb{E}\int_0^{\tau_n} H_\mu(t)\pi'_\mu(t)\big(\nu(t) - \mu(t)\big)\, dt \geq 0, \qquad \forall\, n \in \mathbb{N}.$$

Indeed, recall the equations $dN(t) = \big(\sigma^{-1}(t)\big(\nu(t) - \mu(t)\big)\big)'\, dW^{(\mu)}(t)$ as well as $d\big(\gamma(t)X_\mu(t)\big) = -\gamma(t)c_\mu(t)\, dt + \gamma(t)\pi'_\mu(t)\sigma(t)\, dW^{(\mu)}(t)$ from (5.3.10) and (4.2.9), apply the product-rule to $\gamma(t)X_\mu(t) \cdot N(t)$, and integrate on $[0, \tau_n]$ to obtain

$$(5.3.18) \qquad \gamma(\tau_n)X_\mu(\tau_n)N(\tau_n) + \int_0^{\tau_n} \gamma(t)c_\mu(t)N(t)\, dt$$

$$= \int_0^{\tau_n} \gamma(t)\big(\nu(t) - \mu(t)\big)'\pi_\mu(t)\, dt$$

$$+ \int_0^{\tau_n} \gamma(t)\big[N(t)\pi'_\mu(t)\sigma(t)$$

$$+ X_\mu(t)\big(\sigma^{-1}(t)\big(\nu(t) - \mu(t)\big)\big)'\big]\, dW^{(\mu)}(t).$$

Now take expectations in this expression, with respect to the probability measure $\tilde{\mathbb{P}}_n$ of (5.3.16); because of the way we constructed the stopping time τ_n in (5.3.11), the expectation of the stochastic integral in (5.3.18) is zero, and thus

$$\mathbb{E}\int_0^{\tau_n} H_\mu(t)\big(\nu(t) - \mu(t)\big)'\pi_\mu(t)\, dt$$

$$= \mathbb{E}\left[H_\mu(\tau_n)X_\mu(\tau_n)N(\tau_n) + \int_0^{\tau_n} H_\mu(t)c_\mu(t)N(t)\, dt\right]$$

$$= \mathbb{E}\left[\left\{H_\mu(T)X_\mu(T) + \int_{\tau_n}^T H_\mu(t)c_\mu(t)\, dt\right\}N(\tau_n) + \int_0^{\tau_n} H_\mu(t)c_\mu(t)N(t)\, dt\right]$$

$$= \mathbb{E}\left[H_\mu(T)X_\mu(T)N(\tau_n) + \int_0^T H_\mu(t)c_\mu(t)N(t \wedge \tau_n)\, dt\right].$$

This last term is equal to the left-hand side of (5.3.15), and thus (5.3.17) follows.

STEP 4. For an arbitrary process $\eta(\cdot)$ in $\mathcal{D}$, take $\nu(\cdot) \equiv \mu(\cdot) + \eta(\cdot)$ in (5.3.6) to obtain

$$(5.3.19) \qquad \mathbb{E}\int_0^T H_\mu(t)\eta'(t)\pi_\mu(t)\, dt \geq 0 \qquad \forall\, \eta \in \mathcal{D}$$

from (5.3.17); on the other hand, taking $\nu(\cdot) \equiv 0$ in (5.3.6) we get

$$(5.3.20) \qquad \mathbb{E}\int_0^T H_\mu(t)\mu'(t)\pi_\mu(t)\, dt \leq 0$$

in (5.3.17). Now (5.3.19) leads to the stronger statement

$$(5.3.21) \qquad \eta'(\cdot)\pi_\mu(\cdot) \geq 0, \quad (\lambda \otimes \mathbb{P}) - \text{a.e. on } [0,T] \times \Omega; \qquad \forall \eta \in \mathcal{D}.$$

Indeed, suppose that the set $A = \{(t,w) \in [0,T] \times \Omega \ / \ \eta'(t,w)\pi_\mu(t,w) < 0\}$ had positive product measure for some $\eta \in \mathcal{D}$; then by selecting $\rho \triangleq \eta 1_{A^c} + k\eta 1_A$ and choosing $k \in \mathbb{N}$ large enough, we could make $\mathbb{E} \int_0^T H_\mu(t)\rho'(t)\pi_\mu(t) \, dt < 0$, contradicting (5.3.19) for this $\rho \in \mathcal{D}$.

Taking $\eta(\cdot) \equiv r$ in (5.3.21) for arbitrary $r \in \tilde{K}$, we obtain (4.4.14), and thus also (5.2.18) from Theorem 13.1, p. 112 of Rockafellar (1970); taking $\eta(\cdot) \equiv \mu(\cdot)$ in (5.3.21) we obtain (5.2.19) in conjunction with (5.3.20). $\qquad \square$

It is fairly straightforward to compute the process $\mu \in \mathcal{D}_0$ of (5.3.2)–(5.3.4), as well as the optimal pair $(\hat{\pi}, \hat{C})$ of (5.3.1), in the case of *logarithmic utility functions*.

5.3.2. EXAMPLE. $U_1(t,x) = e^{-\beta_1 t} \log x$, $U_2(x) = e^{-\beta_2 T} \log x$, $(t,x) \in [0,T] \times (0,\infty)$ for some $\beta_1 \in \mathbb{R}$, $\beta_2 \in \mathbb{R}$.

Then we have from (5.2.3)–(5.2.16) that $\mathcal{X}_\nu(y) = \frac{k}{y}$,

$$\xi_\nu = \frac{xe^{-\beta_2 T}}{kH_\nu(T)}, \quad c_\nu(t) = \frac{xe^{-\beta_1 t}}{kH_\nu(t)},$$

where we have set $k(t) \triangleq \int_t^T e^{-\beta_1 u} \, du + e^{-\beta_2 T}$, $k \equiv k(0)$ and $\ell \triangleq \beta_1 \int_0^T e^{-\beta_1 u} u \, du + \beta_2 T e^{-\beta_2 T}$.

In particular, $\mathcal{D}_0 = \mathcal{D}$ in (5.2.4), and from (5.2.7)–(5.2.12): $M_\nu(\cdot) \equiv x$, $\psi_\nu(\cdot) \equiv 0$, $X_\nu(t) = xk(t)/kH_\nu(t)$, as well as

$$(5.3.22) \quad \pi_\nu(t) = \left(\sigma^{-1}(t)\right)' \theta_\nu(t) X_\nu(t) = \left(\sigma(t)\sigma'(t)\right)^{-1} \left[b(t) + \nu(t) - r(t)\mathbf{1}_d\right] X_\nu(t),$$

$$(5.3.23) \quad V_\nu(x) = k \log\left(\frac{x}{k}\right) - \ell + f(\nu), \quad \tilde{V}_\nu(y) = -k \log y - (k + \ell) + f(\nu),$$

where we have set, for every $\nu \in \mathcal{D}$,

$$(5.3.24) \quad f(\nu) \triangleq \mathbb{E}\left[\int_0^T e^{-\beta_1 t} \left(\int_0^t \left\{r(u) + \frac{\|\theta^{(\nu)}(u)\|^2}{2}\right\} du\right) dt \right.$$
$$\left. + e^{-\beta_2 T} \int_0^T \left(r(u) + \frac{\|\theta^{(\nu)}(u)\|^2}{2}\right) du\right].$$

It develops now from (5.3.23), (5.3.24) that finding a process $\mu(\cdot)$ in the class $\mathcal{D}_0 = \mathcal{D}$ which satisfies the conditions (5.3.3) or (5.3.4), amounts to minimizing pointwise the convex function $z \mapsto \|\theta(t,w) + \sigma^{-1}(t,w)z\|$ over $\tilde{K}$, namely

$$(5.3.25) \qquad \mu(t,w) = \arg\min_{z \in \tilde{K}} \|\sigma^{-1}(t,w)[b(t,w) + z - r(t,w)\mathbf{1}_d]\|.$$

This defines a progressively measurable process $\mu \colon [0,T] \times \Omega \to \tilde{K}$ with

$$\mathbb{E} \int_0^T \|\mu(t)\|^2 \, dt \leq C \cdot \mathbb{E} \int_0^T \left(\|\theta^{(\mu)}(t)\|^2 + \|\theta(t)\|^2\right) dt \leq 2C \cdot \mathbb{E} \int_0^T \|\theta(t)\|^2 \, dt < \infty$$

for some real $C > 0$ thanks to (4.1.3), (4.1.4) and (5.3.25), so that $\mu(\cdot)$ belongs to the class $\mathcal{D} = \mathcal{D}_0$ of (4.2.2). From this, (3.2.4) and (4.1.4) again, we obtain

$f(\mu) < \infty$ (in other words, the condition (5.3.5) is satisfied as well). We apply Theorem 5.3.1, to obtain the *optimal wealth, consumption-rate and portfolio processes, and the value-function of* Problem 5.1.1, as

$$(5.3.26) \qquad \hat{X}(t) \equiv X_\mu(t) = \frac{k(t)}{k}\frac{x}{H_\mu(t)}, \qquad 0 \le t \le T$$

$$(5.3.27) \qquad \hat{c}(t) \equiv c_\mu(t) = \frac{e^{-\beta_1 t}}{k(t)}\hat{X}(t), \qquad 0 \le t \le T$$

$$(5.3.28) \quad \hat{\pi}(t) \equiv \pi_\mu(t) = \big(\sigma(t)\sigma'(t)\big)^{-1}\big[b(t) + \mu(t) - r(t)\mathbf{1}_d\big]\hat{X}(t), \qquad 0 \le t \le T$$

$$(5.3.29) \qquad V(x) = k\log\left(\frac{x}{k}\right) - \ell + f(\mu) < \infty, \qquad 0 < x < \infty,$$

respectively, where $\mu(\cdot)$ is the process of (5.3.25).

> **5.3.3. REMARK.** (i) In particular, in the case of Example 4.1.2 (Incomplete Market) we have $\tilde{K} = \{x \in \mathbb{R}^d \ / \ x_1 = \cdots = x_n = 0\}$ and thus (5.3.25), (5.3.28) become

$$(5.3.30) \quad \mu(t) = \arg\min_{\substack{z\in\mathbb{R}^d \\ z_1=\cdots=z_n=0}} \big\|\sigma^{-1}(t)\big(b(t) + z - r(t)\mathbf{1}_d\big)\big\| = \begin{pmatrix} \mathbf{0}_n \\ r(t) - b_{n+1}(t) \\ \vdots \\ r(t) - b_d(t) \end{pmatrix}$$

> and

$$(5.3.31) \qquad \hat{\pi}_i(t) = \left\{ \begin{array}{ll} \big(\big(\tilde{\sigma}(t)\tilde{\sigma}'(t)\big)^{-1}\big[\tilde{b}(t) - r(t)\mathbf{1}_n\big]\big)_i; & i = 1,\ldots,n \\ 0; & i = n+1,\ldots,d \end{array} \right\},$$

> where

$$(5.3.32) \qquad \tilde{b}(\cdot) = \big\{b_i(\cdot)\big\}_{1\le i\le n}, \quad \tilde{\sigma}(\cdot) = \big\{\sigma_{ij}(\cdot)\big\}_{\substack{1\le i\le n \\ 1\le j\le d}}.$$

(ii) In the case of Example 4.1.3 (Incomplete Market with prohibition of short-selling of stocks) we have $\tilde{K} = \{x \in \mathbb{R}^d \ / \ x_1 \ge 0,\ldots,x_n \ge 0\}$ and the processes of (5.3.25), (5.3.28) take the form

$$(5.3.33) \quad \mu(t) = \arg\min_{\substack{z\in\mathbb{R}^d \\ z_1\ge 0,\ldots z_n\ge 0}} \big\|\sigma^{-1}(t)\big(b(t) + z - r(t)\mathbf{1}_d\big)\big\| = \begin{pmatrix} \tilde{\mu}(t) \\ r(t) - b_{n+1}(t) \\ \vdots \\ r(t) - b_d(t) \end{pmatrix}$$

and

$$(5.3.34) \quad \hat{\pi}_i(t) = \left\{ \begin{array}{ll} \big(\big(\tilde{\sigma}(t)\tilde{\sigma}'(t)\big)^{-1}\big[\tilde{b}(t) + \tilde{\mu}(t) - r(t)\mathbf{1}_n\big]\big)_i; & i = 1,\ldots,n \\ 0; & i = n+1,\ldots,d \end{array} \right\},$$

respectively, in the notation of (5.3.32), where we have set

$$(5.3.35) \qquad \tilde{\mu}(t) \triangleq \arg\min_{\xi\in\mathbb{R}^n_+} \big\|\tilde{\sigma}(t)\big(\tilde{\sigma}(t)\tilde{\sigma}'(t)\big)^{-1}\big(\tilde{b}(t) + \xi - r(t)\mathbf{1}_n\big)\big\|.$$

5.4. Duality

Let us introduce now, in addition to our "primal" constrained optimization Problem 5.1.1, a "*dual optimization problem*" with value function

(5.4.1) $$\tilde{V}(y) \triangleq \inf_{\nu \in \mathcal{D}} \tilde{V}_\nu(y), \qquad 0 < y < \infty$$

in the notation of (5.2.11). We call this problem "dual" because, as it will be shown in Proposition 5.4.1 below, the value function $\tilde{V}(\cdot)$ of (5.4.1) is the *convex dual* of the concave value function $V(\cdot)$ of (5.1.3) for Problem 5.1.1:

(5.4.2) $$\tilde{V}(y) = \max_{0<\xi<\infty} \left[V(\xi) - \xi y \right], \qquad 0 < y < \infty.$$

The problem of (5.4.1) is of course suggested by the condition (5.3.4) of Theorem 5.3.1, which amounts to the statement:

$$\tilde{V}(y) = \tilde{V}_\mu(y) \quad \text{for some} \quad \mu \in \mathcal{D}_0 \quad \text{and} \quad y = \mathcal{Y}_\mu(x).$$

It will be assumed, throughout this section and the next, that *the condition* (5.3.5) *holds* so that, in particular,

$$\tilde{V}(y) < \infty, \qquad \forall \, y \in (0, \infty)$$

(see Exercise 5.4.3 below). Our method will be to show that, under reasonably general conditions, the infimum in (5.4.1) is attained by some process $\mu_y(\cdot)$ in $\mathcal{D}_0$, for every $y \in (0, \infty)$, that is,

(5.4.3) $$\forall \, y \in (0, \infty), \quad \exists \, \mu_y \in \mathcal{D}_0 \quad \text{s.t.} \quad \tilde{V}(y) = \tilde{V}_{\mu_y}(y)$$

(cf. Theorem 5.5.1); and then to use (5.4.3) in conjunction with Theorem 5.3.1, in order to establish the existence of an optimal pair $(\hat{\pi}, \hat{C}) \in \mathcal{A}_*(x; K)$ for the "primal" Problem 5.1.1 (Theorem 5.5.2).

5.4.1. PROPOSITION (Weak Duality). *Under conditions* (5.3.5) *and* (5.4.3), *there exists an optimal pair* $(\hat{\pi}, \hat{C}) \in \mathcal{A}_*\big(\mathcal{X}_{\mu_y}(y); K\big)$ *for Problem 5.1.1 and* (5.4.2) *holds, for any given* $y \in (0, \infty)$.

PROOF. The assumption (5.4.3) is equivalent to $\tilde{V}_{\mu_y}(y) \le V_\nu(y)$, $\forall \, \nu \in \mathcal{D}$ which, with $x \triangleq \mathcal{X}_{\mu_y}(y)$ and $\mu(\cdot) \equiv \mu_y(\cdot)$, amounts to the condition (5.3.4) of Theorem 5.3.1. Now the implications (5.3.4) $\Longrightarrow$ (5.3.2) $\Longrightarrow$ (5.3.1) of this theorem give an optimal pair $(\hat{\pi}, \hat{C}) \in \mathcal{A}_*(x; K)$ for Problem 5.1.1, in the form

$$\hat{c}(t) = c_\mu(t) = I_1\big(t, yH_\mu(t)\big), \quad X^{x, \hat{\pi}, \hat{C}}(t) = X_\mu(t); \qquad 0 \le t \le T$$

and such that

$$\hat{\pi}(\cdot) = \pi_\mu(\cdot) \in K, \quad \mu'(\cdot)\hat{\pi}(\cdot) = 0, \quad \lambda \otimes \mathbb{P} - \text{ a.e. on } [0, T] \times \Omega.$$

In particular, $X^{x, \hat{\pi}, \hat{C}}(T) = I_2\big(yH_\mu(T)\big) = \xi_\mu$, a.s. It follows from Exercise 5.2.4 that

(5.4.4) $$\tilde{V}(y) = \tilde{V}_{\mu_y}(y) = V(x) - xy \le \sup_{0<\xi<\infty} \left[V(\xi) - y\xi \right].$$

As for the reverse inequality, observe from (5.2.21) that $\tilde{V}_\nu(y) \ge V(\xi) - y\xi$, $\forall \, 0 < \xi < \infty$ holds for every $\nu \in \mathcal{D}$, and thus $\tilde{V}(y) = \inf_{\nu \in \mathcal{D}} \tilde{V}_\nu(y) \ge \sup_{0<\xi<\infty} \left[V(\xi) - y\xi \right]$; in conjunction with (5.4.4), this leads to (5.4.2). $\qquad \square$

5.4.2. PROPOSITION (Strong Duality). *Suppose that* (5.3.5), (5.4.3) *and*

(5.4.5) $U_2(\infty) = \infty;$ $U_1(t,x), U_2(x) \geq -k$ *for all* $(t,x) \in [0,T] \times (0,\infty)$

hold, for some $k \in [0,\infty)$. *Then, for any given* $x \in (0,\infty)$, *we have the analogue*

(5.4.6) $$V(x) = \inf_{0 < \eta < \infty} \big[\tilde{V}(\eta) + x\eta \big]$$

of (2.1.14), *and the infimum of* (5.4.6) *is attained at some* $y = y(x) \in (0,\infty)$ *which satisfies*

(5.4.7) $$x = \mathcal{X}_{\mu_y}(y).$$

PROOF. The convexity and decrease of $\tilde{U}_1(t,\cdot)$, $\tilde{U}_2(\cdot)$ show that

$$\tilde{V}_\nu(y) \geq \int_0^T \tilde{U}_1\big(t, y\mathbb{E}\, H_\nu(t)\big)\, dt + \tilde{U}_2\big(y\mathbb{E}\, H_\nu(T)\big) \geq \int_0^T \tilde{U}_1\big(t, ye^{\eta t}\big)\, dt + \tilde{U}_2(ye^{\eta T})$$

holds for every $\nu \in \mathcal{D}$, in conjunction with Jensen's inequality, the supermartingale property of $Z_\nu(\cdot)$, and (4.1.4). It develops then that the convex function $f_x(\eta) \triangleq \tilde{V}(\eta) + \eta x$, $0 < \eta < \infty$ satisfies $f_x(\infty) = \infty$ and $f_x(0+) \geq \text{constant} + \tilde{U}_2(0+) = \infty$, since $\tilde{U}_2(0+) = U_2(\infty) = \infty$. Therefore, $f_x(\cdot)$ attains its infimum over $(0,\infty)$ at some $y = y(x) \in (0,\infty)$ which, we have to show, satisfies (5.4.7).

In order to see this, observe that the function $u \mapsto \tilde{V}_{\mu_y}(uy) + xuy$ attains its infimum over $(0,\infty)$ at $u = 1$:

$$\inf_{0 < u < \infty} \big[\tilde{V}_{\mu_y}(uy) + xuy\big] = \inf_{0 < \eta < \infty}\big[\tilde{V}_{\mu_y}(\eta) + \eta x\big] \geq \inf_{0 < \eta < \infty}\big[\tilde{V}(\eta) + \eta x\big]$$
$$= \tilde{V}(y) + xy = \tilde{V}_{\mu_y}(y) + xy,$$

where $\mu_y \in \mathcal{D}_0$ is the process of (5.4.3). Consequently

$$0 = \frac{d}{du}\big(\tilde{V}_{\mu_y}(uy) + xuy\big)\bigg|_{u=1} = y\big(-\mathcal{X}_{\mu_y}(uy) + x\big)\bigg|_{u=1}$$

from (5.2.14), and (5.4.7) follows.

Now the proof of (5.4.6) is easy: for any $\eta \in (0,\infty)$, $\nu \in \mathcal{D}$ we have from (5.2.21) the inequality $V(x) \leq \tilde{V}_\nu(\eta) + x\eta$,   whence also $V(x) \leq \inf_{0 < \eta < \infty}\big[\tilde{V}(\eta) + x\eta\big]$; on the other hand, the first two equalities of (5.4.4) give $V(x) = \tilde{V}(y) + xy \geq \inf_{0 < \eta < \infty}\big[\tilde{V}(\eta) + x\eta\big]$.   □

5.4.3. EXERCISE. Show that the *assumption* (5.3.5) is valid for utility functions that satisfy either the conditions of Example 5.3.2 (logarithmic), or those of Exercise 2.2.6.

$\bigg($ *Hint*: The condition (2.2.22) gives $\tilde{U}_1(t,y), \tilde{U}_2(y) \leq \tilde{K}(1 + y^{-\rho})$, $\forall\, 0 < y < \infty$

for some $\tilde{K} \in (0,\infty)$ and $\rho = \alpha/(1-\alpha)$; from this, and the boundedness of $r(\cdot)$, $\theta(\cdot)$, we deduce

$$\tilde{V}_0(y) \leq \tilde{K}\left[\int_0^T \big\{1 + y^{-\rho} \cdot \mathbb{E}\,(H_0(t))^{-\rho}\big\}\, dt + \big\{1 + y^{-\rho} \cdot \mathbb{E}\,(H_0(T))^{-\rho}\big\}\right] < \infty.\bigg)$$

5.5. Existence

We shall provide in this section sufficiently general conditions, which guarantee the validity of the assumption (5.4.3).

5.5.1. THEOREM (Existence in the "dual" problem). *Under the conditions of* (5.3.5), (5.4.5), (3.6.2), *and those of* Exercise 2.2.8 *there exists, for every* $y \in (0, \infty)$, *a process* $\mu_y(\cdot)$ *in the class* $\mathcal{D}_0$ *of* (5.2.4) *that satisfies*

$$(5.5.1) \qquad \qquad \tilde{V}_\nu(y) \geqq \tilde{V}_{\mu_y}(y), \qquad \forall \nu \in \mathcal{D}.$$

This result allows us to obtain a fairly general existence result for an optimal pair $(\hat{\pi}, \hat{C}) \in \mathcal{A}_*(x; K)$ in the constrained optimization Problem 5.1.1, by putting Theorem 5.5.1 together with Propositions 5.4.1 and 5.4.2.

5.5.2. THEOREM (Existence in the "primal" problem). *Suppose that the conditions of* Theorem 5.5.1 *hold; then for every* $x \in (0, \infty)$, *there exists a pair* $(\hat{\pi}, \hat{C}) \in \mathcal{A}_*(x; K)$ *which attains the supremum in* (5.1.3), *and is thus optimal for* Problem 5.1.1.

The second condition of (5.4.5) excludes logarithmic utility functions; for these, however, we have not only existence of an optimal pair, but actually explicit computations, in Example 5.3.2.

The rest of this section will be devoted to the proof of Theorem 5.5.1. Let us begin with the observation that, for any utility function $U(\cdot)$ with $x \mapsto xU'(x)$ increasing on $(0, \infty)$, as in (3.6.2), the function

$$z \mapsto \left(\tilde{U}(e^z) \right)' = e^z \tilde{U}'(e^z) = -e^z I(e^z) = -\eta U'(\eta) \big|_{\eta = I(e^z)}$$

is increasing, or equivalently the function

$$(5.5.2) \qquad \qquad z \mapsto \tilde{U}(e^z) \text{ is convex (and decreasing) on } \mathbb{R}.$$

On the other hand, for every fixed $y \in (0, \infty)$ let us define the functional $\nu \mapsto \tilde{V}_\nu(y)$ of (5.2.11) on the entirety of the Hilbert space $\mathcal{H}$ in Section 4.2, not just on its (closed, convex) subset $\mathcal{D}$ of (4.2.2):

$(5.5.3) \;\; \tilde{V}_\nu(y)$

$$\triangleq \begin{cases} \mathbb{E}\left[\int_0^T \tilde{U}_1\big(t, y\gamma(t)e^{-\zeta_\nu(t)}\big) \, dt + \tilde{U}_2\big(t, y\gamma(T)e^{-\zeta_\nu(T)}\big) \right]; & \nu \in \mathcal{D} \\ \infty; & \nu \in (\mathcal{H} \backslash \mathcal{D}) \end{cases},$$

where

$$(5.5.4) \;\; \zeta_\nu(t) \triangleq \log \frac{1}{Z_\nu(t)} = \int_0^t \big(\theta^{(\nu)}(u) \big)' \, dW(u) + \frac{1}{2} \int_0^t \big\| \theta^{(\nu)}(u) \big\|^2 \, du, \; 0 \leq t \leq T.$$

5.5.3. EXERCISE. Under the conditions of Theorem 5.5.1, the functional $\nu \mapsto \tilde{V}_\nu(y)$ of (5.5.3) is bounded from below, convex, coercive

$$(5.5.5) \qquad \qquad \lim \tilde{V}_\nu(y) = \infty, \quad \text{as} \quad [\![\nu]\!] \to \infty,$$

and lower-semi-continuous:

$(5.5.6) \;\; \tilde{V}_\nu(y) \leq \varliminf_{n \to \infty} \tilde{V}_{\nu_n}(y), \text{ for any } \nu \in \mathcal{H}, \quad \text{and}$

$$\{\nu_n\} \subseteq \mathcal{H} \text{ with } [\![\nu_n - \nu]\!]_{n \to \infty} \to 0.$$

(*Hint*: From (5.4.5) we have the lower bound $-k(1+T)$; the convexity is a consequence of (5.5.2), and of the convexity of the mapping $\nu \mapsto \zeta_\nu(\cdot)$ in (5.5.4). Now from Jensen's inequality and (4.1.4) we have, for any $\nu \in \mathcal{H}$,

$$\tilde{V}_\nu(y) \geq \mathbb{E}\left[\int_0^T \tilde{U}_1\left(t, y\gamma(T)e^{-\zeta_\nu(t)}\right) dt + \tilde{U}_2\left(y\gamma(t)e^{-\zeta_\nu(T)}\right)\right]$$

$$\geq \int_0^T \tilde{U}_1\left(t, ye^{\eta t - \mathbb{E}\,\zeta_\nu(t)}\right) dt + \tilde{U}_2\left(ye^{\eta T - \mathbb{E}\,\zeta_\nu(T)}\right) \geq -kT + \tilde{U}_2(ye^{\eta T - [\theta^{(\nu)}]^2/2}).$$

The last term in this expression tends to infinity as $[\![\nu]\!] \to \infty$, in view of (4.1.3), and of (5.4.5) — which implies $\tilde{U}_2(0+) = U_2(\infty) = \infty$. This proves (5.5.5); the lower-semi-continuity (5.5.6) is a consequence of the fact that $\tilde{U}_1(t, \cdot)$, $\tilde{U}_2(\cdot)$ are bounded from below, and of Fatou's lemma.)

Now a basic result in Convex Analysis (Proposition 2.12 in Ekeland & Temam (1976)) states that the convex, coercive and lower-semi-continuous functional of (5.5.3) *attains its infimum over the Hilbert space* $\mathcal{H}$; and in view of the assumption (5.3.5), this statement is equivalent to guaranteeing the existence of a process $\mu_y(\cdot)$ in the class $\mathcal{D}$ of (4.2.2), such that (5.5.1) holds:

(5.5.7) $\tilde{V}_{\mu_y}(y) < \infty$ and $\tilde{V}_{\mu_y}(y) \leq \tilde{V}_\nu(y)$, $\forall\, \nu \in \mathcal{D}$.

It remains to show that the process $\mu_y(\cdot)$ belongs actually to the subclass $\mathcal{D}_0$ of (5.2.4); and in view of Exercise 2.2.8, it is enough to prove $\mathcal{X}_{\mu_y}(y) < \infty$. To do this, observe that (2.1.13) and (2.2.24') imply

$$\tilde{U}(\eta) - \tilde{U}(\infty) \geq \tilde{U}(\eta) - \tilde{U}\left(\frac{\eta}{\beta}\right) = \int_\eta^{\eta/\beta} I(\xi)\,d\xi \geq \left(\frac{\eta}{\beta} - \eta\right)I\left(\frac{\eta}{\beta}\right)$$

$$= \eta\frac{1-\beta}{\beta}I\left(\frac{\eta}{\beta}\right) \geq \frac{1-\beta}{\beta\gamma}\eta I(\eta),   \forall\, 0 < \eta < \infty$$

for some $0 < \beta < 1 < \gamma < \infty$; thus, the assumptions of Theorem 5.5.1 give

$$y\mathcal{X}_{\mu_y}(y) = \mathbb{E}\left[\int_0^T yH_{\mu_y}(t)I_1\left(t, yH_{\mu_y}(t)\right) dt + yH_{\mu_y}(T)I_2\left(yH_{\mu_y}(T)\right)\right]$$

$$\leq \frac{\beta\gamma}{1-\beta}\left\{\mathbb{E}\left[\int_0^T \tilde{U}_1\left(t, yH_{\mu_y}(t)\right) dt + \tilde{U}_2\left(yH_{\mu_y}(T)\right)\right]\right.$$

$$\left. - \left(\int_0^T \tilde{U}_1(t, \infty)\,dt + \tilde{U}_2(\infty)\right)\right\}$$

$$\leq \frac{\beta\gamma}{1-\beta}\left(\tilde{V}_{\mu_y}(y) + k(1+T)\right) < \infty.$$

The proof of Theorem 5.5.1 is complete.

5.5.4. REMARK. The conditions (5.4.5), (3.6.2), as well as those of Exercise 2.2.8, are all satisfied by utility functions of the type

(5.5.8) $U_1(t, x) = e^{-\beta_1 t}\dfrac{x^{\alpha_1}}{\alpha_1}$, $U_2(x) = e^{-\beta_2 T}\dfrac{x^{\alpha_2}}{\alpha_2}$; $0 \leq t \leq T$, $0 < x < \infty$

for some real numbers β_1, β_2 and $0 < \alpha_1, \alpha_2 < 1$.

5.5.5. EXERCISE (Maximizing expected utility from terminal wealth). All the results of this chapter go through without change, if you take formally $U_1(\cdot, \cdot) \equiv 0$ throughout, and consider the analogue

$$(5.5.9) \qquad V(x) \triangleq \sup_{(\pi, C) \in \mathcal{A}_*(x; K)} \mathbb{E}\, U\big(X^{x, \pi, C}(T)\big), \qquad 0 < x < \infty$$

of Problem 2.1.5 *with constrained portfolios*, for some utility function $U \colon (0, \infty) \to \mathbb{R}$. Repeat the developments in Sections 5.2–5.5 to show that, for a utility function that satisfies

$$(5.5.10) \qquad \left\{ \begin{array}{l} U(0+) > -\infty \quad \text{or} \quad U(x) = \log x, \quad U(\infty) = \infty \\ \text{as well as } (5.3.5),\ (2.2.24) \text{ and } (3.6.2) \end{array} \right\},$$

there exist, for every given $x \in (0, \infty)$, a process $\mu(\cdot) \equiv \mu_x(\cdot)$ in $\mathcal{D}_0$, and a portfolio $\hat{\pi}_x \colon [0, T] \times \Omega \to K$ with corresponding wealth process

$$(5.5.11) \quad X^{x, \hat{\pi}_x, 0}(t) = \frac{1}{H_{\mu_x}(t)} \mathbb{E}\left[H_{\mu_x}(T) I\big(\mathcal{Y}_{\mu_x}(x) H_{\mu_x}(T)\big) \mid \mathcal{F}(t) \right], \qquad 0 \le t \le T,$$

such that: $\mu_x'(\cdot)\hat{\pi}_x(\cdot) \equiv 0$ a.e. on $[0, T] \times \Omega$. The pair $(\hat{\pi}_x, 0)$ attains the supremum in (5.5.9), i.e.

$$(5.5.12) \quad V(x) = \mathbb{E}\, U\big(X^{x, \hat{\pi}_x, 0}(T)\big) \ge \mathbb{E}\, U\big(X^{x, \pi, C}(T)\big), \qquad \forall\, (\pi, C) \in \mathcal{A}_*(x; K);$$

and

$$(5.5.13) \qquad\qquad\qquad V'(x) = \mathcal{Y}_{\mu_x}(x) > 0.$$

We have denoted by $\mathcal{Y}_{\mu_x}(\cdot)$ the inverse of the continuous, strictly decreasing function $\mathcal{X}_{\mu_x}(y) \triangleq \mathbb{E}\left[H_{\mu_x}(T) I\big(y H_{\mu_x}(T)\big) \right]$, $0 < y < \infty$.

5.6. Relative entropy

Let us suppose now that the relative-risk process $\theta(\cdot) = \sigma^{-1}(\cdot)\big[b(\cdot) - r(\cdot)\mathbf{1}_d\big]$ of Theorem 0.2.4 satisfies the so-called *Novikov condition*

$$(5.6.1) \qquad\qquad \mathbb{E}\left[\exp\left\{ \frac{1}{2} \int_0^T \|\theta(t)\|^2\, dt \right\} \right] < \infty.$$

Then the relative-risk process $\theta^{(\mu)}(\cdot) \equiv \theta(\cdot) + \sigma^{-1}(\cdot)\mu(\cdot)$, in the auxiliary market $\mathcal{M}_\mu$ of Section 4.2 corresponding to the process

$$(5.6.2) \qquad \mu(t) \triangleq \arg\min_{z \in \tilde{K}} \|\theta(t) + \sigma^{-1}(t)z\|$$

$$= \arg\min_{z \in \tilde{K}} \|\sigma^{-1}(t)\big(b(t) - r(t)\mathbf{1}_d + z\big)\|, \qquad 0 \le t \le T$$

of (5.3.25), also satisfies the analogue of the condition (5.6.1), namely

$$\mathbb{E}\left[\exp\left\{ \frac{1}{2} \int_0^T \|\theta^{(\mu)}(t)\|^2\, dt \right\} \right] \le \mathbb{E}\left[\exp\left\{ \frac{1}{2} \int_0^T \|\theta(t)\|^2\, dt \right\} \right] < \infty.$$

And the theorem of Novikov (pp. 198–200 in Karatzas & Shreve (1991)) guarantees then that the exponential process $Z_\mu(\cdot)$ of (4.2.7) is a martingale. Thus, $\mathbb{P}^\mu(A) \triangleq \mathbb{E}\left[Z_\mu(T)\mathbf{1}_A \right]$ defines a probability measure on $\mathcal{F}(T)$, and the process $\mu(\cdot)$ of (5.6.2) belongs to the class $\mathcal{D}_m$ of (4.3.2).

Now for any process $\nu(\cdot)$ in this class $\mathcal{D}_m$, consider the *relative entropy* of the probability measure $\mathbb{P}$ with respect to the probability measure $\mathbb{P}^\nu$ of (4.3.3):

$$(5.6.3) \qquad H(\mathbb{P} \mid \mathbb{P}^\nu) \triangleq \mathbb{E}\left(\log \frac{d\mathbb{P}}{d\mathbb{P}^\nu}\right) = \mathbb{E}\left(\log \frac{1}{Z_\nu(T)}\right)$$

$$= \mathbb{E}\left[\int_0^T \left(\theta^{(\nu)}(t)\right)' dW(t) + \frac{1}{2}\int_0^T \left\|\theta^{(\nu)}(t)\right\|^2 dt\right]$$

$$= \frac{1}{2}\mathbb{E}\int_0^T \left\|\theta^{(\nu)}(t)\right\|^2 dt = \frac{1}{2}\mathbb{E}\int_0^T \left\|\theta(t) + \sigma^{-1}(t)\nu(t)\right\|^2 dt.$$

Consider the problem of *minimizing this quantity*, over $\nu \in \mathcal{D}_m$. It is clear that this is achieved by the process $\mu(\cdot)$ of (5.6.2); in other words,

$$(5.6.4) \qquad \left\{\begin{array}{l} \text{under the condition (5.6.1) the process } \mu(\cdot) \in \mathcal{D}_m \text{ of (5.6.2), the} \\ \text{``dual-optimal process'' in the problem of maximizing expected log-} \\ \text{arithmic utility, also minimizes the relative entropy } H(\mathbb{P} \mid \mathbb{P}^\nu) \text{ over} \\ \nu(\cdot) \in \mathcal{D}_m. \end{array}\right.$$

Consider now the relative entropy of the probability measure $\mathbb{P}^\nu$, $\nu \in \mathcal{D}_m$ with respect to the original probability measure $\mathbb{P}$:

$$(5.6.5) \qquad H(\mathbb{P}^\nu \mid \mathbb{P}) \triangleq \mathbb{E}^\nu\left(\log \frac{d\mathbb{P}^\nu}{d\mathbb{P}}\right) = \mathbb{E}^\nu\left(\log Z_\nu(T)\right)$$

$$= \mathbb{E}^\nu\left[-\int_0^T \left(\theta^{(\nu)}(t)\right)' dW(t) - \frac{1}{2}\int_0^T \left\|\theta^{(\nu)}(t)\right\|^2 dt\right]$$

$$= \mathbb{E}^\nu\left[-\int_0^T \left(\theta^{(\nu)}(t)\right)' dW^{(\nu)}(t) + \frac{1}{2}\int_0^T \left\|\theta^{(\nu)}(t)\right\|^2 dt\right]$$

$$= \frac{1}{2}\mathbb{E}^\nu\int_0^T \left\|\theta^{(\nu)}(t)\right\|^2 dt$$

$$= \frac{1}{2}\mathbb{E}^\nu\int_0^T \left\|\theta(t) + \sigma^{-1}(t)\nu(t)\right\|^2 dt, \quad \nu \in \mathcal{D}_m.$$

If the coefficients $\sigma(\cdot)$ and $\theta(\cdot)$ are deterministic, then $\mu(\cdot)$ of (5.6.2) is also a deterministic (non-random) function $\mu\colon [0,T] \to \tilde{K}$ in $\mathbb{L}^2([0,T])$, and thus so is $\theta^{(\mu)}(\cdot) = \theta(\cdot) + \sigma^{-1}(\cdot)\mu(\cdot)$. Again, this $\mu(\cdot)$ minimizes the quantity of (5.6.5); in other words,

$$(5.6.6) \qquad \left\{\begin{array}{l} \text{if } \sigma(\cdot) \text{ and } \theta(\cdot) \text{ are deterministic, the function } \mu\colon [0,T] \to \tilde{K} \text{ of} \\ \text{(5.6.2) — again ``dual-optimal'' in the problem of maximizing ex-} \\ \text{pected logarithmic utility — also minimizes the relative entropy} \\ H(\mathbb{P}^\nu \mid \mathbb{P}) \text{ over processes } \nu(\cdot) \in \mathcal{D}_m. \end{array}\right.$$

5.7. Constant coefficients

Let us specialize now the results of Sections 5.2–5.5 to the case of *constant coefficients*

$$(5.7.1) \qquad r(\cdot) \equiv r \in \mathbb{R}^+, \quad b(\cdot) \equiv b \in \mathbb{R}^d, \quad \sigma(\cdot) \equiv \sigma \in L(\mathbb{R}^d; \mathbb{R}^d) \text{ nonsingular},$$

and utility functions

$$(5.7.2) \qquad U_1(t,x) = e^{-\beta t}u_1(x), \quad U_2(x) = e^{-\beta T}u_2(x), \quad (t,x) \in [0,T] \times (0,\infty)$$

as in (2.4.1), (2.4.5), under the conditions of (2.4.6). For every process $\nu(\cdot) \in \mathcal{D}$, we recall $\theta^{(\nu)}(\cdot) \triangleq \theta + \sigma^{-1}\nu(\cdot) = \sigma^{-1}\big(b - r\mathbf{1}_d + \nu(\cdot)\big)$ of (4.2.5) and introduce, by analogy with the notation of Section 2.4, the processes

$$Z_\nu(t,s) \triangleq \frac{Z_\nu(s)}{Z_\nu(t)} = \exp\left[-\int_t^s \big(\theta^{(\nu)}(u)\big)' \, dW(u) - \frac{1}{2}\int_t^s \big\|\theta^{(\nu)}(u)\big\|^2 \, du\right],$$

(5.7.3)
$$H_\nu(t,s) \triangleq \frac{H_\nu(s)}{H_\nu(t)} = e^{-r(s-t)} Z_\nu(t,s),$$

$$Y_\nu^{(t,y)}(s) \triangleq y e^{\beta(s-t)} H_\nu(t,s), \qquad t \le s \le T,$$

and the functions

(5.7.4) $\quad S_\nu(t,y) \triangleq \mathbb{E}\left[\int_t^T e^{-\beta(s-t)} Y_\nu^{(t,y)}(s) i_1\big(Y_\nu^{(t,y)}(s)\big) \, ds\right.$

$$\left. + e^{-\beta(T-t)} Y_\nu^{(t,y)}(T) i_2\big(Y_\nu^{(t,y)}(T)\big)\right]$$

(5.7.5) $\quad G_\nu(t,y) \triangleq \mathbb{E}\left[\int_t^T e^{-\beta(s-t)} (u_1 \circ i_1)\big(Y_\nu^{(t,y)}(s)\big) \, ds\right.$

$$\left. + e^{-\beta(T-t)} (u_2 \circ i_2)\big(Y_\nu^{(t,y)}(T)\big)\right], \quad \mathcal{X}_\nu(t,y) \triangleq \frac{1}{y} S_\nu(t,y)$$

defined for $(t,y) \in [0,T] \times (0,\infty)$. Then the value-function $V_\nu(t,\cdot)$ of the unconstrained problem (5.2.1) on the horizon $[t,T]$ is given by

(5.7.6) $\qquad V_\nu(t,x) = G_\nu\big(t, \mathcal{Y}_\nu(t,x)\big), \qquad 0 < x < \infty$

where $\mathcal{Y}_\nu(t,\cdot)$ is the inverse of $\mathcal{X}_\nu(t,\cdot)$; and the convex dual of the function $V_\nu(t,\cdot)$ in (5.7.6), namely $\tilde{V}_\nu(t,y) \triangleq \sup_{0<x<\infty}\big[V_\nu(t,x) - xy\big]$, is given, by analogy with (2.4.12), (2.4.13), as

(5.7.7) $\quad \tilde{V}_\nu(t,y) = G_\nu(t,y) - S_\nu(t,y)$

$$= \mathbb{E}\left[\int_t^T e^{-\beta(s-t)} \tilde{u}_1\big(Y_\nu^{(t,y)}(s)\big) \, ds + e^{-\beta(T-t)} \tilde{u}_2\big(Y_\nu^{(t,y)}(T)\big)\right].$$

In addition, *for every constant vector $\nu \in \tilde{K}$*, this function can be written explicitly as

(5.7.8) $\quad \tilde{V}_\nu(t,y) = h_\nu(y) + \left(u_2(0) - \frac{u_1(0)}{\beta}\right) e^{-\beta(T-t)}$

$$+ \int_0^\infty \big(\tilde{u}_2(q) - h_\nu(q)\big)'' v_\nu(t,y;q) \, dq$$

and solves the Cauchy problem for the linear, second-order partial differential equation

(5.7.9)
$$\frac{\partial \tilde{V}_\nu}{\partial t} + \frac{y^2}{2}\|\theta + \sigma^{-1}\nu\|^2 \frac{\partial^2 \tilde{V}_\nu}{\partial y^2} + (\beta - r)y\frac{\partial \tilde{V}_\nu}{\partial y} - \beta\tilde{V}_\nu + \tilde{u}_1(y) = 0;$$

$$0 \le t < T, \quad 0 < y < \infty$$

$$\tilde{V}_\nu(T,y) = \tilde{u}_2(y); \qquad 0 < y < \infty$$

(from (2.4.24)–(2.4.33) with θ replaced by $\theta_\nu \triangleq \theta + \sigma^{-1}\nu$). Similarly, for constant $\nu \in \tilde{K}$, the value-function $V_\nu(\cdot, \cdot)$ solves the *nonlinear Cauchy problem*

$$(5.7.10) \quad \begin{cases} \dfrac{\partial V_\nu}{\partial t} + \max\limits_{\substack{c \geq 0 \\ \pi \in \mathbb{R}^d}} \left[\dfrac{1}{2}\|\sigma'\pi\|^2 \dfrac{\partial^2 V_\nu}{\partial x^2} + \{rx - c + \pi'(b + \nu - r\mathbf{1}_d)\}\dfrac{\partial V_\nu}{\partial x} \right. \\ \left. \qquad\qquad + u_1(c) \right] = \beta V_\nu(t,x); \qquad 0 \leq t < T,\ 0 < x < \infty, \\ V_\nu(T,x) = u_2(x); \qquad 0 < x < \infty, \end{cases}$$

where the maximum is attained at

$$(5.7.11) \quad \begin{aligned} \mathcal{C}_\nu(t,x) &\triangleq i_1\big(\mathcal{Y}_\nu(t,x)\big), \\ \Pi_\nu(t,x) &\triangleq -(\sigma\sigma')^{-1}[b - r\mathbf{1}_d + \nu]\dfrac{\mathcal{Y}_\nu(t,x)}{(\partial/\partial x)\mathcal{Y}_\nu(t,x)}. \end{aligned}$$

Furthermore, the optimal wealth, consumption-rate and portfolio processes (for this unconstrained optimization problem in $\mathcal{M}_\nu$) are given as

$$(5.7.12) \quad \begin{aligned} X_\nu^{(t,x)}(s) &= \mathcal{X}_\nu\big(s, Y_\nu^{(t,y)}(s)\big)\big|_{y=\mathcal{Y}_\nu(t,x)}, \quad \mathcal{C}_\nu\big(s, X_\nu^{(t,x)}(s)\big), \\ &\qquad \Pi_\nu\big(s, X_\nu^{(t,x)}(s)\big), \end{aligned}$$

respectively, for $t \leq s \leq T$, by analogy with (2.4.19)–(2.4.23).

Let us consider now the analogue of the *dual value function*

$$(5.7.13) \qquad \tilde{V}(t,y) \triangleq \inf_{\nu \in \mathcal{D}} \tilde{V}_\nu(t,y), \quad (t,y) \in [0,T] \times (0,\infty)$$

in (5.4.1). We expect this function to satisfy the "nonlinear version"

$$(5.7.14) \quad \begin{cases} \dfrac{\partial \tilde{V}}{\partial t} + \dfrac{y^2}{2} \inf\limits_{\nu \in \tilde{K}} \left[\|\theta + \sigma^{-1}\nu\|^2 \dfrac{\partial^2 \tilde{V}}{\partial y^2} \right] + (\beta - r)y\dfrac{\partial \tilde{V}}{\partial y} \\ \qquad\qquad - \beta\tilde{V} + \tilde{u}_1(y) = 0; \quad 0 \leq t < T,\ 0 < y < \infty, \\ \tilde{V}(T,y) = \tilde{u}_2(y); \qquad 0 < y < \infty, \end{cases}$$

of the equation (5.7.9). Suppose, in fact, that *there exists a vector $\mu \in \tilde{K}$ with*

$$(5.7.15) \qquad \|\theta_\mu\| \equiv \|\theta + \sigma^{-1}\mu\| = \inf_{\nu \in \tilde{K}} \|\theta + \sigma^{-1}\nu\| > 0;$$

then from the linear equation (5.7.9) and the (strict) convexity of $\tilde{V}_\mu(t, \cdot)$ we deduce that $\tilde{V}_\mu(\cdot, \cdot)$ *solves the nonlinear Cauchy problem* (5.7.14) *as well*, and thus we expect

$$(5.7.16) \qquad \tilde{V}(t,y) = \tilde{V}_\mu(t,y), \quad (t,y) \in [0,T] \times (0,\infty).$$

We also expect that the concave dual $V_\mu(t,x) = \inf_{0<y<\infty}\big[\tilde{V}_\mu(t,y) + xy\big]$ of this function will give, in fact, the value function for the constrained optimization Problem 5.1.1 as

$$(5.7.17) \qquad V(x) = V_\mu(0,x), \qquad 0 < x < \infty,$$

and that it will satisfy the *Hamilton-Jacobi-Bellman* (HJB) equation

$$(5.7.18) \quad \begin{cases} \dfrac{\partial V_\mu}{\partial t} + \max_{\substack{c \geq 0 \\ \pi \in K}} \left[\dfrac{1}{2}\|\sigma'\pi\|^2 \dfrac{\partial^2 V_\mu}{\partial x^2} + u_1(c) + \{rx - c + \pi'(b - r\mathbf{1}_d)\}\dfrac{\partial V_\mu}{\partial x}\right] \\ \qquad\qquad\qquad\qquad = \beta V_\mu; \qquad 0 \leq t < T, \ 0 < x < \infty, \\ \qquad\qquad V_\mu(T,x) = u_2(x); \qquad 0 < x < \infty, \end{cases}$$

associated with Problem 5.1.1.

5.7.1. THEOREM. *Under the assumptions* (5.7.1), (5.7.2), (2.4.6), *and* (5.7.15) *for some vector* $\mu \in \tilde{K}$, *we have:*

$$(5.7.19) \qquad \tilde{V}_\mu(t,y) \leq \tilde{V}_\nu(t,y) \text{ on } [0,T] \times (0,\infty), \qquad \forall \ \nu \in \mathcal{D}$$

$$(5.7.20) \qquad \tilde{V}(t,y) = \tilde{V}_\mu(t,y) \text{ solves the Cauchy problem } (5.7.14), \text{ and}$$

$$(5.7.21) \qquad V_\mu(t,y) \text{ solves the HJB equation } (5.7.18).$$

The value function of Problem 5.1.1 *is given by* $V(x) = V_\mu(0,x)$, $x \in (0,\infty)$; *the optimal wealth, consumption-rate and portfolio processes are as in* (5.7.12), (5.7.11) *with* $\nu = \mu$; *and we have the "complementary slackness" property*

$$(5.7.22) \qquad \mu'\Pi_\mu(t,x) = 0, \text{ on } [0,T] \times (0,\infty).$$

PROOF. In order to prove (5.7.19), it suffices to show

$$(5.7.23) \qquad \mathbb{E} f(Z_\mu(s)) \leq \mathbb{E} f(Z_\nu(s)), \qquad \forall \ s \in [0,T]$$

for any given process $\nu(\cdot)$ in the class $\mathcal{D}$, and for any function

$$(5.7.24) \qquad f\colon (0,\infty) \to \mathbb{R} \quad \text{convex, decreasing, and bounded from below.}$$

To see (5.7.23), write $\theta_\nu(t,w) = O(t,w)\theta_\mu\|\theta_\nu(t,w)\| \, / \, \|\theta_\mu\|$, a.e. on $[0,T] \times \Omega$, for some progressively measurable process $O\colon [0,T] \times \Omega \to \mathfrak{N}(\mathbb{R}^d;\mathbb{R}^d)$ with values in the space of orthonormal $(d \times d)$-matrices, and introduce the random time-change

$$\Lambda(\tau) \triangleq \int_0^\tau \frac{\|\theta_\nu(v)\|^2}{\|\theta_\mu\|^2} \, dv \geq \tau, \qquad 0 \leq \tau \leq T$$

and its inverse $\Gamma(s) \triangleq \inf\{\tau \in [0,T] \, / \, \Lambda(\tau) > s\}$. For every $s \in [0,T]$, $\Gamma(s)$ is an $\mathbb{F}$-stopping time with values in $[0,s]$. Consider also the $\mathbb{F}$-martingale

$$M(\tau) \triangleq \int_0^\tau \frac{\|\theta_\nu(v)\|}{\|\theta_\mu\|} O'(v) \, dW(v), \qquad 0 \leq \tau \leq T.$$

The time-changed process $B(s) \triangleq M(\Gamma(s))$, $0 \leq s \leq T$ is then a continuous local martingale with respect to the time-changed filtration $\mathcal{G}(s) \triangleq \mathcal{F}(\Gamma(s))$, $0 \leq s \leq T$, and we have

$$\langle B_j, B_k \rangle(s) = \delta_{jk} \int_0^{\Gamma(s)} \frac{\|\theta_\nu(v)\|^2}{\|\theta_\mu\|^2} \, dv = \delta_{jk}s; \qquad 1 \leq j, \ k \leq d.$$

P. Lévy's characterization (cf. Karatzas & Shreve (1991), Theorem 3.3.16) implies now that $B(\cdot)$ is a d-dimensional Brownian motion, and the equation $Z_\nu(\tau) = 1 - \int_0^\tau Z_\nu(v)\theta_\nu'(v) \, dW(v)$, $0 \leq \tau \leq T$ becomes

$$Z_\nu(\Gamma(s)) = 1 - \int_0^s Z_\nu(\Gamma(u))\theta_\mu' \, dB(u), \qquad 0 \leq s \leq T.$$

On the other hand, we have $Z_\mu(s) = 1 - \int_0^s Z_\mu(u)\theta'_\mu \, dW(u)$, $0 \leq s \leq T$. Comparison of these two equations shows that $Z_\mu(\cdot)$, $Z_\nu(\Gamma(\cdot))$ *have the same distributions.* From this, the submartingale property of $f(Z_\nu(\cdot))$ (cf. Exercise 5.7.2), and the optional sampling theorem, we deduce

$$\mathbb{E} f(Z_\mu(s)) \equiv \mathbb{E} f(Z_\nu(\Gamma(s))) \leq \mathbb{E} f(Z_\nu(s))$$

for any function $f(\cdot)$ as in (5.7.24), and (5.7.23) follows. The property (5.7.21) is checked in Exercise 5.7.3 below; the remaining properties are consequences of Theorem 5.3.1, and of the theory developed in Sections 5.4 and 2.4. The property (5.7.22) is a corollary of (5.2.19) or (5.3.2). □

5.7.2. EXERCISE. Let $\xi(s)$, $0 \leq s \leq T$ be a positive, continuous local martingale, and $f(\cdot)$ a function as in (5.7.24) with $\mathbb{E} f(\xi(s)) < \infty$, $\forall s \in [0,T]$. Then $f(\xi(s))$, $0 \leq s \leq T$ is a submartingale.

$\big($*Hint*: Observe that, for any $\varepsilon > 0$, the function

$$f_\varepsilon(x) \triangleq \begin{cases} f(\varepsilon) + (x - \varepsilon) \cdot D^+ f(\varepsilon); & 0 < x < \varepsilon \\ f(x); & \varepsilon \leq x < \infty \end{cases}$$

is convex, decreasing and bounded, so that $f_\varepsilon(\xi(\cdot \wedge \tau_n))$ is a bounded submartingale, for any sequence $\{\tau_n\} \subseteq \mathcal{S}_{0,T}$ that localizes $\xi(\cdot)$:

$$\int_A f_\varepsilon(\xi(s \wedge \tau_n)) \, d\mathbb{P} \leq \int_A f_\varepsilon(\xi(t \wedge \tau_n)) \, d\mathbb{P}$$

for every $0 \leq s \leq t \leq T$, $A \in \mathcal{F}(s)$, $n \in \mathbb{N}$. Let $n \to \infty$ and then $\varepsilon \downarrow 0$, and employ respectively the bounded and monotone convergence theorems.$\big)$

5.7.3. EXERCISE. Verify the property (5.7.21).

$\big($*Hint*: Compare the HJB equations of (5.7.18), (5.7.10), for $V_\mu(t,x)$, to see that we have to prove

$$(5.7.25) \quad \max_{\pi \in \mathbb{R}^d} \left[\frac{1}{2} \|\sigma'\pi\|^2 \frac{\partial^2 V_\mu}{\partial x^2} + \pi'(\sigma\theta + \mu) \frac{\partial V_\mu}{\partial x} \right]$$

$$= \max_{\pi \in K} \left[\frac{1}{2} \|\sigma'\pi\|^2 \frac{\partial^2 V_\mu}{\partial x^2} + \pi'\sigma\theta \frac{\partial V_\mu}{\partial x} \right].$$

From $\mu \in \tilde{K}$ we have $\pi'\mu \geq 0$ for every $\pi \in K$ and, since $(\partial/\partial x)V_\mu(t,x) = \mathcal{Y}_\mu(t,x) > 0$ from (5.2.14), the left-hand-side dominates the right-hand side in (5.7.25). For the reverse inequality, observe that the left-hand side equals

$$\frac{1}{2} \|\sigma'\Pi_\mu(t,x)\|^2 \frac{\partial^2 V_\mu}{\partial x^2} + \Pi'_\mu(t,x)(\sigma\theta + \mu) \frac{\partial V_\mu}{\partial x}$$

$$= \frac{1}{2} \|\sigma'\Pi_\mu(t,x)\|^2 \frac{\partial^2 V_\mu}{\partial x^2} + \Pi'_\mu(t,x)\sigma\theta \frac{\partial V_\mu}{\partial x}$$

and is thus dominated by the right-hand side, thanks to (5.7.22) and to the fact that $\Pi_\mu(t,x) \in K$.$\big)$

CHAPTER 6

Pricing

6.1. Introduction

In the case of a standard, *complete* market model $\mathcal{M}$, we saw that the principle of "excluding arbitrage opportunities" leads to a unique price $p > 0$ for any contingent claim Y, namely

$$p = u_0 = \mathbb{E}^0 \big[\gamma(T) Y \big]$$

as in Theorem 1.2.1; and that this price coincides with the upper- and lower- hedging prices of (0.4.2) and (0.4.4).

For an *incomplete*, or more generally a constrained market $\mathcal{M}(K)$, however, the situation is different: based on arbitrage considerations alone, one obtains an entire *interval*

$$(6.1.1) \qquad\qquad h_{\text{low}}(K) \le p \le h_{\text{up}}(K)$$

of admissible values for the price $p > 0$ of the contingent claim at time $t = 0$, the so-called *arbitrage-free interval* $\big[h_{\text{low}}(K), h_{\text{up}}(K) \big]$ of Exercise 4.3.3. Here

$$(6.1.2) \qquad\qquad h_{\text{low}}(K) = \inf_{\nu \in \mathcal{D}_b} u_\nu, \quad h_{\text{up}}(K) = \sup_{\nu \in \mathcal{D}_b} u_\nu$$

are the upper- and lower-hedging prices of (4.3.6) and (4.3.7), respectively, and the inequality $h_{\text{up}}(K) > h_{\text{low}}(K)$ is typically strict; recall the theory and the examples of Sections 4.4 and 4.6.

How does then one select a unique price in the interval $[h_{\text{low}}(K), h_{\text{up}}(K)]$? As we have seen, there is no "preference-independent" way for doing this, based only on the principle of excluding arbitrage opportunities. Buying or selling a contingent claim, such as an option, is genuinely risky within an incomplete or constrained market, and in order to come up with a unique price one has to specify the investor's attitude towards *risk*.

Several ways have been suggested to accomplish this, and perhaps none is entirely satisfactory. We shall present in this chapter the approach of Davis (1994), which fits well with the utility maximization theory that we developed in Chapter 5. It measures the investor's attitude towards risk by means of a *utility function*, and singles out a *fair price* $\hat{p} > 0$ based on the following "zero marginal rate of substitution" principle: the fair price $\hat{p}$ is determined in such a way that, diversion of a small amount of funds into the contingent claim at time $t = 0$, has a neutral effect on the maximal expected utility from total wealth that the investor can achieve at the terminal time $t = T$; see (6.2.1), (6.2.2) and Definition 6.2.1 below for more precise statements.

We show in Section 6.2 that this principle leads, very naturally, to the explicit formula for the fair price

$$(6.1.3) \qquad \hat{p} = u_{\hat{\nu}} = \mathbb{E}\left[H_{\hat{\nu}}(T)Y\right] \in \left[h_{\text{low}}(K), h_{\text{up}}(K)\right],$$

where $\hat{\nu}(\cdot) \in \mathcal{D}$ is determined as in Theorem 5.3.1 and Exercise 5.5.5. In the context of an incomplete market, and provided that $\hat{\nu}(\cdot)$ belongs to the class $\mathcal{D}_m$ of (4.3.2), this amounts to *selecting an equivalent martingale measure from the family* $\{\mathbb{P}^\nu\}_{\nu \in \mathcal{D}_m}$ of Remark 4.3.1. In the case of logarithmic utility functions, or of general utility functions but with constant coefficients, this selection also amounts to relative entropy minimization.

Explicit computations are carried out in Section 6.3, and demonstrate that in several circumstances the fair price $\hat{p}$ actually does not depend on the particular form of the utility function under consideration.

6.2. A fair price

Let us consider a European Contingent Claim Y, as in Sections 4.3 and 4.5, *in the market model* $\mathcal{M}(K)$ *of* (4.1.1)–(4.1.6). For a given utility function $U \colon (0, \infty) \to \mathbb{R}$ as in Definition 2.1.2, and setting formally $U(\cdot) \equiv -\infty$ on $(-\infty, 0)$, consider the stochastic optimization problem with value

$$(6.2.1) \quad Q(\delta, p, x) \triangleq \sup_{(\pi, C) \in \mathcal{A}_*(x - \delta; K)} \mathbb{E}\, U\left(X^{x-\delta,\pi,C}(T) + \frac{\delta}{p}Y\right), \qquad -x < \delta < x$$

for every given $x \in (0, \infty)$, $p \in (0, \infty)$. In words, suppose that an agent with initial wealth x, diverts at time $t = 0$ an amount δ $(|\delta| < x)$ of money and acquires $\frac{\delta}{p}$ units of the contingent claim at the price p. He then tries to find a portfolio/consumption strategy $(\hat{\pi}, \hat{C})$ in the class $\mathcal{A}_*(x - \delta; K)$ of (5.1.1), which will maximize his expected utility, from the terminal wealth $X^{x-\delta,\pi,C}(T)$ plus the value $\frac{\delta}{p}Y$ at time $t = T$ of the acquired units of the contingent claim. Clearly, $Q(0, p, \cdot)$ coincides with $V(\cdot)$, the value function of (5.5.9).

Suppose that, at time $t = 0$, we can select the price $\hat{p} > 0$ of the Contingent Claim in such a way that this diversion of funds has a neutral effect

$$(6.2.2) \qquad\qquad \left.\frac{\partial Q}{\partial \delta}(\delta, \hat{p}, x)\right|_{\delta=0} = 0$$

on the attainable expected utility of (6.2.1). Then we are entitled to call this $\hat{p} > 0$ a "fair price" for the Contingent Claim at $t = 0$, in the sense that the "marginal rate of substitution" $(\partial Q/\partial \delta)(\cdot, \hat{p}, x)$ vanishes at the origin $\delta = 0$. Unfortunately, the differentiability of the function $Q(\cdot, p, x)$ in (6.2.1) is very hard to check directly; thus, we adopt a weaker requirement, reminiscent of the notion of "viscosity solution" from Crandall & Lions (1983) (see also Fleming & Soner (1993)).

6.2.1. DEFINITION. For every given $x \in (0, \infty)$, we call $p \in (0, \infty)$ a *weak solution of* (6.2.2) if, for every function $\varphi \colon (-x, x) \to \mathbb{R}$ of class C^1 which satisfies

$$(6.2.3) \qquad \left\{ \begin{array}{ll} \varphi(\delta) \geq Q(\delta, p, x), & \forall\, \delta \in (-x, x) \\ \varphi(0) = Q(0, p, x) = V(x) & \end{array} \right\},$$

we have $\varphi'(0) = 0$.

If there is only one weak solution $p \equiv \hat{p}(x) \in (0, \infty)$ of (6.2.2), then this is called *the fair price* of the contingent claim at time $t = 0$.

It turns out that, under fairly general conditions, there is indeed a unique weak solution $p \equiv \hat{p}(x) > 0$ of (6.2.2) for every given $x \in (0, \infty)$, and that it is even possible to obtain a useful representation for it. To this end, let us recall the notation of Exercise 5.5.5 and let, for convenience of notation,

$$(6.2.4) \qquad X_*^x(T) \triangleq I\big(\mathcal{Y}_{\mu_x}(x) H_{\mu_x}(T)\big) \equiv X^{x, \hat{\pi}_x, 0}(T)$$

denote the optimal level of terminal wealth in the problem of (5.5.9).

6.2.2. THEOREM. *Under the conditions of* (5.5.10), *the fair price of Definition 6.2.1 exists and is given as*

$$(6.2.5) \qquad \hat{p}(x) = \frac{\mathbb{E}\big[U'\big(X_*^x(T)\big)Y\big]}{V'(x)} = \mathbb{E}\big[H_{\mu_x}(T)Y\big],$$

in the notation of (5.5.9)–(5.5.13).

PROOF. Fix $0 < x < \infty$, $0 < p < \infty$, and recall that the concave function $U(\cdot)$ satisfies

$$(6.2.6) \quad U(z) + (y - z)U'(y) \leq U(y) \leq U(z) + (y - z)U'(z),$$

$$\text{for any } 0 < z < y < \infty.$$

Consider also a function $\varphi \colon (-x, x) \to \mathbb{R}$ of class C^1, which satisfies the conditions of (6.2.3).

Then from (6.2.1), the first inequality in (6.2.6), and the fact that

$$(6.2.7) \qquad z \mapsto X_*^z(T) \text{ is a.s. increasing,}$$

we have for any $0 < \delta < x$:

$$\varphi(\delta) \geq Q(\delta, p, x) \geq \mathbb{E}\, U\bigg(X_*^{x-\delta}(T) + \frac{\delta}{p}Y\bigg)$$

$$\geq \mathbb{E}\, U\big(X_*^{x-\delta}(T)\big) + \frac{\delta}{p} \cdot \mathbb{E}\bigg[U'\bigg(X_*^{x-\delta}(T) + \frac{\delta}{p}Y\bigg) \cdot Y\bigg],$$

whence also

$$\frac{\varphi(\delta) - \varphi(0)}{\delta} \geq \frac{V(x - \delta) - V(x)}{\delta} + \frac{1}{p}\mathbb{E}\bigg[U'\bigg(X_*^x(T) + \frac{\delta}{p}Y\bigg) \cdot Y\bigg].$$

Letting $\delta \downarrow 0$ in this expression, we obtain by monotone convergence

$$(6.2.8) \qquad \varphi'(0) \geq \frac{1}{p}\mathbb{E}\big[U'\big(X_*^x(T)\big)Y\big] - V'(x).$$

Similarly, with $-x < \delta < 0$, we obtain from the second inequality of (6.2.6), (6.2.1) and (6.2.7):

$$\varphi(\delta) \geq Q(\delta, p, x) \geq \mathbb{E}\, U\bigg(X_*^{x-\delta}(T) + \frac{\delta}{p}Y\bigg)$$

$$\geq \mathbb{E}\, U\big(X_*^{x-\delta}(T)\big) + \frac{\delta}{p}\mathbb{E}\bigg[U'\bigg(X_*^{x-\delta}(T) + \frac{\delta}{p}Y\bigg) \cdot Y\bigg],$$

as well as

$$\frac{\varphi(\delta) - \varphi(0)}{\delta} \leq \frac{V(x - \delta) - V(x)}{\delta} + \frac{1}{p}\mathbb{E}\bigg[U'\bigg(X_*^x(T) + \frac{\delta}{p}Y\bigg) \cdot Y\bigg],$$

where we are setting formally $U'(z) \equiv U'(0+) = \infty$ for $z < 0$. Letting $\delta \uparrow 0$ in the above inequality, we get

$$(6.2.9) \qquad \varphi'(0) \leq \frac{1}{p} \mathbb{E}\left[U'\big(X_*^x(T)\big)Y\right] - V'(x),$$

again from the monotone convergence theorem.

Now it is clear from (6.2.8), (6.2.9) that the given $p \in (0,\infty)$ is a weak solution of equation (6.2.2) (i.e., we have $\varphi'(0) = 0$ for any function $\varphi(\cdot)$ of class C^1 which satisfies (6.2.3)), if and only if

$$p = \hat{p}(x) \triangleq \frac{\mathbb{E}\left[U'\big(X_*^x(T)\big)Y\right]}{V'(x)}.$$

And from (5.5.13), (5.2.5) this number is equal to

$$\frac{\mathbb{E}\left[V'(x)H_{\mu_x}(T)Y\right]}{V'(x)} = \mathbb{E}\left[H_{\mu_x}(T)Y\right].$$

$\square$

6.2.3. EXERCISE. Prove the property (6.2.7).

(*Hint:* For some $0 < x < y < \infty$, suppose that the event $A = \{X_*^x(T) > X_*^y(T)\}$ has positive probability. Introduce the stopping time $\tau \triangleq \inf\{t \in [0,T] \ / \ X_*^x(t) = X_*^y(t)\}\wedge T$ and the process $\hat{\pi}(t) \triangleq \hat{\pi}_y(t)1_{[0,\tau]}(t) + \hat{\pi}_x(t)1_{(\tau,T]}(t)$, and observe that $X^{y,\hat{\pi},0}(t) = X_*^y(t)1_{[0,\tau]}(t) + X_*^x(t)1_{(\tau,T]}(t)$, $0 \leq t \leq T$ holds a.s. We have $\tau < T$ on A, and $V(y) \geq \mathbb{E}U\big(X^{y,\hat{\pi},0}(T)\big) = \mathbb{E}\left[U\big(X_*^x(T)\big)1_A + U\big(X_*^y(T)\big)1_{A^c}\right] > \mathbb{E}U\big(X_*^y(T)\big) = V(y)$, a contradiction.)

6.2.4. REMARK. If the process $\mu_x(\cdot)$ in (6.2.5) belongs to the class $\mathcal{D}_b$ of (5.3.2), then we have

$$(6.2.10) \qquad \hat{p}(x) = \mathbb{E}\left[H_{\mu_x}(T)Y\right] = \mathbb{E}^{\mu_x}\left[\gamma(T)Y\right] \in \left[h_{\mathrm{low}}(K), h_{\mathrm{up}}(K)\right],$$

from Theorems 4.4.1, 4.6.1: *the fair price belongs to the arbitrage-free interval.* This can, in fact, be established in great generality, without assuming $\mu_x \in \mathcal{D}_b$; see Karatzas & Kou (1996), Theorem 7.1.

6.3. Examples

An advantage of the Definition 6.2.1 is that it leads to a very explicit formula (6.2.5), (6.2.10) for the fair price, which permits exact computation in several concrete examples. We present some such cases below.

6.3.1. EXAMPLE. *Logarithmic utility function* $U(x) = \log x$; *general random adapted, bounded coefficients.* From Example 5.3.2, the process $\mu_x(\cdot)$ of Theorem 6.2.2 is given by

$$(6.3.1) \qquad \begin{aligned} \mu(t) &= \arg\min_{z \in \tilde{K}}\big\|\theta(t) + \sigma^{-1}(t)z\big\| \\ &= \arg\min_{z \in \tilde{K}}\big\|\sigma^{-1}(t)\big(b(t) + z - r(t)\mathbf{1}_d\big)\big\|, \qquad 0 \leq t \leq T \end{aligned}$$

as in (5.6.2), and is uniformly bounded on $[0,T] \times \Omega$, thus $\mu \in \mathcal{D}_b$. It is also *independent of the initial wealth* $x \in (0,\infty)$, and minimizes the relative entropy $H(\mathbb{P} \mid \mathbb{P}^\nu)$ over $\nu \in \mathcal{D}_m$ as in (5.6.4).

6.3.2. EXAMPLE. *General utility function; constant coefficients.* Under the conditions of Theorem 5.7.1, the process $\mu_x(\cdot)$ of Theorem 6.2.2 becomes

$$(6.3.2) \qquad \mu(\cdot) \equiv \hat{\nu} \triangleq \arg\min_{z \in \tilde{K}} \|\theta + \sigma^{-1}z\| = \arg\min_{z \in \tilde{K}} \|\sigma^{-1}(b - r\mathbf{1}_d + z)\|$$

a constant vector in $\tilde{K}$, *independently of both the utility function $U(\cdot)$ and the initial wealth*. This $\mu(\cdot) \equiv \hat{\nu}$ minimizes, not only the relative entropy $H(\mathbb{P} \mid \mathbb{P}^\nu)$, but also the relative entropy $H(\mathbb{P}^\nu \mid \mathbb{P})$, over $\nu \in \mathcal{D}_m$ as in (5.6.4) and (5.6.6).

Suppose, moreover, that $Y = \varphi(P(T))$ as in Example 1.3.1. Then the fair price of (6.2.10) becomes

$$(6.3.3) \qquad \hat{p} = \mathbb{E}^{\hat{\nu}}\big[e^{-rT}\varphi(P(T))\big] = U^{(\hat{\nu})}(T, P(0)),$$

where

$$(6.3.4) \qquad U^{(\hat{\nu})}(s,p) \triangleq \begin{cases} e^{-rs}\int_{\mathbb{R}^d}(\varphi \circ H^{(\hat{\nu})})(s,p,\sigma\xi)G_s(\xi)\,d\xi; & s > 0, \\ & p \in (0,\infty)^d \\ \varphi(p); & s = 0, \\ & p \in (0,\infty)^d \end{cases},$$

$$(6.3.5) \quad H_i^{(\hat{\nu})}(s,p,y) \triangleq p_i \exp\left[\left(r - \hat{\nu}_i - \frac{1}{2}a_{ii}\right) + y_i\right], \qquad i = 1,\ldots,d, \quad y \in \mathbb{R}^d$$

are the analogues of (1.3.4)–(1.3.7), and $a = \sigma\sigma'$. The function of (6.3.4) is the solution of the Cauchy problem for the linear equation

$$(6.3.6) \qquad \frac{\partial U^{(\hat{\nu})}}{\partial s} = \frac{1}{2}\sum_{i=1}^d\sum_{j=1}^d a_{ij}p_ip_j\frac{\partial^2 U^{(\hat{\nu})}}{\partial p_i\partial p_j} + \sum_{i=1}^d(r - \hat{\nu}_i)p_i\frac{\partial U^{(\hat{\nu})}}{\partial p_i} - rU^{(\hat{\nu})};$$
$$s > 0, \quad p \in (0,\infty)^d$$
$$U^{(\hat{\nu})}(0,p) = \varphi(p); \qquad s = 0, \quad p \in (0,\infty)^d$$

as in (1.3.9); recall the equations (4.3.4).

6.3.3. EXAMPLE. *General utility function; constant coefficients; European call option on the mth stock*, $Y = (P_m(T) - q)^+)$, for some $m = 1,\ldots d$.

In this case the formulae of (6.3.3), (6.3.4) become

$$(6.3.7) \qquad \hat{p} = \hat{U}(T, P_m(0); q)$$

and

$$(6.3.8) \qquad \hat{U}(s,p;q) \triangleq \begin{cases} pe^{-\hat{\nu}_m s}\Phi(\hat{\mu}_+(s,p;q)) \\ \quad - qe^{-rs}\Phi(\hat{\mu}_-(s,p;q)); & s > 0, \\ & 0 < p < \infty, \\ (p-q)^+; & s = 0, \\ & 0 < p < \infty, \end{cases}$$

$$(6.3.9) \qquad \hat{\mu}_\pm(s,p;q) \triangleq \frac{1}{\sigma\sqrt{s}}\left[\log\left(\frac{p}{q}\right) + \left(r - \hat{\nu}_m \pm \frac{\sigma^2}{2}\right)s\right], \qquad \sigma = \sigma_{mm}.$$

These are the analogues of the Black & Scholes formula of (1.3.13), (1.3.14).

For instance, in the case of an *Incomplete Market* with $K = \{\pi \in \mathbb{R}^d/\pi_{n+1} = \cdots = \pi_d = 0\}$ and thus $\tilde{K} = \{x \in \mathbb{R}^d/x_1 = \cdots = x_n = 0\}$, for some $n \in \{1,\ldots,d-1\}$ as in Example 4.1.2, we can distinguish the following two cases.

(i) $m = 1$, *i.e.*, m^{th} *stock available for investment*. Then $\hat{\nu}_m = 0$ in (6.3.2) (recall Remark 5.3.3 (i)), and the fair price $\hat{p}$ of (6.3.7)–(6.3.9) coincides with the classical Black-Scholes formula (1.3.13), (1.3.14):

$$(6.3.10) \qquad \hat{p} = h_{\text{up}}(K) = h_{\text{low}}(K) = U\big(T, P_1(0); q\big).$$

(ii) $n + 1 \leq m \leq d$, *i.e.*, m^{th} *stock unavailable for investment*. Then (5.3.30) gives $\hat{\nu}_m = r - b_m$, and we obtain

$$(6.3.11) \qquad h_{\text{low}}(K) = 0 < \hat{p} = \hat{U}\big(T, P_m(0); q\big) < \infty = h_{\text{up}}(K)$$

from Exercises 4.5.6 and 4.6.4. Notice that (6.3.8), (6.3.9) now take the form

$$(6.3.12) \qquad \hat{U}(s, p; q) = p e^{-(r-b_m)s} \Phi\big(\hat{\mu}_+(s, p; q)\big) - q e^{-rs} \Phi\big(\hat{\mu}_-(s, p; q)\big)$$

$$(6.3.13) \qquad \hat{\mu}_\pm(s, p; q) = \frac{1}{\sigma\sqrt{s}}\left[\log\left(\frac{p}{q}\right) + \left(b_m \pm \frac{\sigma^2}{2}\right)s\right], \qquad \text{for } s > 0,$$

respectively. Unlike the classical Black-Scholes formulae, these expressions now depend on the stock appreciation rate b_m.

In the case $d = m = 1$ with the *No-Short-Selling Constraint* $K = [0, \infty)$ as in Example 4.1.1, we have from (6.3.2) that $\hat{\nu} = (r-b)^+$, and thus from (6.3.7)–(6.3.9)

$$(6.3.14) \qquad h_{\text{low}}(K) = 0 < \hat{p} = \left\{\begin{array}{ll} U\big(T, P_1(0); q\big), & \text{if } r \leq b \\ \hat{U}\big(T, P_1(0); q\big), & \text{if } r > b \end{array}\right\}$$

$$< U\big(T, P_1(0); q\big) = h_{\text{up}}(K)$$

in the notation of (6.3.10), (6.3.12). We have used the results of Exercises 4.6.4 and 4.5.7.

6.3.4. EXAMPLE. *Path-dependent option* $Y = \max_{0 \leq t \leq T} P_1(t)$ in a model with constant coefficients, and general utility function.

In this case (1.3.29) gives

$$(6.3.15) \qquad \hat{p} = P_1(0) e^{-rT} \int_0^\infty f(T, \xi; \rho) e^{\sigma\xi}\, d\xi,$$

in the notation of (1.3.28) with $\rho = (r - \hat{\nu}_1)/\sigma - \frac{\sigma}{2}$.

CHAPTER 7

Transaction costs

7.1. The model

We shall consider in this chapter the market-model $\mathcal{M}$ of (0.1.1)–(0.1.2) with $d = 1$, namely, with prices-per-share governed by

$$(7.1.1) \qquad dB(t) = B(t)r(t)\,dt, \quad B(0) = 1$$

for the *bond* (bank account), and

$$(7.1.2) \qquad dP(t) = P(t)\big[b(t)\,dt + \sigma(t)\,dW(t)\big], \quad P(0) = p \in (0, \infty)$$

for the *stock*. Here $W = \{W(t), 0 \le t \le T\}$ is a one-dimensional standard Brownian motion on the finite horizon $[0, T]$, and the scalar processes $r(\cdot)$, $b(\cdot)$, $\sigma(\cdot)$ are assumed to be *bounded* uniformly in $(t, w) \in [0, T] \times \Omega$ and progressively measurable with respect to the augmentation $\mathbb{F}$ of the Brownian filtration in (0.1.3). Furthermore, it will be assumed that $\sigma(\cdot) > 0$ is also bounded away from zero, uniformly in $(t, w) \in [0, T] \times \Omega$.

Consider now a small investor, who faces *proportional transaction costs* each time he transfers funds from one asset to the other. More precisely, let us denote by x and y his initial "holdings" (amounts of money) in the bond and the stock, respectively; and by $L(t)$ (resp., $M(t)$) the cumulative amount of money that he has transferred, by time t, from bond to stock (respectively, from stock to bond).

7.1.1. DEFINITION. A *trading strategy* for this investor is a pair (L, M) of $\mathbb{F}$-adapted processes with increasing left-continuous paths and $L(0) = M(0) = 0$, $L(T) + M(T) < \infty$ a.s.

Corresponding to such a trading strategy, the processes of *holdings in bond* $X(\cdot) \equiv X^{x,L,M}(\cdot)$ *and in stock* $Y(\cdot) \equiv Y^{y,L,M}(\cdot)$ for this small investor, are then governed by the equations

$$(7.1.3) \qquad X(t) = x - (1 + \lambda)L(t) + (1 - \mu)M(t) + \int_0^t X(u)r(u)\,du,$$

$$(7.1.4) \quad Y(t) = y + L(t) - M(t) + \int_0^t Y(u)\big[b(u)\,du + \sigma(u)\,dW(u)\big], \; 0 \le t \le T.$$

Here λ and μ are two given numbers in the interval $(0, 1)$, which capture the effect of *proportional transaction costs*. As (7.1.3), (7.1.4) show, in order to transfer \$$\ell$ to the stock you need to withdraw \$$(1 + \lambda)\ell$ from the bank account; and if you withdraw \$$m$ from stock holdings, only \$$(1 - \mu)m$ are credited to the bank account. In either case, the bank account is debited with a transaction cost proportional to the amount transferred (and equal to \$$\lambda\ell$ in the former case, \$$\mu m$ in the latter).

Quite unlike anything that we have discussed in Chapters 0–6, the investor's wealth is here inherently *two-dimensional*, described as it is by the vector of processes $\left(X^{x,L,M}(\cdot), Y^{y,L,M}(\cdot)\right)$ with dynamics as in (7.1.3), (7.1.4). These equations can be written equivalently as

$$(7.1.5) \qquad d\left(\frac{X(t)}{B(t)}\right) = \frac{1}{B(t)}\left[(1-\mu)\,dM(t) - (1+\lambda)\,dL(s)\right], \quad X(0) = x$$

$$(7.1.6) \qquad d\left(\frac{Y(t)}{P(t)}\right) = \frac{1}{P(t)}\left[dL(t) - dM(t)\right], \quad Y(0) = y$$

in terms of "numbers-of-shares", rather than amounts, held at each instant in each of the assets.

In the absence of transaction costs (i.e., with $\lambda = \mu = 0$), when our wealth-process $X^{x,\pi,0}(\cdot)$ was one-dimensional, we introduced in (0.2.11) a positive martingale $Z_0(\cdot)$ with $Z_0(0) = 1$ and such that

$$(7.1.7) \qquad H_0(\cdot)X^{x,\pi,0}(\cdot) = Z_0(\cdot)\frac{X^{x,\pi,0}(\cdot)}{B(\cdot)} \quad \text{became a } \mathbb{P}\text{-local martingale;}$$

and we constrained the portfolio process $\pi(\cdot)$ in such a way that this local martingale was also a $\mathbb{P}$-*supermartingale* (recall (2.1.5)–(2.1.7) and the subsequent discussion). Thus, the process $H_0(\cdot) = Z_0(\cdot)/B(\cdot)$ played, in (7.1.7) and in the developments of Chapters 1–3, the role of a *state-price-density process*.

Now that we have to deal with an inherently two-dimensional wealth process $(X(\cdot), Y(\cdot)) = \left(X^{x,L,M}(\cdot), Y^{y,L,M}(\cdot)\right)$, what can we expect the analogue of the state-price-density process to be? Presumably, we shall need now a *pair of positive martingales* $\left(Z_0(\cdot), Z_1(\cdot)\right)$ with $Z_0(0) = 1$ and such that

$$(7.1.8) \quad Z_0(\cdot)\frac{X(\cdot)}{B(\cdot)} + Z_1(\cdot)\frac{Y(\cdot)}{P(\cdot)} = H_0(\cdot)X(\cdot) + H_1(\cdot)Y(\cdot) \text{ is a } \mathbb{P}\text{-supermartingale}$$

by analogy with (7.1.7); here now $H_0(\cdot) \triangleq (Z_0(\cdot)/B(\cdot))$, $H_1(\cdot) \triangleq (Z_1(\cdot)/P(\cdot))$ play the role of *state-price-density processes*, corresponding to the holdings in bond and stock, respectively.

To see if we can accomplish (7.1.8), and how, let us write the positive martingales $Z_0(\cdot)$, $Z_1(\cdot)$ in their exponential-integral representation

$$(7.1.9) \qquad \begin{cases} Z_i(t) = z_i \exp\left[-\int_0^t \theta_i(s)\,dW(s) - \frac{1}{2}\int_0^t \theta_i^2(s)\,ds\right], \quad 0 \le t \le T, \\ i = 0, 1 \quad \text{with} \quad z_0 = 1, \ p(1-\mu) \le z_1 = z \le p(1+\lambda) \end{cases}$$

for appropriate $\mathbb{F}$-progressively measurable processes $\theta_i: [0,T] \times \Omega \to \mathbb{R}$ which satisfy $\int_0^T \theta_i^2(t)\,dt < \infty$, a.s. $(i = 0, 1)$. From (7.1.5), (7.1.6), (7.1.9) and the product rule, we obtain then

$$(7.1.10) \quad Z_0(t)\frac{X(t)}{B(t)} + Z_1(t)\frac{Y(t)}{P(t)}$$

$$= x + \frac{yz}{p} - \int_{[0,t)} \frac{Z_0(s)}{B(s)}\big(1 + \lambda - R(s)\big)\, dL(s)$$

$$- \int_{[0,t)} \frac{Z_0(s)}{B(s)}\big(R(s) - (1 - \mu)\big)\, dM(s)$$

$$- \int_0^t \frac{Z_0(s)}{B(s)}\big[X(s)\theta_0(s) + R(s)Y(s)\theta_1(s)\big]\, dW(s),$$

$$0 \le t \le T,$$

where we have set

$$(7.1.11) \qquad R(t) \triangleq \frac{H_1(t)}{H_0(t)} = \frac{Z_1(t)}{P(t)}\frac{B(t)}{Z_0(t)}, \qquad 0 \le t \le T.$$

What does it take for (7.1.8) *to hold?* The stochastic integral in (7.1.10) is a local martingale, so we need both $\int_{[0,\cdot)}(Z_0(s)/B(s))\big(1 + \lambda - R(s)\big)\, dL(s)$ and $\int_{[0,\cdot)}(Z_0(s)/B(s))\big[R(s) - (1 - \mu)\big]\, dM(s)$ to be increasing; in other words, we need that the ratio-process $R(\cdot)$ of (7.1.11) satisfy a.s.

$$(7.1.12) \qquad 1 - \mu \le R(t) \le 1 + \lambda, \qquad \forall\, 0 \le t \le T.$$

This constraint on the ratio of the two state-price-density processes reflects the frictions induced, in the market $\mathcal{M}$ of (7.1.1)–(7.1.2), by the presence of the proportional transaction costs as in (7.1.3)–(7.1.4). Furthermore, if we introduce the probability measure

$$(7.1.13) \qquad \mathbb{P}_0(A) \triangleq \mathbb{E}\big[Z_0(T)1_A\big], \qquad A \in \mathcal{F}(T)$$

and the $\mathbb{P}_0$-Brownian motion

$$(7.1.14) \qquad W_0(t) \triangleq W(t) + \int_0^t \theta_0(s)\, ds, \qquad 0 \le t \le T$$

as in (0.2.12)–(0.2.13), we may equivalently re-write (7.1.10) in the form

$$(7.1.15) \quad \frac{X(t) + R(t)Y(t)}{B(t)} + \int_{[0,t)} \frac{1 + \lambda - R(s)}{B(s)}\, dL(s)$$

$$+ \int_{[0,t)} \frac{R(s) - (1 - \mu)}{B(s)}\, dM(s)$$

$$= x + \frac{yz}{p} - \int_0^t \frac{R(s)Y(s)}{B(s)}\big(\theta_1(s) - \theta_0(s)\big)\, dW_0(s),$$

$$0 \le t \le T$$

and require that

$$(7.1.16) \qquad \text{the process} \quad \frac{X(\cdot) + R(\cdot)Y(\cdot)}{B(\cdot)} \quad \text{be a } \mathbb{P}_0 - \text{supermartingale.}$$

We are now in a position to make some precise definitions.

7.1.2. DEFINITION. We denote by $\mathcal{D}$ the class of pairs (Z_0, Z_1) of positive martingales as in (7.1.9), for which the ratio-process $R(\cdot)$ of (7.1.11) satisfies the a.s. constraint (7.1.12).

7.1.3. REMARK. The process $R(\cdot)$ of (7.1.11) obeys the linear equation

$$(7.1.17) \quad dR(t) = R(t)\big[\sigma^2(t) + r(t) - b(t) - \big(\theta_0(t) - \theta_1(t)\big)\big(\sigma(t) - \theta_0(t)\big)\big]\,dt$$
$$+ R(t)\big(\theta_0(t) - \sigma(t) - \theta_1(t)\big)\,dW(t), \quad R(0) = \frac{z}{p}.$$

We obtain a special pair (Z_0^*, Z_1^*) in $\mathcal{D}$, by selecting an arbitrary $z^* \in \big[(1-\mu)p, (1+\lambda)p\big]$ and requiring that both the drift and the diffusion terms in (7.1.17) should vanish; that is, by selecting $\theta_0(\cdot)$, $\theta_1(\cdot)$ equal respectively to

$$(7.1.18) \qquad \theta_0^*(t) \triangleq \frac{b(t) - r(t)}{\sigma(t)}, \quad \theta_1^*(t) \triangleq \theta_0^*(t) - \sigma(t); \qquad 0 \le t \le T.$$

Then $R^*(\cdot) \equiv (z^*/p)$ is a constant in $[1-\mu, 1+\lambda]$; in fact, if $\lambda = \mu = 0$, the choices of (7.1.18) and $z^* = p$ lead to the *only* element (Z_0^*, Z_1^*) in $\mathcal{D}$.

We shall denote in the sequel by $\mathbb{P}_0^*$, W_0^* the counterparts of (7.1.13), (7.1.14) with $\theta_0(\cdot) \equiv \theta_0^*(\cdot)$ as in (7.1.18).

7.1.4. DEFINITION. We shall say that a given trading strategy (L, M) is *admissible for the pair of initial holdings* (x, y), if the requirement (7.1.16) holds for every pair (Z_0, Z_1) of positive martingales in the class

$$(7.1.19) \qquad \mathcal{D}_\infty \triangleq \left\{ (Z_0, Z_1) \in \mathcal{D} \ \Big/ \ \frac{Z_0(T)}{Z_0^*(T)} \text{ is essentially bounded} \right\}.$$

We note by $\mathcal{A}(x, y)$ the class of such admissible strategies.

Consider, for example, a strategy (L, M) that keeps the vector of holdings

$$(7.1.20) \qquad \big(X(t), Y(t)\big) = \big(X^{x,L,M}(t), Y^{y,L,M}(t)\big) \in \mathcal{S}, \qquad \forall\, 0 \le t \le T$$

a.s. inside the region

$$(7.1.21) \qquad \mathcal{S} \triangleq \big\{ (x, y) \in \mathbb{R}^2 \ / \ x + (1+\lambda)y \ge 0, \ x + (1-\mu)y \ge 0 \big\}.$$

Clearly, then: $X(\cdot) + R(\cdot)Y(\cdot) \ge 0$, a.s.; the process of (7.1.15) is a nonnegative $\mathbb{P}^0$-local martingale; and thus (7.1.16) holds, for every $(Z_0, Z_1) \in \mathcal{D}$. The admissibility condition of Definition 7.1.4 is actually a weaker requirement, since it postulates the validity of (7.1.16) only for (Z_0, Z_1) in the class $\mathcal{D}_\infty$ of (7.1.19).

7.1.5. REMARK. For obvious reasons, the set $\mathcal{S}$ in (7.1.21) is called the *solvency region*. Indeed, suppose that $(x, y) \in \mathcal{S}$; if $x \ge 0$, $y \ge 0$ you are clearly not in debt; if $x < 0$, you can sell stock to cover your negative position in the bank, receive $(1 - \mu)y$, and end up with $x + (1 - \mu)y \ge 0$ in the account; if $y < 0$, you can cover your short position in the stock by transferring $(1 + \lambda)(-y)$ from the bank account, which leaves the account with $x - (1 + \lambda)(-y) \ge 0$.

7.2. Contingent claims

Just as we had to extend our notion of "wealth-process", in the presence of proportional transaction costs, we also have to revise what we understand by "contingent claim". Again, this notion has to accommodate the holdings in both bond and stock; that is, it has to become two-dimensional.

7.2.1. DEFINITION. A *contingent claim* (Γ_0, Γ_1) is a pair of $\mathcal{F}(T)$-measurable random variables. We say that a trading strategy $(L, M) \in \mathcal{A}(x, y)$ *hedges the contingent claim* (B_0, B_1) *starting with initial holdings* x, y if

$$(7.2.1) \qquad X^{x,L,M}(T) + (1-\mu)Y^{y,L,M}(T) \geq \Gamma_0 + (1-\mu)\Gamma_1$$

$$(7.2.2) \qquad X^{x,L,M}(T) + (1+\lambda)Y^{y,L,M}(T) \geq \Gamma_0 + (1+\lambda)\Gamma_1$$

holds a.s. We shall denote by $\mathcal{H}(\Gamma_0, \Gamma_1; x, y)$ the class of all such (admissible) trading strategies.

The random variable Γ_0 (respectively, Γ_1) has to be understood as a "target position" in the bank account (respectively, the stock) — holdings, at the terminal time $t = T$. For example, in the case of a *European call-option* (Example 1.3.2) with exercise price $q \geq 0$,

$$(7.2.3) \qquad \Gamma_0 = -q1_{\{P(T)>q\}}, \quad \Gamma_1 = P(T)1_{\{P(T)>q\}};$$

and in the case of a *European put-option* (Example 1.3.3),

$$(7.2.4) \qquad \Gamma_0 = q1_{\{P(T)<q\}}, \quad \Gamma_1 = -P(T)1_{\{P(T)<q\}}.$$

Hedging, in the sense of (7.2.1) and (7.2.2), means that *one is able to cover these positions at time $t = T$*; it is thus the two-dimensional analogue of the requirement (0.4.1).

Indeed, (7.2.1)–(7.2.2) are equivalent to the statement that the random vector $\left(X^{x,L,M}(T) - \Gamma_0, Y^{y,L,M}(T) - \Gamma_1\right)$ belongs to the solvency region $\mathcal{S}$ of (7.1.21), with probability one; in other words, it requires that "one should be solvent at the terminal time $t = T$, after the debts (positions) Γ_0, Γ_1 have been covered".

Suppose now that we fix the initial holdings y in the stock, and ask the following question, by analogy with (0.4.2): what is the smallest holding x in the bank-account at $t = 0$, that allows us to hedge the contingent claim in the sense of Definition 7.2.1? In other words, we would like to compute the *upper hedging price*

$$(7.2.5) \qquad h_{\text{up}}(\Gamma_0, \Gamma_1; y) \triangleq \inf\left\{x \in \mathbb{R} \,/\, \exists (L, M) \in \mathcal{H}(\Gamma_0, \Gamma_1; x, y)\right\}$$

of the Contingent Claim (Γ_0, Γ_1). We shall address this question in the next section.

7.3. Hedging

Let us characterize now the upper hedging price of (7.2.5) for a contingent claim (Γ_0, Γ_1), in the spirit of a suitable optimization problem similar to that of Section 4.4; we shall need the conditions

$$(7.3.1) \qquad \Gamma_0 + (1+\lambda)\Gamma_1 \geq -K \quad \text{and} \quad \Gamma_0 + (1-\mu)\Gamma_1 \geq -K, \text{ a.s.}$$

for some $0 \leq K < \infty$, as well as

$$(7.3.2) \qquad \mathbb{E}_0^*(\Gamma_0^2 + \Gamma_1^2) < \infty.$$

Here, $\mathbb{E}_0^*$ denotes expectation under the probability measure $\mathbb{P}_0^*$ of Remark 7.1.3; and it is not hard to verify both these conditions (7.3.1), (7.3.2) for the European call- and put-options of (7.2.3) and (7.2.4), respectively.

Here is the fundamental result of this section.

7.3.1. THEOREM. *Let* (Γ_0, Γ_1) *be a contingent claim as in* Definition 7.2.1, *and suppose that the conditions* (7.3.1), (7.3.2) *are satisfied. Then the upper hedging price of* (7.2.5) *is given by*

$$(7.3.3) \qquad h_{\mathrm{up}}(\Gamma_0, \Gamma_1; y) = \sup_{\mathcal{D}} \mathbb{E}\left[\frac{Z_0(T)}{B(T)} \cdot \Gamma_0 + \frac{Z_1(T)}{P(T)} \cdot \Gamma_1 - \frac{y}{p} z\right]$$

$$= \sup_{\mathcal{D}_\infty} \mathbb{E}\left[\frac{Z_0(T)}{B(T)}(\Gamma_0 + R(T)\Gamma_1) - \frac{y}{p} Z_1(T)\right].$$

The reader should not fail to notice that (7.3.3) is a direct generalization of the Black-Scholes formula (1.2.4); indeed, with $\lambda = \mu = 0$ we have $\mathcal{D} = \{(Z_0^*, Z_1^*)\}$ as in Remark 7.1.3, and for $\Gamma_1 \equiv 0$, $y = 0$ the formula (7.3.3) becomes

$$h_{\mathrm{up}}(\Gamma_0, 0; 0) = \mathbb{E}\left[Z_0^*(T) \cdot \gamma(T)\Gamma_0\right] = \mathbb{E}_0^*[\gamma(T)\Gamma_0], \text{ as in (1.2.4)}.$$

The formula (7.3.3) also brings out the interpretation of the processes $H_0(\cdot) = (Z_0(\cdot)/B(\cdot))$, $H_1(\cdot) = (Z_1(\cdot)/P(\cdot))$ as state-price-densities for the holdings in bond and stock, respectively, that we mentioned already in the discussion of (7.1.8).

Clearly, (7.3.3) will follow as soon as we have established the string of inequalities

$$(7.3.4) \qquad h_{\mathrm{up}}(\Gamma_0, \Gamma_1; y) \geq \sup_{\mathcal{D}_\infty} \mathbb{E}\left[\frac{Z_0(T)}{B(T)}(\Gamma_0 + R(T)\Gamma_1) - \frac{y}{p} Z_1(T)\right]$$

$$\geq \sup_{\mathcal{D}} \mathbb{E}\left[\frac{Z_0(T)}{B(T)}(\Gamma_0 + R(T)\Gamma_1) - \frac{y}{p} Z_1(T)\right]$$

$$\geq h_{\mathrm{up}}(\Gamma_0, \Gamma_1; y).$$

PROOF OF THE FIRST INEQUALITY (7.3.4). This is obvious, if $h_{\mathrm{up}} = \infty$; if not, let x be an arbitrary member in the set of (7.2.5) and (Z_0, Z_1) an arbitrary member of $\mathcal{D}_\infty$. From the Definitions 7.1.4, 7.2.1 and Remark 7.3.2 below, we have

$$x + \frac{y}{p}\mathbb{E}\, Z_1(T) = x + \frac{y}{p} z \geq \mathbb{E}_0\left[\frac{X(T) + R(T)Y(T)}{B(T)}\right]$$

$$\geq \mathbb{E}_0\left(\frac{\Gamma_0 + R(T)\Gamma_1}{B(T)}\right)$$

$$= \mathbb{E}\left[\frac{Z_0(T)}{B(T)}(\Gamma_0 + R(T)\Gamma_1)\right].$$

We obtain

$$x \geq \sup_{\mathcal{D}_\infty} \mathbb{E}\left[\frac{Z_0(T)}{B(T)}(\Gamma_0 + R(T)\Gamma_1) - \frac{y}{p} Z_1(T)\right],$$

and the inequality follows from the arbitrariness of x. □

7.3.2. REMARK. If $x + (1-\mu)y \geq \gamma_0 + (1-\mu)\gamma_1$ and $x + (1+\lambda)y \geq \gamma_0 + (1+\lambda)\gamma_1$ then $x + ry \geq \gamma_0 + r\gamma_1$ for every $1 - \mu \leq r \leq 1 + \lambda$.

PROOF OF THE SECOND INEQUALITY (7.3.4), UNDER (7.3.1). To simplify notation, we take $y = 0$. For an arbitrary $(Z_0, Z_1) \in \mathcal{D}$, introduce the stopping times $\tau_n \triangleq \inf\{t \in [0, T] \,/\, (Z_0(t)/Z_0^*(t)) \geq n\} \wedge T$, the processes

$$(7.3.5) \qquad \theta_i^{(n)}(t) \triangleq \left\{\begin{array}{ll} \theta_i(t); & 0 \leq t < \tau_n \\ \theta_i^*(t); & \tau_n \leq t \leq T \end{array}\right\},$$

and the positive martingales

$$(7.3.6) \quad Z_i^{(n)}(t) \triangleq Z_i(0) \exp\left\{ -\int_0^t \theta_i^{(n)}(s)\,dW(s) - \frac{1}{2}\int_0^t \left(\theta_i^{(n)}(s)\right)^2 ds \right\},$$

$$0 \le t \le T$$

(for $i = 0, 1$). For every $n \in \mathbb{N}$, the ratio process

$$(7.3.7) \qquad R^{(n)}(\cdot) \triangleq \frac{Z_1^{(n)}(\cdot)}{P(\cdot)} \frac{B(\cdot)}{Z_0^{(n)}(\cdot)} = R(\cdot \wedge \tau_n)$$

takes values in $[1 - \mu, 1 + \lambda]$ from Remark 7.1.3, and $(Z_0^{(n)}(\cdot)/Z_0^*(\cdot)) \le n$ a.s. , so that $(Z_0^{(n)}, Z_1^{(n)}) \in \mathcal{D}_\infty$. With k denoting an upper bound on $(K/B(T))$, we obtain then from condition (7.3.1) and Fatou's lemma

$$(7.3.8) \quad \mathbb{E}\left[\frac{Z_0(T)}{B(T)}(\Gamma_0 + R(T)\Gamma_1)\right] + k = \left[Z_0(T)\left\{\frac{\Gamma_0 + R(T)\Gamma_1}{B(T)} + k\right\}\right]$$

$$= \mathbb{E}\left[\lim_n Z_0^{(n)}(T)\left\{\frac{\Gamma_0 + R^{(n)}(T)\Gamma_1}{B(T)} + k\right\}\right]$$

$$\le \varliminf_n \mathbb{E}\left[\frac{Z_0^{(n)}(T)}{B(T)}(\Gamma_0 + R^{(n)}(T)\Gamma_1)\right] + k$$

which establishes the inequality. With $\mathbb{E}_0$, $\mathbb{E}_0^{(n)}$ denoting expectations with respect to the probability measures $\mathbb{P}_0$ of (7.1.13) and $\mathbb{P}_0^{(n)}(\cdot) \triangleq \mathbb{E}\left[Z_0^{(n)}(T)1.\right]$, respectively, (7.3.8) also gives

$$(7.3.9) \qquad \mathbb{E}_0\left(\frac{\Gamma_0 + R(T)\Gamma_1}{B(T)}\right) \le \varliminf_n \mathbb{E}_0^{(n)}\left(\frac{\Gamma_0 + R^{(n)}(T)\Gamma_1}{B(T)}\right).$$

$$\square$$

PROOF OF THE LAST INEQUALITY (7.3.4) UNDER (7.3.1), (7.3.2). In order to simplify notation somewhat, we shall take $p = 1$, $r(\cdot) \equiv 0$ (so $B(\cdot) \equiv 1$) without any loss of generality. For *an arbitrary* $b < h(\Gamma_0, \Gamma_1; y)$ consider the sets

$$(7.3.10) \qquad C \triangleq \left\{(V_0, V_1) \in (\mathbb{L}_2^*)^2 \, / \, \exists (L, M) \in \mathcal{H}(V_0, V_1; 0, 0)\right\}$$

$$(7.3.11) \qquad D \triangleq \left\{(\Gamma_0 - b, \Gamma_1 - yP(T))\right\}$$

with the notation $\mathbb{L}_2^* = \mathbb{L}_2(\Omega, \mathcal{F}(T), \mathbb{P}_0^*)$. We show below, in Exercises 7.3.3 and 7.3.4, that

$$(7.3.12) \qquad C \text{ is a convex cone in } (\mathbb{L}_2^*)^2, \text{ which contains the origin } (0, 0)$$

$$(7.3.13) \qquad\qquad\qquad C \cap D = \varnothing.$$

It is also true, though much harder to show (cf. Appendix A in Cvitanić & Karatzas (1996) for the lengthy proof), that

$$(7.3.14) \qquad\qquad\qquad C \text{ is closed in } (\mathbb{L}_2^*)^2.$$

From (7.3.12)–(7.3.14) and the Hahn-Banach theorem, there exists a pair of random variables $(\rho_0^*, \rho_1^*) \in (\mathbb{L}_2^*)^2$, $(\rho_0^*, \rho_1^*) \neq (0, 0)$ such that

$$(7.3.15) \qquad \mathbb{E}_0^*[\rho_0^* V_0 + \rho_1^* V_1] = \mathbb{E}[\rho_0 V_0 + \rho_1 V_1] \leq 0, \quad \forall\, (V_0, V_1) \in C$$

$$(7.3.16) \qquad \mathbb{E}_0^*\left[\rho_0^*(\Gamma_0 - b) + \rho_1^*\left(\Gamma_1 - y P(T)\right)\right]$$
$$= \mathbb{E}\left[\rho_0(\Gamma_0 - b) + \rho_1\left(\Gamma_1 - y P(T)\right)\right] \geq 0,$$

where we have set $\rho_i \triangleq \rho_i^* Z_0^*(T)$, $i = 0, 1$. Some properties of the pair (ρ_0, ρ_1) are derived in Lemma 7.3.5 below; in particular from (7.3.20) we may take $\mathbb{E}(\rho_0) = 1$, so that (7.3.16) implies

$$(7.3.17) \qquad \mathbb{E}\left[\rho_0 \Gamma_0 + \rho_1\left(\Gamma_1 - y P(T)\right)\right] \geq b.$$

Now for *an arbitrary pair* $(Z_0, Z_1) \in \mathcal{D}$ and $0 < \varepsilon < 1$, consider the positive martingales

$$(7.3.18) \qquad \begin{aligned} Z_0^{(\varepsilon)}(t) &\triangleq \varepsilon Z_0(t) + (1 - \varepsilon)\mathbb{E}\left[\rho_0 \mid \mathcal{F}(t)\right], \\ Z_1^{(\varepsilon)}(t) &\triangleq \varepsilon Z_1(t) + (1 - \varepsilon)\mathbb{E}\left[\rho_1 P(T) \mid \mathcal{F}(t)\right] \end{aligned}$$

on $[0, T]$ with $Z_0^{(\varepsilon)}(0) = 1$. Multiply the inequality (7.3.19) of Lemma 7.3.5 by $1 - \varepsilon$, and the inequality (consequence of (7.1.12))

$$(1 - \mu) Z_0(t) \leq \frac{Z_1(t)}{P(t)} \leq (1 + \lambda) Z_0(t), \qquad 0 \leq t \leq T$$

by ε, and add the resulting inequalities up, to conclude that $(Z_0^{(\varepsilon)}, Z_1^{(\varepsilon)}) \in \mathcal{D}$. Therefore, from (7.3.17):

$$\begin{aligned} \sup_{\mathcal{D}} \mathbb{E}\left[Z_0(T)\Gamma_0 + Z_1(T)\left(\frac{\Gamma_1}{P(T)} - y\right)\right] &\geq \mathbb{E}\left[Z_0^{(\varepsilon)}(T)\Gamma_0 + Z_1^{(\varepsilon)}(T)\left(\frac{\Gamma_1}{P(T)} - y\right)\right] \\ &= (1 - \varepsilon) \cdot \mathbb{E}\left[\rho_0 \Gamma_0 + \rho_1\left(\Gamma_1 - y P(T)\right)\right] \\ &\quad + \varepsilon \cdot \mathbb{E}\left[Z_0(T)\Gamma_0 + Z_1(T)\left(\frac{\Gamma_1}{P(T)} - y\right)\right] \\ &\geq b(1 - \varepsilon) + \varepsilon \cdot \mathbb{E}\left[Z_0(T)\Gamma_0 + Z_1(T)\left(\frac{\Gamma_1}{P(T)} - y\right)\right]. \end{aligned}$$

Letting $\varepsilon \downarrow 0$ and then $b \uparrow h(\Gamma_0, \Gamma_1; y)$, the last inequality of (7.3.4) follows. $\qquad \square$

7.3.3. EXERCISE. Establish the claim of (7.3.9).

(*Hint*: Let $(U_i, V_i) \in C$ and suppose $(L_i, M_i) \in \mathcal{H}(U_i, V_i; 0, 0)$, $i = 1, 2$; for $\zeta \geq 0$, $\eta \geq 0$ check that the pair $(U, V) = (\zeta U_1 + \eta U_2, \zeta V_1 + \eta V_2)$ is hedged by $(L, M) = (\zeta L_1 + \eta L_2, \zeta M_1 + \eta M_2) \in \mathcal{H}(U, V; 0, 0)$. The convexity of C follows by taking $0 < \eta < 1$, $\zeta = 1 - \eta$; it is seen easily that $(0, 0) \in C$, and taking $\eta > 0$, $\zeta = 0$ shows that C is a cone.)

7.3.4. EXERCISE. Establish the claim of (7.3.10).

(*Hint*: Suppose that the contingent claim $\left(\Gamma_0 - b, \Gamma_1 - y P(T)\right)$ belongs to C, i.e. that it can be hedged by some trading strategy $(L, M) \in \mathcal{H}(\Gamma_0 - b, \Gamma_1 - y P(T); 0, 0)$; show that this then implies $(L, M) \in \mathcal{H}(\Gamma_0, \Gamma_1; b, y)$, contradicting the assumption $b < h_{\text{up}}(\Gamma_0, \Gamma_1; y)$ and the definition (7.2.5).)

7.3.5. LEMMA. *For the random variables ρ_0, ρ_1 of (7.3.15) and (7.3.16), we have* a.s.

$$(7.3.19) \quad (1-\mu)\mathbb{E}\left[\rho_0 \mid \mathcal{F}(t)\right] \leq \frac{\mathbb{E}\left[\rho_1 P(T)|\mathcal{F}(t)\right]}{P(t)} \leq (1+\lambda)\mathbb{E}\left[\rho_0 \mid \mathcal{F}(t)\right],$$

$$0 \leq t \leq T$$

as well as

$$(7.3.20) \qquad \rho_1 \geq 0, \quad \rho_2 \geq 0, \quad \text{and} \quad \mathbb{E}\left(\rho_0\right) > 0, \quad \mathbb{E}\left(\rho_1 P(T)\right) > 0.$$

PROOF. For fixed $t \in [0,T]$ and a bounded, $\mathcal{F}(t)$-measurable $\xi \colon \Omega \to [0,\infty)$, consider the "buy-and-hold" strategy (L^ξ, M^ξ) of starting with initial holdings $(0,0)$ and "buying ξ shares of stock at time $s = t$, otherwise doing nothing"; more precisely, $M^\xi(s) \equiv 0$, $L^\xi(s) = \xi P(t)1_{(t,T]}(s)$ and

$$X^\xi(s) \triangleq X^{0,L^\xi,M^\xi}(s) = -\xi(1+\lambda)P(t)1_{(t,T]}(s),$$
$$Y^\xi(s) \triangleq Y^{0,L^\xi,M^\xi}(s) = \xi P(s)1_{(t,T]}(s)$$

for $0 \leq s \leq T$. It is not hard to see that $X^\xi(\cdot) + R(\cdot)Y^\xi(\cdot)$ is a $\mathbb{P}_0$-supermartingale for every $(Z_0, Z_1) \in \mathcal{D}_\infty$, so that $(L^\xi, M^\xi) \in \mathcal{A}(0,0)$ and $\left(X^\xi(T), Y^\xi(T)\right)$ belongs to the set C of (7.3.7).

Consequently, we obtain from (7.3.15)

$$0 \geq \mathbb{E}\left[\rho_0 X^\xi(T) + \rho_1 Y^\xi(T)\right] = \mathbb{E}\left[\xi\left(\rho_1 P(T) - (1+\lambda)\rho_0 P(t)\right)\right]$$
$$= \mathbb{E}\left[\xi\left(\mathbb{E}\left(\rho_1 P(T) \mid \mathcal{F}(t)\right) - (1+\lambda)P(t)\cdot\mathbb{E}\left(\rho_0 \mid \mathcal{F}(t)\right)\right)\right],$$

and the arbitrariness of ξ leads to the a.s. inequality on the right-hand side of (7.3.19); a dual argument, based on selling rather than buying at time t, leads to the left-hand inequality. Thus (7.3.19) follows, first for fixed $t \in [0,T]$, and then for all $0 \leq t \leq T$ simultaneously, thanks to the a.s. continuity of the processes involved.

Reading (7.3.19) with $t = T$ yields $(1-\mu)\rho_0 \leq \rho_1 \leq (1+\lambda)\rho_0$ whence also $\rho_0 \geq 0$, $\rho_1 \geq 0$ almost surely; reading it with $t = 0$ we obtain $(1-\mu)\mathbb{E}\,\rho_0 \leq \mathbb{E}\left[\rho_1 P(T)\right] \leq (1+\lambda)\mathbb{E}\,\rho_0$ and since $(\rho_0, \rho_1) \neq (0,0)$ we deduce $\mathbb{E}\left(\rho_0\right) > 0$, $\mathbb{E}\left[\rho_1 P(T)\right] > 0$. □

7.3.6. EXAMPLE. Consider the *European call-option* of (7.2.3) for which, if at time $t = T$ the stock price $P(T)$ exceeds the exercise price $q \geq 0$, the seller has to deliver one share of the stock (i.e., $\Gamma_1 = P(T)1_{\{P(T)>q\}}$) but can cover the position in the bank account $\Gamma_0 = -q1_{\{P(T)>q\}}$ from the buyer's payment of the exercise price. With $y = 0$, the formula (7.3.3) gives then

$$(7.3.21) \quad h(\Gamma_0,\Gamma_1) \equiv h(\Gamma_0,\Gamma_1;0) = \sup_{\mathcal{D}} \mathbb{E}\left[Z_1(T)1_{\{P(T)>q\}} - q\frac{Z_0(T)}{B(T)}1_{\{P(T)>q\}}\right].$$

Clearly, $h(\Gamma_0,\Gamma_1) \leq \sup_{\mathcal{D}}\mathbb{E}\,Z_1(T) = \sup_{\mathcal{D}} Z_1(0) \leq p(1+\lambda)$; this number represents the cost of a "buy-and-hold" strategy which acquires one share of the stock at time $t = 0$ (at price $p(1+\lambda)$, due to the transaction cost) and holds on to it until the end of the horizon $t = T$. It was conjectured by Davis & Clark (1994), and proved by Soner, Shreve & Cvitanić (1995), that this is actually the cheapest way to hedge the European call-option, in the sense

$$(7.3.22) \qquad\qquad\qquad h(\Gamma_0,\Gamma_1) = p(1+\lambda).$$

It would be nice to compute the upper hedging prices of other interesting contingent claims, as in Section 1.2 for example, using the representation (7.3.3).

7.3.7. REMARK. For a contingent claim (Γ_0, Γ_1) that satisfies the conditions (7.3.1)–(7.3.2), the methods of Appendix A in Cvitanić & Karatzas (1996) show that *the infimum of* (7.2.5) *is actually attained*: for every given $y \in \mathbb{R}$, and with $h \equiv h_{\mathrm{up}}(\Gamma_0, \Gamma_1; y)$, there exists a pair (L, M) in the class $\mathcal{H}(\Gamma_0, \Gamma_1; h, y)$ of Definition 7.2.1.

7.4. Optimization

Let us discuss now, in the context of the market-model with transaction costs (7.1.1)–(7.1.4), a utility maximization problem for an agent with utility $U(X(T+))$ from his *terminal wealth*

$$(7.4.1) \qquad X(T+) \triangleq X(T) + f(Y(T)) \quad \text{where} \quad f(x) \triangleq \begin{cases} (1+\lambda)x; & x \le 0 \\ (1-\mu)x; & x > 0 \end{cases}.$$

In other words, at the end of the horizon $[0, T]$ the agent liquidates his position in the stock, his bank-account is debited by the appropriate transaction costs, and all his money is then collected in the bank-account.

7.4.1. PROBLEM. For a given utility function $U: (0, \infty) \to \mathbb{R}$ as in Definition 2.1.2, and a given initial position $y \ge 0$ in the stock, find a trading strategy $(\hat{L}, \hat{M})$ in the class

$$(7.4.2) \quad \mathcal{A}^+(x, y) \triangleq \{(L, M) \in \mathcal{A}(x, y) \ / \ X^{x, L, M}(T) + f(Y^{y, L, M}(T)) \ge 0, \ \text{a.s.}\}$$
$$= \{(L, M) \in \mathcal{A}(x, y) \ / \ (X^{x, L, M}(T), Y^{y, L, M}(T)) \in \mathcal{S}, \ \text{a.s.}\}$$

that attains the supremum

$$(7.4.3) \quad V(x; y) \triangleq \sup_{(L, M) \in \mathcal{A}^+(x, y)} \mathbb{E}\, U(X^{x, L, M}(T) + f(Y^{y, L, M}(T))),$$
$$0 < x < \infty.$$

It can be shown (cf. Appendix B in Cvitanić & Karatzas (1996)) that such an optimal trading strategy exists: namely,

$$(7.4.4) \qquad V(x; y) = \mathbb{E}\, U(X^{x, \hat{L}, \hat{M}}(T) + f(Y^{y, \hat{L}, \hat{M}}(T))) < \infty, \qquad \forall\, 0 < x < \infty$$

for some $(\hat{L}, \hat{M}) \in \mathcal{A}^+(x, y)$. We shall try here to describe the properties of this strategy using Theorem 7.3.1 and the *dual problem*

$$(7.4.5) \qquad \tilde{V}(\zeta; y) \triangleq \inf_{(Z_0, Z_1) \in \mathcal{D}} \mathbb{E}\left[\tilde{U}\left(\zeta \frac{Z_0(T)}{B(T)} \right) + \frac{y\zeta}{p} Z_1(T) \right], \qquad 0 < \zeta < \infty$$

by analogy with our results in Chapters 2 and 5.

To simplify matters, we shall impose here the following conditions.

7.4.2. ASSUMPTION. There exists a pair $(\hat{Z}_0, \hat{Z}_1) \in \mathcal{D}$ that attains the infimum in (7.4.5) and satisfies

$$(7.4.6) \qquad \mathbb{E}\left[\frac{\hat{Z}_0(T)}{B(T)} I\left(\zeta \frac{Z_0^*(T)}{B(T)} \right) \right] < \infty, \quad \mathbb{E}\, \tilde{U}\left(\zeta \frac{Z_0^*(T)}{B(T)} \right) < \infty$$

for all $0 < \zeta < \infty$ simultaneously.

OPEN QUESTION. The attainability of the infimum in (7.4.5) is a big assumption; find some general sufficient conditions that guarantee it (but also see Examples 7.4.11–7.4.12 below).

7.4.3. REMARK. The assumption that the minimization in (7.4.5) can be done for all $0 < \zeta < \infty$ simultaneously, is made only for simplicity; duality methods, analogous to those developed in Section 5.4, can be employed to remove it. Note, however, that this assumption *is* satisfied in the case of logarithmic or power-type utility functions:

$$(7.4.7) \qquad U(x) = \log x, \quad \text{or} \quad U(x) = \frac{x^\alpha}{\alpha} \quad \text{for some} \quad 0 < \alpha < 1.$$

7.4.4. REMARK. The second inequality in (7.4.6) implies

$$\tilde{V}(\zeta; y) \leq \mathbb{E}\, \tilde{U}\left(\zeta \frac{Z_0^*(T)}{B(T)}\right) + y\zeta(1 + \lambda) < \infty, \qquad \forall\, 0 < \zeta < \infty;$$

it is satisfied by the utility functions of (7.4.7), as well as under the condition (2.2.22) on $U(\cdot)$; recal Exercise 5.4.3.

7.4.5. LEMMA. *Suppose that the utility function $U(\cdot)$ satisfies*

$$(7.4.8) \qquad xU'(x) \leq \gamma + \delta U(x), \qquad \forall\, 0 < x < \infty$$

for some $\gamma \geq 0$ and $0 \leq \delta < 1$, and that the Assumption 7.4.2 *holds. Then we have*

$$(7.4.9) \quad \mathbb{E}\left[\frac{Z_0(T)}{B(T)} I\left(\zeta \frac{\hat{Z}_0(T)}{B(T)}\right) - \frac{y}{p} Z_1(T)\right]$$

$$\leq \mathbb{E}\left[\frac{\hat{Z}_0(T)}{B(T)} I\left(\zeta \frac{\hat{Z}_0(T)}{B(T)}\right) - \frac{y}{p} \hat{Z}_1(T)\right] < \infty$$

for all $0 < \zeta < \infty$, $(Z_0, Z_1) \in \mathcal{D}$.

We defer the proof of this result to the end of the section, but remark that condition (7.4.8) is satisfied by the utility functions of (7.4.7).

Let us consider now, by direct analogy with (2.2.10), the continuous and strictly decreasing function

$$\mathcal{X}(\zeta) \triangleq \mathbb{E}\left[\frac{\hat{Z}_0(T)}{B(T)} I\left(\zeta \frac{\hat{Z}_0(T)}{B(T)}\right)\right], \qquad 0 < \zeta < \infty$$

with $\mathcal{X}(0+) = \infty$ and $\mathcal{X}(\infty) = 0$. For any given $x > 0$, $y \geq 0$ there exists a unique number $\hat{\zeta} \equiv \hat{\zeta}(x; y, U)$ in $(0, \infty)$ that satisfies $\mathcal{X}(\hat{\zeta}) = x + \frac{y}{p} \mathbb{E}\, \hat{Z}_1(T)$. Therefore, letting

$$(7.4.10) \qquad \hat{\Gamma}_0 \triangleq I\left(\hat{\zeta} \frac{\hat{Z}_0(T)}{B(T)}\right), \qquad \hat{\Gamma}_1 \triangleq 0$$

we obtain

$$(7.4.11) \quad \sup_{(Z_0, Z_1) \in \mathcal{D}} \mathbb{E}\left[Z_0(T) \frac{\hat{\Gamma}_0}{B(T)} + Z_1(T)\left(\frac{\hat{\Gamma}_1}{P(T)} - \frac{y}{p}\right)\right]$$

$$= \mathbb{E}\left[\hat{Z}_0(T) \frac{\hat{\Gamma}_0}{B(T)} + \hat{Z}_1(T)\left(\frac{\hat{\Gamma}_1}{P(T)} - \frac{y}{p}\right)\right] = x$$

from (7.4.9); and if, in addition, we have

(7.4.12) $\mathbb{E}_0^*(\hat{\Gamma}_0^2) < \infty,$

then Theorem 7.3.1 and Remark 7.3.7 guarantee $h(\hat{\Gamma}_0, \hat{\Gamma}_1; y) = x$, and that there exists a pair $(\hat{L}, \hat{M}) \in \mathcal{A}(x, y)$ with

(7.4.13) $\hat{X}(T) + (1+\lambda)\hat{Y}(T) \geq \hat{\Gamma}_0, \quad \hat{X}(T) + (1-\mu)\hat{Y}(T) \geq \hat{\Gamma}_0,$ a.s.

for $\hat{X}(\cdot) \equiv X^{x,\hat{L},\hat{M}}(\cdot)$, $\hat{Y}(\cdot) \equiv Y^{y,\hat{L},\hat{M}}(\cdot)$. In particular, (7.4.13) implies that the pair $(\hat{L}, \hat{M})$ belongs to the class $\mathcal{A}^+(x, y)$ of (7.4.2).

   7.4.6. THEOREM. *Under the* Assumption 7.4.2 *and the conditions* (7.4.8) *and* (7.4.12), *the above pair* $(\hat{L}, \hat{M}) \in \mathcal{A}^+(x, y)$ *is optimal for* Problem 7.4.1, *that is, attains the supremum in* (7.4.3). *We also have*

(7.4.14) $\hat{X}(T+) \equiv \hat{X}(T) + f(\hat{Y}(T)) = \hat{\Gamma}_0,$

(7.4.15) $\displaystyle\int_{[0,T)} \left[(1+\lambda) - \hat{R}(t)\right] d\hat{L}(t) = 0, \quad \int_{[0,T)} \left[\hat{R}(t) - (1-\mu)\right] d\hat{M}(t) = 0,$

(7.4.16) $\dfrac{\hat{X}(t) + \hat{R}(t)\hat{Y}(t)}{B(t)} = \hat{\mathbb{E}}_0\left(\dfrac{\hat{\Gamma}_0}{B(T)} \,\bigg|\, \mathcal{F}(t)\right), \qquad 0 \leq t \leq T,$

almost surely, as well as

(7.4.17) $V(x; y) = \tilde{V}(\hat{\zeta}; y) + x\hat{\zeta} = \displaystyle\inf_{0<\zeta<\infty}\left[\tilde{V}(\zeta; y) + x\zeta\right].$

We have set $\hat{R}(\cdot) \equiv (\hat{Z}_1(\cdot)/\hat{Z}_0(\cdot))(B(\cdot)/P(\cdot))$, *as in* (7.1.11).

   7.4.7. REMARK. In conjunction with (7.1.12), the equalities of (7.4.15) imply that the increasing processes $\hat{L}(\cdot)$, $\hat{M}(\cdot)$ are *flat* away from the sets $\{t \in [0,T] \,/\, \hat{R}(t) = 1+\lambda\}$ and $\{t \in [0,T] \,/\, \hat{R}(t) = 1-\mu\}$, respectively, a.s.

   PROOF OF (7.4.14). From (7.4.13) and Remark 7.3.2, it develops that

(7.4.18) $\hat{X}(T) + \hat{R}(T)\hat{Y}(T) \geq \hat{\Gamma}_0, \quad \hat{X}(T) + f(\hat{Y}(T)) \geq \hat{\Gamma}_0,$ a.s.

On the other hand, we know from Definition 7.1.4 that, in the notation $\hat{R}^{(n)}(\cdot) \triangleq \hat{Z}_1^{(n)}(\cdot)B(\cdot)/\hat{Z}_0^{(n)}(\cdot)P(\cdot)$ of (7.3.5)–(7.3.7), the process $(\hat{X}(\cdot) + \hat{R}^{(n)}(\cdot)\hat{Y}(\cdot))/B(\cdot)$ is a $\hat{\mathbb{P}}_0$-supermartingale, and thus

(7.4.19) $\begin{aligned} x + \dfrac{y}{p}\mathbb{E}\,\hat{Z}_1(T) &= x + \dfrac{yz}{p} \\ &\geq \varliminf_n \hat{\mathbb{E}}_0^{(n)}\left(\dfrac{\hat{X}(T) + \hat{R}^{(n)}(T)\hat{Y}(T)}{B(T)}\right) \\ &\geq \hat{\mathbb{E}}_0\left(\dfrac{\hat{X}(T) + \hat{R}(T)\hat{Y}(T)}{B(T)}\right) \\ &\geq \hat{\mathbb{E}}_0\left(\dfrac{\hat{\Gamma}_0}{B(T)}\right) = \mathbb{E}\left(\dfrac{\hat{Z}_0(T)}{B(T)}\hat{\Gamma}_0\right) = x + \dfrac{y}{p}\mathbb{E}\,\hat{Z}_1(T) \end{aligned}$

from (7.3.9), (7.4.18), (7.4.11) and (7.4.10); consequently,

(7.4.20) $\hat{X}(T) + \hat{R}(T)\hat{Y}(T) = \hat{\Gamma}_0,$ a.s.

$\square$

7.4.8. EXERCISE. Derive (7.4.14) from (7.4.19).

(*Hint:* We have $\hat{R}(T) = 1+\lambda$ on $\{\hat{Y}(T) < 0\}$ and $\hat{R}(T) = 1-\mu$ on $\{\hat{Y}(T) > 0\}$, thanks to (7.4.20) and (7.4.13), whence $\hat{X}(T) + \hat{R}(T)\hat{Y}(T) = \hat{X}(T) + f(\hat{Y}(T))$.)

7.4.9. EXERCISE. Show that the process $(\hat{X}(\cdot) + \hat{R}(\cdot)\hat{Y}(\cdot))/B(\cdot)$ is martingale under $\mathbb{P}^0$ and that (7.4.16) is satisfied.

(*Hint:* Clearly, this process is a $\hat{\mathbb{P}}_0$-supermartingale with constant expectation; cf. (7.4.19). The martingale property gives (7.4.16), in conjunction with (7.4.20).)

PROOF OF (7.4.15). From Exercise 7.4.9 and (7.1.15), the process

$$\hat{Q}(t) \triangleq \frac{\hat{X}(t) + \hat{R}(t)\hat{Y}(t)}{B(t)} + \int_{[0,t)} \frac{1+\lambda - \hat{R}(s)}{B(s)} \, d\hat{L}(s)$$
$$+ \int_{[0,t)} \frac{\hat{R}(s) - (1-\mu)}{B(s)} \, d\hat{M}(s), \qquad 0 \le t \le T$$

is a nonnegative local martingale, hence a supermartingale, under $\hat{\mathbb{P}}^0$; therefore,

$$\hat{\mathbb{E}}_0(\hat{Q}(T)) \le x + \frac{y}{p}\mathbb{E}\hat{Z}_1(T) = \hat{\mathbb{E}}_0\left(\frac{\hat{X}(T) + \hat{R}(T)\hat{Y}(T)}{B(T)}\right)$$

from (7.4.19). It develops that the nonnegative random variables

$$\int_{[0,T)} \frac{1+\lambda - \hat{R}(t)}{B(t)} \, d\hat{L}(t), \quad \int_{[0,T)} \frac{\hat{R}(t) - (1-\mu)}{B(t)} \, d\hat{M}(t)$$

have zero expectations under $\hat{\mathbb{P}}_0$; thus they are a.s. equal to zero and (7.4.15) follows. $\qquad\square$

PROOF OF (7.4.17) AND THE OPTIMALITY OF $(\hat{L}, \hat{M})$. For any pair $(L, M) \in \mathcal{A}^+(x,y)$, let $X(\cdot) \equiv X^{x,L,M}(\cdot)$, $Y(\cdot) \equiv Y^{y,L,M}(\cdot)$ and observe from (2.1.12) that we have the a.s. inequalities

$$U(X(T) + (1-\mu)Y(T)) \le \tilde{U}\left(\zeta\frac{\hat{Z}_0(T)}{B(T)}\right) + \zeta\frac{\hat{Z}_0(T)}{B(T)}[X(T) + (1-\mu)Y(T)]$$

$$U(X(T) + (1+\lambda)Y(T)) \le \tilde{U}\left(\zeta\frac{\hat{Z}_0(T)}{B(T)}\right) + \zeta\frac{\hat{Z}_0(T)}{B(T)}[X(T) + (1+\lambda)Y(T)].$$

Using these, as well as (7.3.9) and Remark 7.3.2, we obtain

(7.4.21) $\mathbb{E}U(X(T) + f(Y(T)))$

$$\le \mathbb{E}\tilde{U}\left(\zeta\frac{\hat{Z}_0(T)}{B(T)}\right) + \zeta\hat{\mathbb{E}}_0\left(\frac{X(T) + \hat{R}(T)Y(T)}{B(T)}\right)$$

$$\le \mathbb{E}\tilde{U}\left(\zeta\frac{\hat{Z}_0(T)}{B(T)}\right) + \zeta\underline{\lim}_{n\to\infty}\hat{\mathbb{E}}_0^{(n)}\left(\frac{X(T) + \hat{R}^{(n)}(T)Y(T)}{B(T)}\right)$$

$$\le \mathbb{E}\tilde{U}\left(\zeta\frac{\hat{Z}_0(T)}{B(T)}\right) + \zeta\left(x + \frac{y}{p}\mathbb{E}\hat{Z}_1(T)\right) = \tilde{V}(\zeta; y) + x\zeta,$$

for every $0 < \zeta < \infty$. On the other hand, (7.4.14) and (7.4.10) yield

$$(7.4.22) \quad \mathbb{E}\,U\big(\hat{X}(T) + f\big(\hat{Y}(T)\big)\big) = \mathbb{E}\,U(\hat{\Gamma}_0)$$

$$= \mathbb{E}\,U\bigg(I\Big(\hat{\zeta}\frac{\hat{Z}_0(T)}{B(T)}\Big)\bigg)$$

$$= \mathbb{E}\,\tilde{U}\Big(\hat{\zeta}\frac{\hat{Z}_0(T)}{B(T)}\Big) + \hat{\zeta}\,\mathbb{E}\,\Big[\frac{\hat{Z}_0(T)}{B(T)}I\Big(\hat{\zeta}\frac{\hat{Z}_0(T)}{B(T)}\Big)\Big]$$

$$= \mathbb{E}\,\tilde{U}\Big(\hat{\zeta}\frac{\hat{Z}_0(T)}{B(T)}\Big) + \hat{\zeta}\Big(x + \frac{y}{p}\mathbb{E}\,\hat{Z}_1(T)\Big)$$

$$= \tilde{V}(\hat{\zeta};y) + x\hat{\zeta}.$$

Both (7.4.17) and the optimality of $(\hat{L}, \hat{M})$ follow from (7.4.21) and (7.4.22). The proof of Theorem 7.4.6 is now complete. $\qquad\square$

7.4.10. EXERCISE. Prove Lemma 7.4.5.

(*Hint*: Assume for simplicity $p = 1$, re-write the condition (7.4.8) in the form $(1 - \delta)\eta I(\eta) \le \gamma + \delta\tilde{U}(\eta)$, $0 < \eta < \infty$ and deduce

$$(1 - \delta)\zeta \cdot \mathbb{E}\,\Big[\frac{\hat{Z}_0(T)}{B(T)}I\Big(\zeta\frac{\hat{Z}_0(T)}{B(T)}\Big) - y\hat{Z}_1(T)\Big]$$

$$\le \gamma + \delta \cdot \mathbb{E}\,\tilde{U}\Big(\zeta\frac{\hat{Z}_0(T)}{B(T)}\Big) - y\zeta(1 - \delta)\hat{Z}_1(0)$$

$$\le \gamma + \delta\big[\tilde{V}(\zeta;y) - y\zeta(1 - \mu)\big] < \infty,$$

which proves the second inequality in (7.4.9). To prove the first inequality, fix arbitrary $0 < \varepsilon < 1$, $(Z_0, Z_1) \in \mathcal{D}$, introduce $\tilde{Z}_i^{(\varepsilon)}(\cdot) \triangleq (1 - \varepsilon)\hat{Z}_i(\cdot) + \varepsilon Z_i(\cdot)$, $i = 0, 1$ and observe that we have $(\tilde{Z}_0^{(\varepsilon)}, \tilde{Z}_1^{(\varepsilon)}) \in \mathcal{D}$, $\mathbb{E}\,G^{(\varepsilon)} \le 0$ where

$$G^{(\varepsilon)} \triangleq \frac{1}{\varepsilon}\Big[\tilde{U}\Big(\zeta\frac{\hat{Z}_0(T)}{B(T)}\Big) - \tilde{U}\Big(\zeta\frac{\tilde{Z}_0^{(\varepsilon)}(T)}{B(T)}\Big)\Big] + \frac{y\zeta}{\varepsilon}\big[\hat{Z}_1(T) - \tilde{Z}_1^{(\varepsilon)}(T)\big].$$

Use Fatou's lemma to argue that

$$\zeta \cdot \mathbb{E}\,\Big[I\Big(\zeta\frac{\hat{Z}_0(T)}{B(T)}\Big)\frac{Z_0(T) - \hat{Z}_0(T)}{B(T)} + y\big(\hat{Z}_1(T) - Z_1(T)\big)\Big] \le \varliminf_{\varepsilon\downarrow 0}\mathbb{E}\,G^{(\varepsilon)} \le 0,$$

first in the case $(Z_0(T)/Z_0^*(T)) \ge \eta$ (for some $0 < \eta < 1$) and then in general (by introducing the stopping times $\tau_n = \inf\{t \ge 0 \,/\, (Z_0(t)/Z_0^*(t)) \ge \frac{1}{n}\} \wedge T$, and imitating the proof of (7.3.8)).)

7.4.11. EXAMPLE. $r(\cdot)$ *deterministic*. In this case

$$(7.4.23) \quad \mathbb{E}\,\Big[\tilde{U}\Big(\zeta\frac{Z_0(T)}{B(T)}\Big) + \frac{y\zeta}{p}Z_1(T)\Big] \ge \tilde{U}\Big(\frac{\zeta}{B(T)}\mathbb{E}\,Z_0(T)\Big) + \frac{y\zeta}{p}\cdot Z_1(0)$$

$$\ge \tilde{U}\Big(\frac{\zeta}{B(T)}\Big) + y\zeta(1 - \mu),$$

$$\forall\,(Z_0, Z_1) \in \mathcal{D}$$

by Jensen's inequality, and we have

$$(7.4.24) \qquad \tilde{V}(\zeta; y) = \tilde{U}\left(\frac{\zeta}{B(T)}\right) + y\zeta(1 - \mu)$$

$$= \mathbb{E}\left[\tilde{U}\left(\zeta \frac{\hat{Z}_0(T)}{B(T)}\right) + \frac{y\zeta}{p}\hat{Z}_1(T)\right], \qquad 0 < \zeta < \infty$$

in each of the following cases:

(i) $y = 0$ and (7.4.26) below. If $y = 0$, then (7.4.24) holds with $\hat{Z}_0(\cdot) \equiv 1$ and any positive martingale $\hat{Z}_1(\cdot)$ that satisfies a.s.

$$(7.4.25) \qquad 1 - \mu \le \hat{R}(\cdot) = \hat{Z}_1(\cdot)\frac{B(\cdot)}{P(\cdot)} \le 1 + \lambda, \qquad 0 \le t \le T.$$

In particular, one may take $\hat{Z}_1(0) = p(1 + \lambda)$ and $\hat{\theta}_1(\cdot) \equiv -\sigma(\cdot)$ in (7.1.9), and in this case (7.4.25) is equivalent to

$$(7.4.26) \qquad 0 \le \int_0^t \big(b(s) - r(s)\big)\, ds \le \log\frac{1 + \lambda}{1 - \mu}, \qquad \forall\, 0 \le t \le T \quad \text{(a.s.)}.$$

We deduce then easily, that *the no-trading strategy $\hat{L} \equiv \hat{M} \equiv 0$ is optimal* (and gives $\hat{X}(T) = xB(T)$, $\hat{Y}(T) = 0$).

The condition (7.4.26) holds, if $r(\cdot) \le b(\cdot) \le r(\cdot) + \frac{1}{T}\log(1 + \lambda)/(1 - \mu)$. If $b(\cdot) \equiv r(\cdot)$, this result is not surprising; even in the absence of transaction costs, it is optimal not to trade at all (recall Examples 2.2.4, 2.2.5, 2.3.4 and the formula (2.4.22)). If $b(\cdot) > r(\cdot)$, however, the optimal investment strategy always engages the stock, in the absence of transaction costs; this is the case even in the presence of such costs, when one maximizes expected discounted utility from consumption, over an infinite horizon and with constant b, r, σ (cf. Shreve & Soner (1994), Theorem 11.6).

Here the situation is different; if the excess-rate-of-return $b(\cdot) - r(\cdot)$ is positive but small relative to the transaction costs, in the sense

$$(7.4.27) \qquad 0 \le b(t) - r(t) \le \frac{1}{T}\log\frac{1 + \lambda}{1 - \mu}, \qquad \forall\, 0 \le t \le T,$$

then it is optimal not to trade.

(ii) $y > 0$, $b(\cdot) \equiv r(\cdot)$. In this case (7.4.24) holds with $\hat{Z}_0(t) \equiv 1$ and $\hat{Z}_1(t) = p(1-\mu)\exp\{\int_0^t \sigma(s)\, dW(s) - \frac{1}{2}\int_0^t \sigma^2(s)\, ds\}$, $0 \le t \le T$ (or equivalently by $\hat{\theta}_0(\cdot) \equiv 0$, $\hat{\theta}_1(\cdot) = -\sigma(\cdot)$ and $\hat{Z}_1(0) = p(1 - \mu)$ in (7.1.9)). The pair $(\hat{Z}_0, \hat{Z}_1)$ belongs to the class $\mathcal{D}_\infty$ of (7.1.19); the conditions of Theorem 7.4.6 hold; and the optimal strategy takes the form

$$(7.4.28) \qquad \hat{L}(t) \equiv 0, \quad \hat{M}(\cdot) = y1_{(0,T]}(t); \qquad 0 \le t \le T$$

("liquidate immediately, at $t = 0$, the position in the stock, and do nothing during the interval $(0, T]$"). This leads to holdings

$$\hat{X}(t) = \big[x + y(1 - \mu)1_{(0,T]}(t)\big]B(t), \quad \hat{Y}(t) = y1_{\{0\}}(t), \qquad 0 \le t \le T$$

in bond and stock, respectively, and $\hat{X}(T+) = \hat{X}(T) + f(\hat{Y}(T)) = \hat{\Gamma}_0 = I(\hat{\zeta}/B(T))$ $= \big(x + y(1 - \mu)\big)B(T)$.

7.4.12. EXAMPLE $(b(\cdot) \equiv r(\cdot), U(x) = \log x)$. In this case the value function of the dual problem in (7.4.5) becomes

$$(7.4.29) \quad \tilde{V}(\zeta; y) = -(1 + \log \zeta) + \mathbb{E} \int_0^T r(t)\, dt$$
$$+ \inf_{(Z_0, Z_1) \in \mathcal{D}} \mathbb{E} \left[\int_0^T \theta_0^2(t)\, dt + \frac{y\zeta}{p} Z_1(T) \right],$$

and the infimum is attained by the same pair $(\hat{Z}_0, \hat{Z}_1) \in \mathcal{D}_\infty$ as in Example 7.4.11, part (ii); furthermore, the strategy pair $(\hat{L}, \hat{M}) \in \mathcal{A}^+(x; y)$ of (7.4.28) is again optimal for Problem 7.4.1 (here, the difference with Example 7.4.11 is that $b(\cdot) \equiv r(\cdot)$ can now be random).

OPEN QUESTION. Solve the minimization problem on the right-hand side of (7.4.29), when the condition $b(\cdot) \equiv r(\cdot)$ fails.

7.5. Pricing

The results of Sections 7.3 and 7.4 suggest the possibility of defining a "fair price" for a given contingent claim (Γ_0, Γ_1) in the presence of transaction costs, in a sense analogous to that of Definition 6.2.1.

More precisely, consider an investor with initial holdings $x > 0$ in the bank-account and $y \geq 0$ in the stock; suppose, further, that this investor's attitude towards risk is measured by a utility function $U(\cdot)$. Then, by analogy with Theorem 6.2.2, it can be argued that the "fair price" of this contingent claim for the investor should be given as

$$(7.5.1) \qquad \hat{p}(x; U) = \mathbb{E} \left[\hat{Z}_0(T) \frac{\Gamma_0}{B(T)} + \hat{Z}_1(T) \left(\frac{\Gamma_1}{P(T)} - \frac{y}{p} \right) \right],$$
$$= \mathbb{E} \left[\frac{\hat{Z}_0(T)}{B(T)} (\Gamma_0 + \hat{R}(T)\Gamma_1) \right] - \frac{y}{p} \hat{Z}_1(0),$$

provided that the dual optimization problem of (7.4.5) has a unique solution pair $(\hat{Z}_0, \hat{Z}_1) \in \mathcal{D}$. This "fair price" does not depend on the initial holdings $x > 0$ in the bank-account if, as in Assumption 7.4.2, the solution of the dual problem (7.4.5) is the same for all $\zeta \in (0, \infty)$; recall Remark 7.4.3.

For instance, if $b(\cdot) \equiv r(\cdot)$, $y > 0$ and the conditions of Theorem 7.4.6 are satisfied, the expression of (7.5.1) for the *European call-option*

$$(7.5.2) \qquad \Gamma_0 = -q\mathbf{1}_{\{P(T)>q\}}, \quad \Gamma_1 = P(T)\mathbf{1}_{\{P(T)>q\}}$$

becomes

$$(7.5.3) \quad \hat{p}(x; U) = (1 - \mu) \cdot \mathbb{E} \left[\frac{P(T)}{B(T)} \mathbf{1}_{\{P(T)>q\}} \right]$$
$$- \mathbb{E} \left[\frac{q}{B(T)} \mathbf{1}_{\{P(T)>q\}} \right] - y(1 - \mu),$$

either for $U(x) = \log x$, or for arbitrary $U(\cdot)$ but $b(\cdot) \equiv r(\cdot)$ deterministic (Examples 7.4.11 (ii) and 7.4.12). In particular, with constant $b = r > 0$ and $\sigma > 0$, the expression of (7.5.3) becomes

$$(7.5.4) \qquad \hat{p}(x; U) = p(1 - \mu)\Phi\big(\mu_+(T, p; q)\big) - qe^{-rT}\Phi\big(\mu_-(T, p; q)\big) - y(1 - \mu)$$

in the notation of (1.3.14), independently of the initial holdings $x > 0$ in the bank-account and of the utility function $U(\cdot)$.

RESEARCH QUESTION. Complement the theory of Section 7.3 by developing a theory for the "lower hedging price" of a contingent claim (Γ_0, Γ_1) in the presence of proportional transaction costs, analogous to that of Section 4.6. Develop the details for the theory of a "fair price" in this context, along the lines of Section 6.2, leading to the expression of (7.5.1).

APPENDIX A

Historical Notes

A.1. Chapter 0

The model of (0.1.1), (0.1.2) with constant coefficients is due to Samuelson (1965), (1973); it is better known today as the "Black-Scholes (1973) model", after the seminal paper which discussed and solved in its context the valuation problem for European options (Section 1.2). Of course, the earliest attempt to use diffusion-based models for stock-price modelling, based on "arithmetic" rather than on "geometric" Brownian motion, goes back to Bachelier's (1900) dissertation, which is also the first mathematical treatment of the Brownian motion—including the diffusion (heat) equation and the distribution of $\max_{0 \le t \le 1} W(t)$. The reader should consult the volume edited by Cootner (1964) for a translation into English of Bachelier's dissertation, and for other early work on the general theme of the "random character of stock-market prices". Models that permit discontinuous components in the equations (0.1.1), (0.1.2) have been employed by Back (1991), Madan & Milne (1991), Mastroeni & Matzeu (1996), Mercurio & Runggaldier (1993), Merton (1976), Jeanblanc-Picqué & Pontier (1990), Pham (1995), Schweizer (1991, 1992), Shirakawa (1990), Xue (1992), Zhang (1993), among others. For the passage from discrete- to continuous-time models of financial markets, see Willinger & Taqqu (1988, 1991) and He (1990, 1991), Cutland et al. (1993).

According to Theorem 0.2.4 (i), the existence of an equivalent martingale measure (under which discounted prices are martingales) rules out arbitrage opportunities; this is a consequence of basic results in martingale theory (Doob (1953), Chung (1974), Neveu (1975)) such as optional sampling and martingale transform theorems, according to which "one cannot win for sure by betting on a martingale". Now if one cannot win for sure by betting on a given process (i.e., if arbitrage is not possible), is this process necessarily a martingale under some equivalent probability? This question was first formulated, in the slightly different context of "coherent subjective probabilities", by de Finetti (1937); see also Heath & Sudderth (1972, 1978) for more general versions. For random sequences, affirmative answers to this question were provided by Ross (1976), Cox & Ross (1976), Harrison & Kreps (1979), Harrison & Pliska (1981) and Taqqu & Willinger (1987) on finite probability spaces, and by Dalang, Morton & Willinger (1990) (later simplified by Kabanov & Kramkov (1993), Rogers (1995a)) on a general probability space.

Theorem 0.2.4 (ii) provides an affirmative answer to this question in the context of continuous-time; for general continuous-time processes, however, the situation is less clear-cut, and we refer to Kreps (1981), Stricker (1990), Back & Pliska (1991), Delbaen (1992), Lakner (1993), Delbaen & Schachermayer (1994a, b, 1995), Fritelli & Lakner (1994), Schachermayer (1992, 1993, 1994), and Leventhal & Skorohod

(1995) for the deep probabilistic and functional-analytic results that have been developed in this context. This literature provides an excellent example of the extent to which high-level mathematical research can be motivated and driven by the applications.

Theorem 0.3.5 relates the completeness of the market model of (0.1.1), (0.1.2) to the uniqueness of the equivalent martingale measure. This relation was apparently first noticed by Harrison & Kreps (1979) and Harrison & Pliska (1981, 1983); see also Ansel & Stricker (1991, 1992), Jacka (1992), Taqqu & Willinger (1987).

Sections 0.1–0.3 are an abridgement of Chapter 1 in the forthcoming research monograph by Karatzas & Shreve (1997), to which we refer the reader who is motivated to pursue the subject-matter of these lectures further. I am indebted to Ali Lazrak for stimulating conversations that led to Exercise 0.3.8. *Section* 0.4 follows Karatzas & Kou (1996). Hedging problems for a "large investor", whose actions can affect asset prices, are discussed in Cvitanić & Ma (1996) using the theory of forward-backward stochastic differential equations.

Detailed expositions and surveys of issues in Finance can be found in the books by Cox & Rubinstein (1985), Duffie (1988, 1989, 1992), Huang & Litzenberger (1988), Hull (1993), Ingersoll (1987), Jarrow (1988), Lamberton & Lapeyre (1991), Merton (1990), Müller (1985), Musiela & Rutkowski (1997), Wilmott et al. (1993). Among topics that are not covered in these lectures, we should mention the area of *Futures Contracts* (cf. Duffie (1989), Duffie (1992) Sections 7.B-D, Hull (1993), Karatzas & Shreve (1997) Section 2.3), as well as the vast area of the *Term-Structure of Interest Rates* (cf. Rogers (1995b), Musiela & Rutkowski (1997), Duffie (1992) Sections 7.G-L, as well as Heath, Jarrow & Morton (1992), El Karoui et al. (1992), for reviews).

A.2. Chapter 1

The material of *Section* 1.2 is standard; we have followed the exposition in the survey article Karatzas (1989). The theory of pricing contingent claims in a complete market begins with the seminal papers of Samuelson (1965), Black & Scholes (1973) and Merton (1973a); see Smith (1976) for a survey of work in this "early" period. The theory found its "proper" exegesis, in terms of arbitrage and its connections with the equivalent martingale measure, in the papers of Harrison & Kreps (1979), Harrison & Pliska (1981, 1983); earlier work in this vein includes Ross (1976), Cox & Ross (1979) and Cox, Ross & Rubinstein (1979).

Section 1.3. The Examples 1.3.1–1.3.4 are standard; see, for instance, Harrison & Pliska (1981), Karatzas (1989), Föllmer (1991). The Examples 1.3.6–1.3.9 constitute instances of "Exotic Options", an excellent compilation of which can be found in Rubinstein (1991). The formulae of Example 1.3.9 on the "exchange option" are due to Margrabe (1978); we have followed the methodology of Davis (1996). The "path-dependent" option of Example 1.3.7 was first studied by Goldman et al. (1979). There are numerous "barrier-options"—depending on the relative location of the barrier with respect to the initial price, and on its function—of which that of Example 1.3.6 is only one case; see Merton (1973), Cox & Rubinstein (1985), Rubinstein (1991), Broadie et al. (1995) for an interesting numerical method involving a "continuity correction", and Geman & Yor (1996) for discussion of the "double barrier option", which is activated only if both an upper and a lower barrier are attained during the interval $[0, T]$. The extensive literature on the "Asian Option" includes Kemna & Vorst (1990), Conze & Viswanathan (1991), Turnbull

& Wakeman (1991), Bouaziz et al. (1992), Geman & Yor (1992, 1993); in our Example 1.3.8 we have followed the approach of Rogers & Shi (1994). Let us also mention the "compound option" (a standard European call-option, except that its underlying asset is itself a standard call-option; see Geske (1979), Selby & Hodges (1987)), the "quantile option" (Akahori (1995), Dassios (1995)) and the "Parisian option" (which is like the "barrier option" of Example 1.3.6 with the additional feature that, in order for the option to be activated, the stock-price not only has to reach the prescribed barrier but also to stay long enough above it; see Chesney et al. (1995)).

The valuation theory for American Contingent Claims, based on hedging and absence of arbitrage arguments and using the tool of equivalent martingale measure, began with Bensoussan (1984) and Karatzas (1988); our presentation in *Section* 1.4 follows Karatzas & Kou (1997). The origins of this theory can be traced to Samuelson (1965), and to McKean (1965) who treated the valuation problem as a question in optimal stopping. Remark 1.4.6 and Example 1.4.7 are due to Merton (1973a), which contains a plethora of examples. The results of Example 1.4.8 are very similar to those in McKean (1965), who treats the American call-option on a dividend-paying stock and on an infinite-horizon. For the measure-theoretic subtleties that one has to face when dealing with infinite-horizon problems as in Example 1.4.8 (and Proposition 2.3.5, Section 2.5) the reader should consult Section 1.7 in Karatzas & Shreve (1997). Example 1.4.9 on the American call-option is based on the paper by Jacka (1991); related results appear in Kim (1990), Carr, Jarrow & Myneni (1992) and in the references cited in the survey article of Myneni (1992). Example 1.4.10 is due to X. Zhao. For numerical methods related to American options, see Barles et al. (1993, 1995), Barone-Adesi & Whalley (1987), Barraquand & Pudet (1996), Boyle et al. (1989), Brennan & Schwartz (1977), Broadie & Detemple (1995), Broadie & Glasserman (1993), Carr & Faguet (1994), Carverhill & Webber (1990), Geske & Johnson (1984), Jaillet et al. (1990), Lamberton (1993, 1995), Meyer & Van der Hoek (1995), Mulinacci & Pratelli (1995), Wilmott et al. (1993).

Finally, some remarks of "general" interest: contingent claims, such as options, have been traded for a long time, primarily as a means of hedging the risks inherent in economic activities, but it is only in the last thirty years that they have become important. Call-options on stocks began to be traded in a systematic way in 1973, at the Chicago Board of Trade and soon thereafter at all the other major stock-exchanges; the trading of put-options started in 1977, whereas path-dependent options were introduced in 1982. Already in the early 80s, call- and put-options could be traded on over 400 stocks, and options were also available on several other financial assets (foreign currencies, futures contracts, treasury bonds). I take this information from, among other sources, the survey paper by Ingersoll (1989). By the early 90s, the volume of trade in the world-wide contingent-claim market was estimated at four trillion dollars.

A.3. Chapter 2

Portfolio optimization under uncertainty originates with the static models of Markowitz (1952, 1958) and Tobin (1958), who developed the notions of "efficient portfolios" and "separation" (mutual-fund theorem). Similar problems, in the context of discrete multi-period models and based on utility maximization and dynamic programming, go back at least to Samuelson (1969) and Hakansson (1970); they have the drawback that it is typically very hard to obtain explicit solutions in their context. Continuous-time models of the type (2.1.1), (2.1.2) are more amenable to explicit solutions. Such models with constant coefficients and with logarithmic or power-type utility functions (as in Examples 2.2.4, 2.2.5), were introduced in the famous papers by Merton (1969, 1971) and were treated by the methods of *continuous-time stochastic control*; see Fleming & Rishel (1975), Fleming & Soner (1993). Constant-coefficient models were studied for general utility functions, on an infinite time-horizon and with general patterns of behavior upon bankruptcy, by Karatzas, Lehoczky, Sethi & Shreve (1986).

The introduction of the notion of the "equivalent martingale measure" opened the door to the possibility of treating utility maximization problems, in the general context of the model in (2.1.1), (2.1.2), by martingale methods and without the need of imposing any Markovian assumptions. This possibility is implicit in Bismut (1975), who obtained the formula (2.3.3) for the optimal consumption using his theory of *stochastic duality* as in Bismut (1973), and explicit in Pliska (1986) and in Karatzas, Lehoczky & Shreve (1987); we follow this latter paper throughout *Sections 2.1–2.4*. Related results were obtained by Cox & Huang (1989). An alternative but related methodology, based on backwards stochastic differential equations, is expounded in El Karoui, Peng & Quenez (1994). Proposition 1.3.5 comes from Karatzas (1989) and is inspired by results of Cover (1984), Algoet & Cover (1988); for the related concept of "universal portfolios" and their properties, see Cover (1991) and Jamshidian (1992). For models with partial observations and/or unknown parameters in a Bayesian framework, see Karatzas & Xue (1991) and Kuwana (1995); for models with side-information, we refer to Pikovsky & Karatzas (1996). Utility maximization problems for a "large investor", with both an initial capital and a random endowment stream, are studied by martingale and duality techniques in Cuoco & Cvitanić (1995).

The notion of utility function in Definition 2.1.2 was kept deliberately simple, in order to simplify our analysis in this and subsequent chapters. It can be extended considerably, and in such a way as to cover models of "portfolio insurance", which require terminal wealth and/or consumption above a certain given positive threshold; see Karatzas & Shreve (1997), Chapter 3 for the details. For extensions of utility theory that take into account "habit formation" (by allowing explicit dependence on past consumption, as well as present) see Sundaresan (1989), Detemple & Zapatero (1991, 1992), Duffie & Epstein (1992).

An approach similar to that of *Section* 2.4, based on partial differential equations, can be carried out for time-varying but deterministic coefficients and, with less explicit results, even for coefficients that are functions of time and of the current value of a Markov diffusion process; we leave the details to the care of the diligent reader. *Section* 2.5 is based on the paper of Cvitanić & Karatzas (1995), which extends results of Grossman & Zhou (1993). *Section* 2.6 follows Heath's (1993) rendition of the continuous-time results of Kulldorff (1993), while Remark 2.6.6 is due to Föllmer (1995). I am grateful to F. Delbaen for correcting an error in Exercise 2.6.5.

A.4. Chapter 3

The results in this chapter are drawn from the paper Karatzas, Lehoczky & Shreve [KLS] (1990); the existence proof in Theorem 3.6.1 is due to Ph. Dybvig, and improves the original argument in [KLS]. The exposition adopted in this Chapter is based on the less general but much simplified version Karatzas, Lakner, Lehoczky & Shreve (1991) of the paper [KLS].

Historically, the first attempts at developing equilibrium models for capital asset-pricing (CAPM) under uncertainty, go back to Sharpe (1964) and Lintner (1965), who worked with static models. The dynamic model presented in *Sections* 2 and 4 was inspired by Duffie (1986), Duffie & Huang (1985), Duffie & Zame (1989). For related work, the reader is referred to Merton (1973b), Lucas (1978), Breeden (1979), Cox, Ingersoll & Ross (1985), Mas-Colell (1986), Huang (1987), Araujo & Monteiro (1989), Lakner (1989), Back (1991), Duffie (1992) Chapter 9, Föllmer & Schweizer (1993). Dana & Pontier (1990) offer some sharpenings and extensions of these results. Karatzas, Lehoczky & Shreve (1991) present an equilibrium analysis that allows for utility functions with finite marginal utility at the origin; in this context, they show that the equilibrium bond-price might not be absolutely continuous with respect to Lebesgue measure, but instead will typically exhibit "singular" components governed by local time. The reader should consult this paper, as well as [KLS], for additional examples. For a variant of the model of this chapter with different agents possessing different filtrations (information structure) on which to base their decisions, see Pikovsky & Karatzas (1995).

A.5. Chapter 4

The material in this Chapter is taken from Cvitanić & Karatzas (1993) and Karatzas & Kou (1996). These papers deal with general closed, convex constraint sets, and their methodologies can also be applied to the case of different interest rates for borrowing and lending (see also Bergmann (1995) in this regard); for simplicity, we have confined ourselves here to the case of cone constraints. For related results in the case of short-sale constraints, see Jouini & Kallal (1995a).

For the special case of incomplete markets, Theorem 4.4.1 and Proposition 4.4.2 were established by El Karoui & Quenez (1991, 1995) in the context of our model in Section 4.1; for similar results in the context of more general models for the stock-price processes, see Kramkov (1994) and Föllmer & Kramkov (1995). The proof of Theorem 4.4.1 is reminiscent of the "classical" martingale treatment of general stochastic control problems, as in Davis & Varaiya (1973), Davis (1979), and Chapter 16 of Elliott (1982); the additional feature here is the presence of an entire family of equivalent probability measures, which leads to the "simultaneous Doob-Meyer decomposition" (4.4.8) (valid for all these probability measures simultaneously). The result of (4.5.10) vindicates a conjecture of Harrison & Pliska (1983); see Ansel & Stricker (1994), Jacka (1992) for related results.

Similar results, for the problem of hedging *American* contingent claims in the presence of constraints on portfolio choice, are presented in Karatzas & Kou (1997).

A.6. Chapter 5

The material in this Chapter is drawn from Cvitanić and Karatzas (1992), who deal also with general closed, convex constraints on portfolio proportions, as well as with different interest rates for borrowing and lending. Related "martingale-type" methodologies, based on Bismut's (1973) convex duality approach to stochastic control, were first developed by Xu (1990) for short-selling prohibition, and then by Karatzas, Lehoczky, Shreve & Xu (1991) for incomplete markets and by He &

Pearson (1991) for incomplete markets and short-sale constraints. Earlier results, using models with deterministic coefficients and employing mostly partial differential equation methodologies, appeared in Zariphopoulou (1989) and Fleming & Zariphopoulou (1991). For optimization problems with constraints on portfolio and in the presence of a random adapted endowment *stream*, see Cuoco (1996) and the references therein; Browne (1995) solves explicitly a special case with exponential utility function and unconstrained portfolios in an incomplete market. Equilibrium problems for incomplete markets, in the spirit of Chapter 3, are discussed in Cuoco & He (1994). The proof of Theorem 5.7.1 is due to Xu & Shreve (1992).

In the case of an incomplete market, the equivalent martingale measure obtained through relative entropy minimization (or equivalently, through maximization of expected logarithmic utility) as in *Section* 5.6, coincides with the "minimal equivalent martingale measure" of Föllmer & Schweizer (1991), Hofmann et al. (1992). For the concept of "mean-variance hedging" in incomplete markets, and its relation to the minimal equivalent martingale measure, we refer to Duffie & Richardson (1991), Schweizer (1992) as well as Schweizer (1990, 1991, 1994).

A.7. Chapter 6

The results presented here come from Karatzas & Kou (1996). The Definition 6.2.1 of a "fair price" is due (essentially, in its form (6.2.2)) to Davis (1994), who formulated it in the context of incomplete markets. The methodology in Karatzas & Kou (1996) covers general convex constraint sets, as well as the case of different interest rates for borrowing and lending.

Related approaches to the question of "fair pricing", when there is a continuum of arbitrage-free prices, have been proposed by Föllmer & Sondermann (1986), Foldes (1990), Föllmer & Schweizer (1991), Duffie & Skiadas (1991) in the context of incomplete markets, by Hodges & Neuberger (1989) for transaction costs, and by Barron & Jensen (1990) in the context of different interest rates. This latter is equivalent to Davis's approach, as is shown in Karatzas & Kou (1996).

A.8. Chapter 7

This chapter is an abridgement of Cvitanić & Karatzas (1996). The "adjoint process" interpretation of the positive martingales in (7.1.8), (7.1.10) was inspired by the work of Cadenillas & Haussmann (1994) on the stochastic maximum principle for singular stochastic control problems, whereas the proof of Theorem 7.3.1 was inspired in part by Kusuoka (1995). The conjecture (7.3.22) has also been proved independently by Levental & Skorohod (1995).

For related work on hedging problems with transaction costs as in *Section* 7.3, see Bensaid et al. (1992), Boyle & Vorst (1992), Davis & Panas (1994), Davis, Panas & Zariphopoulou (1993), Edirisinghe et al. (1993), Hodges & Neuberger (1989), Jouini & Kallal (1995b), Leland (1985), Shirakawa & Konno (1995), as well as Barles & Soner (1996) and Avellaneda & Parás (1994) for approximations (as the transaction costs become small, or large). Portfolio optimization problems in the presence of transaction costs, related to the problem of *Section* 7.4, have been treated by Magill & Constantinides (1976), Constantinides (1979, 1986), Taksar, Klass & Assaf (1988), Davis & Norman (1990), Shreve et al. (1991), Shreve & Soner (1994), Zariphopoulou (1992), Akian et al. (1996), Weerasinghe (1996).

Bibliography

1. Akahori, J., *Some formulae for a new type of path-dependent option*, Ann. Appl. Probab. **5** (1995), 383–388.
2. Algoet, P. H. and Cover, T. M., *Asymptotic optimality and asymptotic equipartition properties of log-optimum investment*, Ann. Probab. **16** (1988), 876–898.
3. Ansel, J. P. and Stricker, C., *Lois de martingale, densités, et décomposition de Föllmer-Schweizer*, Ann. Inst. H. Poincaré **28** (1992), 375–392.
4. _____, *Couverture des actifs contingents*, Ann. Inst. H. Poincaré **30** (1994), 303–315.
5. Araujo, A. and Monteiro, P. K., *Equilibrium without uniform conditions*, J. Econom. Theory **48** (1989a), 416–427.
6. Avellaneda, M. and Parás, A., *Dynamic hedging portfolios for derivative securities in the presence of large transaction costs*, Appl. Math. Finance 1 (1994), 165–194.
7. Bachelier, L., *Théorie de la spéculation*, Ann. Sci. École Norm. Sup **17** (1900), 21–86, Reprinted in Cootner, 1964.
8. Back, K., *Asset pricing for general processes*, J. Math. Econom. **20** (1991), 371–395.
9. Back, K. and Pliska, S., *On the fundamental theorem of asset pricing with an infinite state-space*, J. Math. Econom. **20** (1991), 1–18.
10. Barles, G., Burdeau, J., Romano, M., and Sansoen, N., *Estimation de la frontière libre des options américaines au voisinage de l'échéance*, C. R. Acad. Sci. Paris, Sér. I Math. **316** (1993), 171–174.
11. _____, *Critical stock price near expiration*, Math. Finance (to appear), 1995.
12. Barles, G. and Soner, H. M., *Option pricing with transaction costs and a nonlinear Black-Scholes equation*, Preprint, 1996.
13. Barone-Adesi, G. and Whalley, R., *Efficient analytic approximation of American option values*, J. Finance **42** (1987), 301–320.
14. Barraquand, J. and Pudet, Th., *Pricing of American path-dependent contingent claims*, Math. Finance **6** (1996), 17–51.
15. Barron, E. N. and Jensen, R., *A stochastic control approach to the pricing of options*, Math. Oper. Res. **15** (1990), 49–79.
16. Bensaid, B., Lesne, J.-P., Pagès, H., and Scheinkman, J., *Derivative asset pricing with transaction costs*, Math. Finance **2** (1992), 63–86.
17. Bensoussan, A., *On the theory of option pricing*, Acta Appl. Math. **2** (1984), 139–158.
18. Bergmann, Y. Z., *Option pricing with different borrowing and lending rates*, Preprint, 1995.
19. Bismut, J. M., *Conjugate convex functions in optimal stochastic control*, J. Math. Anal. Appl. **44** (1973), 384–404.
20. _____, *Growth and optimal intertemporal allocation of risks*, J. Econom. Theory **10** (1975), 239–257.
21. Black, F. and Scholes, M., *The pricing of options and corporate liabilities*, J. Political Econom. **81** (1973), 637–659.
22. Border, K. C., *Fixed point theorems with applications to economics and game theory*, Cambridge University Press, 1985.
23. Bouaziz, L., Briys, E., and Crouhy, M., *The pricing of forward-starting Asian options*, Preprint, 1992.
24. Boyle, P., Evnine, J., and Gibbs, S., *Numerical evaluation of multivariate contingent claims*, Rev. Financial Studies **2** (1989), 241–250.
25. Boyle, P. and Vorst, T., *Option replication in discrete time with transaction costs*, J. Finance **47** (1992), 272–293.

26. Brennan, M. and Schwartz, E., *The valuation of the American put option*, J. Finance **32** 1977, 449–462.

27. Breeden, D. T., *An intertemporal asset pricing model with stochastic consumption and investment opportunities*, J. Financial Econom. **7**, (1979) 265–296.

28. Broadie, M. and Detemple, J., *American option values: new bounds, approximations and a comparison of existing methods*, Rev. Financial Studies (to appear), 1995.

29. Broadie, M. and Glasserman, P., *Estimating security price derivatives using simulation*, Preprint, Columbia University, 1993.

30. Broadie, M., Glasserman, P., and Kou, S. G., *A continuity correction for discrete barrier options*, Preprint, Columbia University, 1995.

31. Browne, S., *Optimal investment policies for a firm with random risk process: exponential utility and minimization of the probability of ruin*, Math. Oper. Res. **20**, (1995) 937–958.

32. Cadenillas, A. and Haussmann, U. G., *The stochastic maximum principle for a singular stochastic control problem*, Stochastics **49** (1994), 211–238.

33. Carr, P. and Faguet, D., *Fast accurate valuation of American options*, Preprint, Graduate School of Management, Cornell University, 1994.

34. Carr, P., Jarrow, R., and Myneni, R., *Alternative characterizations of American put-options*, Math. Finance **2** (2), 1992 87–106.

35. Carverhill, A. P. and Webber, N., *American options: theory and numerical analysis*, Options: Recent Advances in Theory and Practice, Manchester University Press, 1990.

36. Chesney, M., Jeanblanc-Picqué, M., and Yor, M., *Brownian excursions and Parisian options*, Preprint, Université d'Evry, Val d'Essonne, 1995.

37. Chung, K. L., *Probability theory*, Academic Press, New York, 1974.

38. Constantinides, G. M., *Multiperiod consumption and investment behavior with convex transaction costs*, Management Sci. **25** (1979), 1127–1137.

39. Constantinides, G. M., *Capital market equilibrium with transactions costs*, J. Political Econom. **94** (1986), 842–862.

40. Conze, A. and Viswanathan, R., *European path-dependent options: the case of geometric averages*, Finance **12** (1991).

41. Cootner, P. H. (ed.), *The random character of stock market prices*, MIT Press, Cambridge, MA., 1964.

42. Cover, T. M., *An algorithm for maximizing expected log-investment return*, IEEE Trans. Inform. Theory **30** (1984), 369–373.

43. Cover, T. M., *Universal portfolios*, Math. Finance **1** (1), 1991, 1–29.

44. Cox, J. and Huang, C. F., *Optimal consumption and portfolio policies when asset prices follow a diffusion process*, J. Econom. Theory **49** (1989), 33–83.

45. Cox, J. C., Ingersoll, J. E., and Ross, S., *An intertemporal general equilibrium model of asset prices*, Econometrica **53** (1985), 363–384.

46. Cox, J. C. and Ross, S. A., *The valuation of options for alternative stochastic processes*, J. Financial Econom. **3** (1976), 145–166.

47. Cox, J. C., Ross, S. A, and Rubinstein, M., *Option pricing: a simplified approach*, J. Financial Econom. **7** (1979), 229–263.

48. Cox, J. C. and Rubinstein, M., *Options markets*, Prentice-Hall, Englewood Cliffs, N.J., 1985.

49. Crandall, M. G. and Lions, P. L., *Viscosity solutions of Hamilton-Jacobi equations*, Trans. Amer. Math. Soc. **277** (1983), 1–42.

50. Cuoco, D., *Optimal policies and equilibrium with portfolio constraints and stochastic labor income*, J. Econom. Theory (to appear), 1996.

51. Cuoco, D. & Cvitanić, J., *Optimal consumption choices for a "large investor"*, Preprint, 1995.

52. Cuoco, D. & He, H., *Dynamic equilibrium in infinite-dimensional economies with incomplete financial markets*, Preprint, 1994.

53. Cutland, N. J., Kopp, P. E., and Willinger, W., *From discrete to continuous financial models: new convergence results for option pricing*, Math. Finance **3** (1993), no. 2, 101–123.

54. Cvitanić, J. and Karatzas, I., *Convex duality in convex portfolio optimization*, Ann. Appl. Probab. **2** (1992), 767–818.

55. ———, *Hedging contingent claims with constrained portfolios*, Ann. Appl. Probab. **3** (1993), 652–681.

56. ———, *On portfolio optimization under "drawdown" constraints*, IMA J. Appl. Math. **65**, 35–45.

57. _____, *Hedging and portfolio optimization under transaction costs: a martingale approach*, Math. Finance **6** (1996), 133–165.

58. Cvitanić, J. & Ma, J., *Hedging options for a large investor, and forward-backward SDEs*, Ann. Appl. Prob. (to appear), (1996).

59. Dalang, R. C., Morton, A., and Willinger, W., *Equivalent martingale measures and no-arbitrage in stochastic security market models*, Stochastics **29** (1990), 185–201.

60. Dana, R.-A. and Pontier, M., *On the existence of an Arrow-Radner equilibrium in the case of complete markets. A remark*, Math. Oper. Res. **17** (1990), 148–163.

61. Dassios, A., *The distribution of the quantile of a Brownian motion with drift, and the pricing of path-dependent options*, Ann. Appl. Prob. **5** (1995), 389–398.

62. Davis, M. H. A., *Martingale methods in stochastic control*, Lecture Notes in Control Inform. Sci. **16**, Springer Verlag, Berlin, 1979.

63. _____, *Option pricing in incomplete markets*, Preprint, Imperial College, London, 1994.

64. _____, *The Margrabe formula*, Research Note, Tokyo-Mitsubishi Internaitonal, London, 1996.

65. Davis, M. H. A. and Clark, J. M. C., *A note on super-replicating strategies*, Philos. Trans. Roy. Soc. London Ser. A, **347** (1994), 485–494.

66. Davis, M. H. A. and Panas, V. D., *The writing of a European contingent claim under proportional transaction costs*, Comp. Appl. Math. **13** (1994), 115–157.

67. Davis, M. H. A., Panas, V. G., and Zariphopoulou, Th., *European option pricing with transaction costs*, SIAM J. Control Optim. **31** (1993), 470–493.

68. Davis, M. H. A. and Norman, A. R., *Portfolio selection with transaction costs*, Math. Oper. Res. **15** (1990), 676–713.

69. Davis, M. H. A. and Varaiya, P., *Dynamic programming conditions for partially-observed stochastic systems*, SIAM J. Control Optim. **11** (1973), 226–261.

70. De Finetti, B., *La prévision: ses lois logiques, ses sources subjectives*, Ann. Inst. H. Poincaré **7** (1937), 1–68.

71. Delbaen, F., *Representing martingale measures when asset prices are continuous and bounded*, Math. Finance **2** (1992), no. 2, 107–130.

72. Delbaen, F. and Schachermayer, W., *A general version of the fundamental theorem of asset-pricing*, Math. Ann. **300** (1994a), 463–520.

73. _____, *Arbitrage and free-lunch with bounded risk, for unbounded continuous processes*, Mathematical Finance **4** (4), 1994b, 343–348.

74. _____, *Mathematical theory of arbitrage*, Preprint 1995.

75. Detemple, J. and Zapatero, F., *Asset prices in an exchange economy with habit-formation*, Econometrica **59** (1991), 1633–1657.

76. _____, *Optimal consumption-portfolio policies with habit-formation*, Math. Finance **2** (1992), 251–274.

77. Doob, J. L., *Stochastic processes*, J. Wiley & Sons, New York, 1953.

78. Duffie, D., *Stochastic equilibria: existence, spanning number, and the "no expected financial gain from trade" hypothesis*, Econometrica **54** (1986), 1161–1183.

79. _____, *Security markets: stochastic models*, Academic Press, Orlando, 1988.

80. _____, *Futures markets*, Prentice-Hall, Englewood Cliffs, NJ., 1989.

81. _____, *Dynamic asset pricing theory*, Princeton University Press, Princeton, 1992.

82. Duffie, D. and Epstein, L. G., *Stochastic differential utility and asset pricing*, Econometrica **60** (1992), 353–394.

83. Duffie, D. and Huang, C. F., *Implementing Arrow-Debreu equilibria by continuous trading of few long-lived securities*, Econometrica **53** (1985), 1337–1356.

84. Duffie, D. and Richardson, H. R., *Mean-variance hedging in continuous time*, Ann. Appl. Probab. **1** (1991), 1–15.

85. Duffie, D. and Skiadas, C., *Continuous-time security pricing: a utility-gradient approach*, Preprint, Stanford University, 1991.

86. Duffie, D. and Zame, W., *The consumption-based capital asset pricing model*, Econometrica **57** (1989), 1279–1297.

87. Edirisinghe, C., Naik, V., and Uppal, R., *Optimal replication of options with transaction costs and trading restrictions*, J. Finan. Quant. Anal. **28** (1993), 117–138.

88. Ekeland, I. and Temam, R., *Convex analysis and variational problems*, North Holland, Amsterdam and American Elsevier, New York, 1976.

89. El Karoui, N., *Les aspects probabilistes du contrôle stochastique*, Lecture Notes in Math., vol. 876, Springer Verlag, Berlin, 1981, pp. 73–238.

90. El Karoui, N., Kapoudjian, C., Pardoux, E., Peng, S. G., and Quenez, M. C., *Reflected solutions of backward SPEs, and related obstacle problems for PDEs*, Preprint, 1996.

91. El Karoui, N., Myneni, R. Viswanathan, R., *Arbitrage pricing and hedging of interest rate claims with state variables, I (theory) and II (applications)*, Preprint, 1992.

92. El Karoui, N., Peng, S., and Quenez, M. C., *Backward stochastic differential equations in finance and optimization*, Preprint, Laboratoire de Probabilités, Univ. Paris VI, 1994.

93. El Karoui, N. and Quenez, M. C., *Programmation dynamique et évaluation des actifs contingents en marché incomplet*, C. R. Acad. Sci. Paris, Sér. I **313** (1991), 851–854.

94. _____, *Dynamic programming and pricing of contingent claims in an incomplete market*, SIAM J. Control Optim. **33** (1995), 29–66.

95. Elliott, R. J., *Stochastic calculus and applications*, Springer Verlag, New York, 1982.

96. Fleming, W. H. and Rishel, R. W., *Deterministic and stochastic optimal control*, Springer Verlag, New York, 1975.

97. Fleming, W. H. and Soner, H. M., *Controlled Markov processes and viscosity solutions*, Springer Verlag, New York, 1993.

98. Fleming, W. and Zariphopoulou, Th., *An optimal investment consumption model with borrowing*, Math. Oper. Res. **16** (1991), 802–822.

99. Foldes, L. P., *Conditions for optimality in the infinite-horizon portfolio-cum-savings problem with semi-martingale investments*, Stochastics **29** (1990), 133–171.

100. Föllmer, H., *Probabilistic aspects of options*, Preprint, University of Bonn, 1991.

101. _____, *Talk at the Isaac Newton Institute for the mathematical sciences*, Cambridge University, March 1995.

102. Föllmer, H. and Kramkov, D., *Decomposition theorems for random processes, and applications to hedging with constrained portfolios*, Preprint, University of Bonn, 1995.

103. Föllmer, H. and Schweizer, M., *Hedging of contingent claims under incomplete information*, Applied Stochastic Analysis, (M. H. A. Davis and R. J. Elliott, eds.), Stochastics Monographs **5**, Gordon and Breach, New York, 1991, pp. 389–414.

104. _____, *A microeconomic approach to diffusion models for stock prices*, Math. Finance **3** (1993), 1–23.

105. Föllmer, H. and Sondermann, D., *Hedging of non-redundant contingent claims*, Contributions to Mathematical Economics, (W. Hildenbrand and A. Mas Collel, eds.) pp. 205–223, 1986.

106. Friedman, A., *Partial differential equations of parabolic type*, Prentice-Hall, Englewood Cliffs, NJ., 1964.

107. Fritelli, M. and Lakner, P., *Almost sure characterization of martingales*, Stochastics **49** (1994), 181–190.

108. Geman, H. and Yor, M., *Quelques relations entre processus de Bessel, options asiatiques, et fonctions confluents hypergéometriques*, C. R. Acad. Sci. Paris **314**, Sér. I (1992), 471–474.

109. _____, *Bessel processes, Asian options, and perpetuities*, Math. Finance **3** (1993), 349–375.

110. _____, *Pricing and hedging double barrier options: a probabilistic approach*, Preprint.

111. Geske, R., *The valuation of compound options* J. Financial Econom. **7** (1979), 63–81.

112. Geske, R. and Johnson, H., *The American put-option valued analytically*, J. Finance **39** (1984), 1511–1524.

113. Goldman, M. B., Sosin, H. B., and Gatto, M. A., *Path-dependent options*, J. Finance **34** (1979), 1111–1127.

114. Grossman, S. and Zhou, Z., *Optimal investment strategies for controlling drawdowns*, Math. Finance **3** (1993), 241–276.

115. Hakansson, N., *Optimal investment and consumption strategies under risk, for a class of utility functions*, Econometrica **38** (1970), 587–607.

116. Harrison, J. M. and Kreps, D.M., *Martingales and arbitrage in multiperiod security markets*, J. Econom. Theory, **20** (1979), 381–408.

117. Harrison, J. M. and Pliska, S. R., *Martingales and stochastic integrals in the theory of continuous trading*, Stochastic Processes and Appl. **11** (1981), 215–260.

118. _____, *A stochastic calculus model of continuous trading: complete markets*, Stochastic Processes and Appl. **15** (1983), 313–316.

119. He, H., *Convergence from discrete to continuous-time contingent claim prices*, Rev. Financial Stud. **3** (1990), 523–546.

120. _____, *Optimal consumption/portfolio policies: a convergence from discrete to continuous-time models*, J. Econom. Theory **55** (1991), 34–363.

121. He, H. and Pearson, N. D., *Consumption and portfolio with incomplete markets and short-sale constraints: the finite-dimensional case*, Math. Finance **1** (3) 1991, 1–10.

122. _____, *Consumption and portfolio policies with incomplete markets and short-sale constraints: the infinite-dimensional case*, J. Econ. Theory **54** (1991), 259–304.

123. Heath, D., *A continuous-time version of Kulldorff's result*, Unpublished manuscript, 1993.

124. Heath, D, Jarrow, R., and Morton, A., *Bond pricing and the term structure of interest rates: a new methodology*, Econometrica **60** (1992), 77–105.

125. Heath, D. and Sudderth, W., *On a theorem of de Finetti, oddsmaking, and game theory*, Ann. Mat. Statist. **43** (1972), 2072–2077.

126. _____, *On finitely-additive priors, coherence, and extended admissibility*, Ann. Statist. **6** (1978), 333–345.

127. Hodges, S. D and Neuberger, A., *Optimal replication of contingent claims under transaction costs*, Rev. Futures Markets **8** (1989), 222–239.

128. Hofmann, N., Platen, E., and Schweizer, M., *Option pricing under incompleteness and stochastic volatility*, Math. Finance **2** (1992), 153–188.

129. Huang, C. F., *An intertemporal general equilibrium asset pricing model: the case of diffusion information*, Econometrica, **55** (1987), 117–142.

130. Huang, C. F. and Litzenberger, R., *Foundations for financial economics*, North Holland, Amsterdam, 1988.

131. Hull, J., *Options, Futures, and other Derivative Securities*, 2nd ed., Prentice-Hall, NJ., 1993.

132. Ingersoll, J. E. Jr., *Theory of financial decision making*, Rowman and Littlefield, 1987.

133. _____, *Option pricing theory*, Finance: The New Palgrave, (Eatwell, J., Milgate, M., and Newman, P., eds.), W. W. Norton, New York & London, 1989.

134. Jacka, S. D., *Optimal stopping and the American put*, Math. Finance **1** (1991), no. 2, 1–14.

135. _____, *A martingale representation result and an application to incomplete financial markets*, Math. Finance **2** (1992), no. 4, 239–250.

136. Jaillet, P., Lamberton, D., and Lapeyre, B., *Variational inequalities and the pricing of American options*, Acta Appl. Math. **21** (1990), 263–289.

137. Jamshidian, F., *Asymptotically optimal portfolios*, Math. Finance **2** (1992), no. 2, 131–150.

138. Jarrow, R., *Finance theory*, Prentice-Hall, Englewood Cliffs, NJ., 1988.

139. Jeanblanc-Picqué, M. and Pontier, M., *Optimal portfolio for a small investor in a market model with discountinuous prices*, Appl. Math. Optimiz. **22** (1990), 287–310.

140. Jouini, E. and Kallal, H., *Arbitrage in security markets and short-sale constraints*, Math. Finance **5** (1995a), 197–232.

141. _____, *Martingales and arbitrage in security markets with transaction costs*, J. Econ. Theory **66** (1995b), 178–197.

142. Kabanov, Yu. M. and Kramkov, D. O., *No-arbitrage and equivalent martingale measures: an equivalent proof of the Harrison-Pliska theorem*, Preprint, 1993.

143. Karatzas, I., *On the pricing of American options*, Appl. Math. Optimiz., **17** (1988), 37–60.

144. _____, *Optimization problems in the theory of continuous trading*, SIAM J. Control and Optimization **27** (1989), 1221–1259.

145. _____, *Lectures on optimal stopping and stochastic control*, Department of Statistics, Columbia University, 1993.

146. Karatzas, I. and Kou, S. G., *Pricing contingent claims with constrained portfolios*, Ann. Appl. Probab. **6** (1996), 321–369.

147. _____, *Hedging American contingent claims with constrained portfolios*, Preprint, 1997.

148. Karatzas, I., Lakner, P., Lehoczky, J. P., and Shreve, S. E., *Dynamic equilibrium in a multi-agent economy: construction and uniqueness*, Stochastic Analysis: Liber Amicorum for Moshe Zakai (E. Meyer-Wolf, A. Schwartz and O. Zeitouni, eds.), Academic Press, 1991.

149. Karatzas, I., Lehoczky, J. P., Sethi, S. P., and Shreve, S. E., *Explicit solution of a general consumption/investment problem*, Math. Oper. Res. **11** (1986), 261–294.

150. Karatzas, I., Lehoczky, J. P., and Shreve, S. E., *Optimal portfolio and consumption decisions for a "small investor" on a finite horizon*, SIAM J. Control Optim. **25** (1987), 1157–1586.

151. _____, *Existence and uniqueness of multi-agent equilibrium in a stochastic, dynamic consumption/investment model*, Math. Oper. Res. **15** (1990), 80–128.

152. _____, *Equilibrium models with singular asset prices*, Math. Finance **1** (1991), no. 3, 11–29.

153. Karatzas, I., Lehoczky, J. P., Shreve, S. E., and Xu, G. L., *Martingale and duality methods for utility maximization in an incomplete market*, SIAM J. Control Optim. **29** (1991), 702–730.

154. Karatzas, I. and Shreve, S. E., *Brownian motion and stochastic calculus*, 2nd ed., Springer Verlag, New York, 1991.

155. _____, *Methods of mathematical finance*, Springer Verlag, New York, 1997 (to appear).

156. Karatzas, I. and Xue, X. X., *A note on utility maximization under partial observations*, Math. Finance **1** (1991), no. 2, 57–70.

157. Kemna, A. G. Z. and Vorst, A. C. F., *A pricing method for options based on average asset-value*, J. Banking and Finance **14** (1990), 113–129.

158. Kim, I. J., *The analytic valuation of American options*, Rev. Financial Studies **3** (1990), 547–572.

159. Knaster, B., Kuratowski, K., and Mazurkiewicz, S., *Ein Beweis des Fixpunktsatzes für n-dimensionale Simplexe*, Fundamenta Mathematicae **14** (1929), 132–137.

160. Kramkov, D., *Optional decomposition of supermartingales, and hedging contingent claims in incomplete security markets*, Preprint, 1994.

161. Kulldorff, M., *Optimal control of favorable games with a time- limit*, SIAM J. Control Optim. **31** (1993), 52–69.

162. Kusuoka, S., *Limit theorems on option replication with transaction costs*, Ann. Appl. Prob. **5** (1995), 198–221.

163. Kuwana, Y., *Certainty-equivalence and logarithmic utilities in consumption/investment problems*, Math. Finance **5** (1995), 297–309.

164. Lakner, P., *Consumption/Investment and Equilibrium in the Presence of Several Commodities*. Doctoral Dissertation, Columbia University, 1989.

165. _____, *Martingale measures for a class of right-continuous processes*, Math. Finance **3** (1993), no. 1, 43–53.

166. Lamberton, D., *Convergence of the critical price in the approximation of American options*, Math. Finance **3** (1993), no. 2, 179–190.

167. _____, *Error estimates for the binomial approximation of American put-options*, Preprint, 1995.

168. Lamberton, D. and Lapeyre, B., *Introduction au calcul stochastique appliqué à la finance*, Editions S.M.A.I. Paris, 1991.

169. Lehmann, E., *Testing statistical hypotheses*, 2nd ed., J. Wiley & Sons, New York, 1986.

170. Leland, H., *Option pricing and replication with transaction costs*, J. Finance **40** (1985), 1283–1301.

171. Levental, S. and Skorohod, A. V., *A necessary and sufficient condition for absence of arbitrage with tame portfolios*, Ann. Appl. Probab. **4** (1995), 906–925.

172. _____, *On the possibility of hedging options in the presence of transaction costs*, Preprint, Michigan State University, 1995.

173. Lintner, J., *The valuation of risky assets and the selection of risky investments in stock portfolios and capital budgets*, Rev. Econom. and Stat. **47** (1965), 13–37.

174. Lucas, R., *Asset prices in an exchange economy*, Econometrica, **46**, (1978), 1429–1445.

175. Madan, D. and Milne, F., *Option pricing with V-G martingale components*, Math. Finance **1** (1991), no. 4, 39–56.

176. Magill, M. J. P. and Constantinides, G. M., *Portfolio selection with transaction costs*, J. Econom. Theory **13** (1976), 245–263.

177. Margrabe, W., *The value of an option to exchange one asset for another*, J. Finance **33** (1978), 177–186.

178. Markowitz, H., *Portfolio selection*, J. Finance **7** (1952), 77–91.

179. _____, *Portfolio selection: efficient diversification of investments*, J. Wiley & Sons, New York, 1958.

180. Mas-Colell, A., *The price equilibrium existence problem in topological vector lattices*, Econometrica **54** (1986), 1039–1053.

181. Mastroeni, L. and Matzeu, M., *An integro-differential parabolic variational inequality connected with the problem of American option pricing*, Zeitschrift für Analysis und ihre Anwendungen (to appear), 1996.

182. McKean, H. P. Jr., *A free boundary problem for the heat equation arising from a problem in mathematical economics*, Industr. Manag. Rev., **6** (1965), 32–39.

183. Mercurio, F. and Runggaldier, W., *Option pricing for jump diffusions: approximations and their interpretation*, Math. Finance **3** (1993), no. 2, 191–200.

184. Merton, R. C., *Lifetime portfolio selection under uncertainty: the continuous-time case*, Rev. Econom. Stat., **51** (1969), 247–257.

185. _____, *Optimum consumption and portfolio rules in a continuous-time model*, J. Econom. Theory **3** (1971), 373–413; Erratum, J. Econom. Theory, **6** (1973), 213–214.

186. _____, *Theory of rational option pricing*, Bell J. Econom. Management Sci., **4** (1973a), 141–183.

187. _____, *An intertemporal capital asset pricing model*, Econometrica, **41** (1973b), 867–888.

188. _____, *Option pricing when underlying stock returns are discontinuous*, J. Financial Econom. **3** (1976), 125–144.

189. _____, *Continuous-time finance*, Basil Blackwell, Cambridge and Oxford, 1990.

190. Meyer, G. H. and Van der Hoek, J., *The evaluation of American options with the method of lines*, Preprint, University of Adelaide, 1995.

191. Mulinacci, S. and Pratelli, M., *Functional convergence of Snell envelopes: applications to American options approximations*, Preprint, 1995.

192. Müller, S., *Arbitrage pricing of contingent claims*, Lecture Notes in Econom. and Math. Systems **254**. Springer Verlag, NY., 1985.

193. Musiela, M. and Rutkowski, M., *Book on mathematical finance*, (to appear), 1997.

194. Myneni, R., *The pricing of the American option*, Ann. Appl. Probab. **2** (1992), 1–23.

195. Neveu, J., *Discrete-Parameter Martingales*, English transl., North-Holland, Amsterdam and American Elsevier, New York, 1975.

196. Pham, H., *Optimal stopping, free boundary, and American option in a jump-diffusion model*, Appl. Math. Optim. (to appear), 1995.

197. Pikovsky, I. and Karatzas, I., *Anticipative portfolio optimization*, Adv. Appl. Probab. **28** (1996), 1095–1122.

198. _____, *Equilibrium with differential information*, Preprint, 1995.

199. Pliska, S. R., *A stochastic calculus model of continuous trading: optimal portfolio*, Math. Oper. Res. **11** (1986), 371–382.

200. Protter, Ph., *Stochastic integration and differential equations*, 2nd printing, corrected, Springer Verlag, New York, 1992.

201. Rockafellar, R. T., *Convex analysis*, Princeton University Press, Princeton, NJ., 1970.

202. Rogers, L. C. G., *Equivalent martingale measures and no-arbitrage*, Stochastics **51** (1995a), 41–50.

203. _____, *Which model for term-structure of interest rates should one use?* IMA Vol. Math. Appl. **65** (1995b), 93–115.

204. Rogers, L. C. G. and Shi, Z., *The value of an Asian option*, Preprint, Queen Mary & Westfield College, 1994.

205. Ross, S. A., *The arbitrage theory of capital asset pricing*, J. Econom. Theory **13** (1976), 341–360.

206. Rubinstein, M., *Exotic options*, Preprint, Haas School of Business, University of California, Berkeley, 1991.

207. Samuelson, P. A., *Rational theory of warrant pricing*, Indust. Manag. Rev. **6** (1965a), 13–31.

208. _____, *Proof that properly anticipated prices fluctuate randomly*, Indust. Manag. Rev. **6** (1965b), 41–50.

209. _____, *Lifetime portfolio selection by dynamic stochastic programming*, Rev. Econom. Stat. **51** (1969), 239–246.

210. _____, *Mathematics of speculative prices*, SIAM Rev. **15** (1973), 1–39.

211. Schachermayer, W., *A Hilbert-space proof of the fundamental theorem of asset-pricing in finite discrete time*, Insurance Math. Econom. **11** (1992), 249–257.

212. _____, *A counterexample to several problems in mathematical finance*, Math. Finance **3** (1993), no. 2, 217–229.

213. _____ , *Martingale measures for discrete-time processes with infinite horizon*, Math. Finance **4** (1994), no. 1, 25–56.

214. Schweizer, M., *Risk-minimality and orthogonality of martingales*, Stochastics **30** (1990), 123–131.

215. _____ , *Option hedging for semimartingales*, Stochastic Process. Appl. **37** (1991), 339–363.

216. _____ , *Mean-variance hedging for general claims*, Ann. Appl. Probab. **2** (1992), 171–179.

217. _____ , *On the minimal martingale measure and the Föllmer-Schweizer decomposition*, Stochastic Anal. Appl. (to appear), 1994.

218. Selby, M. and Hodges, S., *On the valuation of compound options*, Management Science **33** (1987), 347–355.

219. Sharpe, W. F., *Capital asset prices: a theory of market equilibrium under conditions of risk*, J. Finance **19** (1964), 425–442.

220. Shirakawa, H., *Optimal dividend and portfolio decisions with Poisson and diffusion-type return processes*, Preprint IHSS 90–20, Tokyo Inst. of Technology, 1990

221. Shirakawa, H. and Konno, H., *Pricing of options under proportional transaction costs*, Preprint, Tokyo Institute of Technology, 1995.

222. Shreve, S. E. and Soner, H. M., *Optimal investment and consumption with transaction costs*, Ann. Appl. Probab. **4** (1994), 609–692.

223. Shreve, S. E., Soner, H. M. and Xu, G.-L., *Optimal investment and consumption with two bonds and transaction costs*, Math. Finance **13** (1991), 53–84.

224. Smith, C. W. Jr., *Option pricing: a review*, J. Financial Econom. **3** (1976), 3–51.

225. Soner, H. M., Shreve, S. E., and Cvitanić, J., *There is no nontrivial hedging portfolio for option pricing with transaction costs*, Ann. Appl. Probab. **5** (1995), 327–355.

226. Stricker, C., *Arbitrage et lois de martingale*, Ann. Inst. Henri Poincaré **26** (1990), 451–460.

227. Sundaresan, S., *Intertemporally dependent preferences and the volatility of consumption and wealth*, Rev. Financial Econom. **2** (1989), 73–89.

228. Taksar, M., Klass, M. J., and Assaf, A., *A diffusion model for optimal portfolio selection in the presence of brokerage fees*, Math. Oper. Res. **13** (1988), 277–294.

229. Taqqu, M. and Willinger, W., *The analysis of finite security markets using martingales*, Adv. Appl. Probab. **19** (1987), 1–25.

230. Tobin, J., *Liquidity preference as behavior towards risk*, Rev. Econom. Stud. **25** (1958), 65–86.

231. Turnbull, S. M. and Wakeman, L. M., *A quick algorithm for pricing European average options*, J. Financial Quant. Anal. **26** (1991), 377–389.

232. Weerasinghe, A., *Singular optimal strategies for investment with transaction costs*, Preprint, Iowa State University, 1996.

233. Willinger, W. and Taqqu, M., *Pathwise approximations of processes based on the fine structure of their filtrations*, Lecture Notes in Math. **1321** (1988), Springer Verlag, Berlin, 1988, pp. 542–559.

234. _____ , *Towards a convergence theory for continuous stochastic securities market models*, Math. Finance **1** (1991), no. 1, 55–99.

235. Wilmott, Dewynne and Howison, *Option Pricing: mathematical models and computation*, Oxford Financial Press, Oxford, 1993.

236. Xu, G. L., *A duality method for optimal consumption and investment under short-selling prohibition*, Doctoral Dissertation, Dept. of Mathematics, Carnegie Mellon University, 1990.

237. Xu, G. L. and Shreve, S. E., *A duality method for optimal consumption and investment under short-selling prohibition*, Ann. Appl. Probab. **2** (1992), 87–112 (Part I); 314–328 (Part II).

238. Xue, X. X., *Martingale representation for a class of processes with independent increments, and its applications*, Lecture Notes in Control and Inform. Sci. **177**, Springer Verlag, Berlin (1992), 279–311.

239. Zariphopoulou, Th., *Optimal investment/consumption models with constraints*, Doctoral Dissertation, Div. Appl. Math., Brown University, Providence, RI, 1989.

240. Zhang, X., *Options américaines et modèles de diffusion avec sauts*, C. R. Acad. Sci. Paris Sér. I Math. **317** (1993), 857–862.

Added in reprint

Akian, M., Menaldi, J. L. & Sulem, A., *On an investment-consumption model with transaction costs.* SIAM J. Control & Optimization **34** (1996), 329–364.

Kreps, D. M., *Arbitrage and equilibrium in economies with infinitely many commodities*, J. Math. Econom. **8** (1981), 15–35.

Zariphopoulou, Th., *Investment-Consumption with transaction fees and Markov chain parameters*, SIAM J. Control & Optimization **30** (1992), 613–636.